contents

DECKS MAKE A GRACEFUL TRANSITION from an indoor to an outdoor environment. They are an invitation to spend time relaxing, dining, and entertaining in the fresh air and sunshine, enjoying the sights and sounds of nature. Building a deck is a satisfying, cost-effective way to add living area to your home.

Decks are adaptable structures that can be designed to fit a house of any size or architectural style. Whether they are simple platforms built low to the ground or multilevel extravaganzas with arbors and curved edges, most decks are straightforward construction projects requiring moderate do-it-yourself skills and simple tools. The ongoing popularity of decks ensures that stylish, easy-to-use deck components and accents are readily available at lumber stores and home improvement centers. Innovative products, such as synthetic lumber and high-performance stains, are engineered to give decks long life with a minimum of maintenance.

Once built, a deck can easily become a favorite living area. Decks are tough, forgiving places designed to withstand kids dripping wet and fresh from a romp through the sprinkler, muddy dog tracks, and the occasional spilled iced tea. Dressed up with outdoor furniture and pots of flowers, they can be serene and elegant or boisterous and casual. Decks are much more than structures—they are great places to enjoy life.

In this chapter

This multiuse deck in the northern suburbs of Chicago, *opposite,* typifies what decks are all about—busy backyard staging areas for every member of the family, often all at once. Check out our portfolio of decks depicting outdoor living at its very best.

A well-designed deck increases living area, offers a comfortable outdoor environment, and looks beautiful for years to come.

Decks are more than just structures; they're summer places embracing all the best that outdoor living offers—lounging in the shade with a glass of lemonade, enjoying a blossom-filled garden, conversing with friends while the smells of savory barbecue waft from the grill, watching children scurrying about catching fireflies at dusk, snoozing in a comfy hammock on a lazy afternoon. Decks are part of an outdoor environment that includes garden spaces, patios, pathways, play areas, fences, and trees all arranged—either by chance or by design—into unique areas.

Just as your home's interior is not a single large space, a backyard is divided into rooms, each with its own personality and distinct characteristics. A deck is one of these outdoor rooms, integrated into the overall setting, connected to other areas with well-positioned stairways and interesting vistas. The best decks play this vital role with ingenuity and artistry while not overwhelming the other facets of the landscape. A good-looking, smartly designed deck encourages the complete use of the property, takes its cues from the personalities of the owners and is an important part of an entire home.

Topping It Off

Sporting comfortable wicker furniture and festooned with flowers, this serene deck in Portland, Oregon, is transformed from a backyard perch to a cozy, intimate tea room. Wisteria hanging from the pergola rafters adds to the charm.

A View-Filled Room

There's no room for worry in this restful suburban backyard retreat. Lush plantings of hostas and pots of impatiens frame this small but inviting deck. Shaded by trees and protected by a privacy fence, a hammock awaits an afternoon daydreamer.

Contemporary and On Course

Only a chip shot away from the fairway, the open-air, contemporary-style house, *above,* backs onto a residential golf course. Designed to keep a low profile, the platform deck offers peaceful vistas without intruding on the view. Built-in bench seating takes advantage of the long outdoor season of the Pacific Northwest.

The Lush Life

Jutting into the lushly landscaped backyard, this 10-foot-diameter octagonal deck and faux gazebo, *right,* is purposely designed for only two. Outfitted with a pair of lounge chairs, the deck offers respite from busy days. The deck overlooks a small koi pond. A larger deck connects the octagon to the house and provides steps to the backyard.

Making a Splash

This small water feature goes a long way toward creating an oasis in the center of this meditative deck. The pond is made from a long plastic tub that can be removed from underneath for cleaning. The edge of the decking boards overlap the tub slightly to disguise it. A small drain allows old water to be drained and replenished throughout the summer, and an electric bubbler creates the soothing sounds of moving water. The owner brings out his cactus collection in May, giving a desertlike appeal to this Minnesota setting.

Dinner for 20

The wraparound deck on this 100-year-old renovated home features a generous 20×24 main area that serves as an open-air dining room and allows table seating for 16 to 20 people. Sliding glass doors from the deck open directly into the kitchen. A simple but stylish railing adds personality.

Privacy, Please

A nearly useless 7-foot space between house and garage, *right,* is transformed into a private breakfast nook adjacent to the kitchen with the addition of a deck and an overhead arbor. Lining the edge of the deck with a potting bench and planters full of annuals and perennials adds bursts of color. Now it's the perfect spot for the homeowners to sit outside in the morning with a cup of coffee and a newspaper.

Upwardly Inclined

Hemmed in by nearby houses in their close-fitting urban neighborhood, the owners of this small house, *below,* sought relief by renovating upward. They turned an unused attic into a light-filled studio and added an upper-story deck at treetop level. Solid railings and a privacy screen ensure peaceful outings on a deck that's ideal for quiet relaxation or for entertaining with a small group of family or friends.

AS TRANSITIONAL SPACES, decks blend elements of both indoor and outdoor living. They offer many of the comforts of interior living areas, such as floors, furnishings, accessories, and even walls and ceilings. At the same time, they are open to the elements. They provide access to other outdoor areas, such as gardens and paths. The best deck designs take all factors into consideration.

The physical characteristics of your property are important elements of design. Good design takes advantage of the best attributes, such as great views and large shade trees, and carefully avoids the pitfalls, such as locating the deck where it's open to the hot summer-afternoon sun. This chapter will show you how to create a site plan that indicates prominent landscaping features, marks the location of underground utilities, notes legal considerations such as setback lines, and shows the slope of your property. This sketch is a key part of your deck-building strategy.

To gain an understanding of your property, walk into your yard at various times of the day and, if time allows, in different seasons to observe the location of sun and shade, views, the proximity of neighbors, and traffic patterns leading to and from gardens, gates, and ancillary structures. Visualizing the location of your deck and sketching it in on your site plan is a first step toward effective project planning.

The best deck design takes advantage of all your property's positive attributes.

property

The physical characteristics of your property—its size, the slope or contours of the land, the location of shade patterns throughout the day, and the availability of views—are important factors in establishing a location and developing a pleasing design. In addition, prominent landscaping features, such as large rocks, beautiful trees, garden areas, and sheds, will determine how your deck is situated. Begin your project by sketching a map of your property that indicates landscaping features and physical characteristics. Creating a property map encourages you to become familiar with your yard and all its characteristics—knowledge you'll use as the basis for your deck design, and to communicate with any design and building professionals that you hire to complete the work.

Beginning sketches

A map of your property doesn't have to be elaborate—a simple sketch will do—so don't worry if you're not an accomplished artist. The main objective is to work out your thoughts on paper. As you develop your ideas, you'll make one of two types of sketches. A *plan view* shows everything as if looking down from directly above. Use a plan view to create a map of your property and to find the right location for your deck. An *elevation* looks at an object from the side.

Elevations add valuable information that isn't shown on a plan view, such as the vertical distance from the decking to the ground and the style of the railing system.

To create a planning map, start with the plat of your property, available at your local planning and zoning offices. Obtaining a plat should be free of charge. A plat is a plan view that shows your surrounding neighborhood, including your lot and neighboring lots. The plat also indicates the size of your lot, its shape, and the location of any easements. By law, these easements must be kept free of any structures or impediments. Examples of easements include the following:

UTILITY EASEMENTS provide space so that crews can access electrical power lines or other utilities to make repairs. Utility easements typically are situated at the rear of a property and may run the length of the neighborhood. They typically are 5 to 10 feet wide.

OVERLAND FLOWAGE EASEMENTS include significant depressions or gullies that may collect running water during rainstorms or snow melts. These physical characteristics of the land must not be altered or blocked by construction. Flowage easements prohibit structures from being built close to runoff areas where foundations may be undermined or damaged.

Drawing Tools

To sketch a planning map, you'll need basic drawing tools. GRAPH PAPER gives your drawings accurate scale. It is divided into squares so you can plot dimensions and locations of objects accurately. Use standard 8½x11-inch paper for rough sketches; larger sizes if you want your drawings to have more detail. Stock up on PENCILS AND ERASERS—altering ideas and fixing mistakes on paper doesn't cost anything! If you prefer, use colored pencils so you can readily distinguish between tree locations and other objects you'll draw. A THREE-SIDED ARCHITECTURAL RULER makes drawing to scale simple. Use a simple, grade school-type COMPASS to position landscape features accurately. Invest in a quality 50- or 100-foot TAPE MEASURE—use this handy tool to measure distances around your yard so your map will be accurate. Tape measures of this length feature tough, flexible tapes and reel-type cases with a hand crank. It's also a valuable tool for construction.

A peninsula deck with a charming gazebo provides a peaceful retreat in the middle of a wooded backyard. Trees, shrubs, foundation plantings, and plants in hanging pots blend the structure with its surroundings.

ACCESSIBILITY EASEMENTS ensure a piece of property has direct access to a main road or byway. Creating these easements is a common practice when property is split into two parcels, creating a front lot adjacent to a road and a separate rear lot. An accessibility easement guarantees main road access with a corridor wide enough for a driveway.

BUFFER EASEMENTS are created when a piece of property is next to a public park. They prevent residential construction from intruding on the character of the park.

Size and setbacks

If your property is large, you may have a choice between morning or evening sun, views to the south or east, and a variety of options for positioning your project. However, if your house is situated on a modest suburban property or an even smaller, narrow urban lot, your options will be limited. Remember that in addition to easements, construction is subject to setbacks. These are distances measured in from the edges of a piece of property. A typical suburban lot may have a front setback of 30 to 40 feet, a side setback of 15 feet, and a rear setback of 10 to 20 feet. New construction cannot take place in the setback shown on your plat.

Copy your plat with a photocopier, enlarging it if necessary to a handy size, such as 8½×11 inches. Once you've outlined your lot and indicated setbacks and easements, draw in the outline of your house. Measure from a fixed starting point, such as the sidewalk or street, to position your house accurately. Transfer the measurements to the scale drawing. Indicate locations of doors and windows. Once this portion of your sketch is finished, make photocopies so that you can try out and compare different ideas.

Drawing in landscaping features

Your map should indicate the location of important landscaping features such as large trees. To do this, you'll need to establish two fixed reference points, such as two corners of your house. Use a long tape to measure out from each corner to the landscaping feature, then record the two distances.

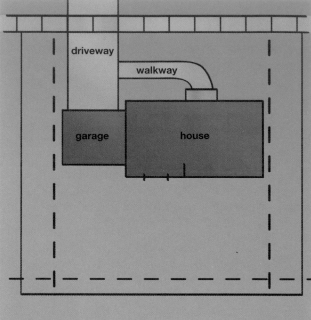

1. PLAT MAP shows street location, property lines, setbacks, and easements. Use the plat as a starting point of your deck design.

2. SITE THE HOUSE on the plat map. Measure from a fixed point, such as the sidewalk or street. Add basic features, such as the driveway and walkways.

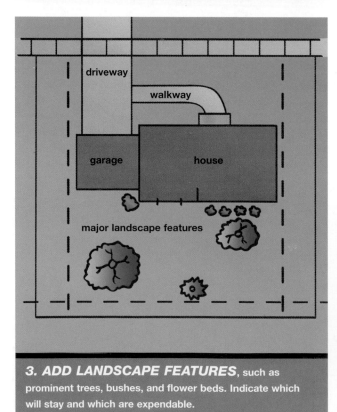

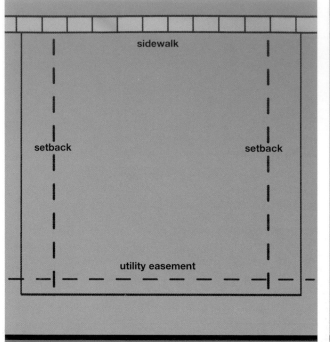

3. ADD LANDSCAPE FEATURES, such as prominent trees, bushes, and flower beds. Indicate which will stay and which are expendable.

4. INDICATE VIEWS that may influence the design of the deck. Small trees and shrubs can be removed to take advantage of a great vista. Show any privacy concerns.

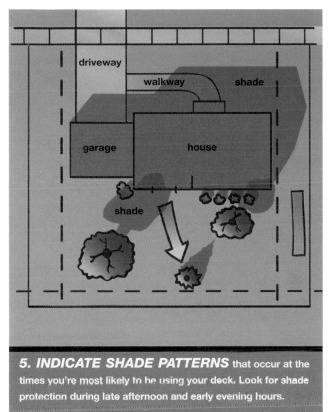

driveway

walkway

shade

garage

house

shade

5. INDICATE SHADE PATTERNS that occur at the times you're most likely to be using your deck. Look for shade protection during late afternoon and early evening hours.

the trunk of a large tree is 20 feet. Set your compass so the gap between the pencil and the steel point is 5 inches (20 divided by 4). Place the steel point at the appropriate corner of your house drawing and use the compass pencil to draw an arc at the approximate location of the tree. Next, take the second measurement—the distance from the other house corner to the same tree. Again, set your compass to scale. For this example, let's say the second measurement is 24 feet. Set the compass gap at 6 inches (24 divided by 4). Place the steel point at the second corner of the house drawing and draw a second arc. The point where the two arcs intersect is the location of the tree.

Indicating views

If you have great views, you may want to orient your deck to take advantage of them. You may even be willing to overcome obstacles in order to enjoy them. For instance, you might expose your deck to harsh western sun so that you'll be able to watch sunsets over the ocean. Or you might decide to build an expensive, two-story deck on a steep lot so that you can face mountain vistas.

On your planning map, use arrows to indicate interesting views. If views are important, consider selectively harvesting some trees in order to create interesting lines of sight. If you are unsure about taking down trees, consult with a landscape architect or designer who can help you make decisions so that you won't destroy rare or important parts of your living

To transfer the measurements to your planning map, use your compass and a simple method called triangulation (see below). You need to figure in the scale of your planning map to calculate properly.

For example, your map is drawn to ¼-inch scale (¼ inch = 1 foot) and the distance from one corner of your house to

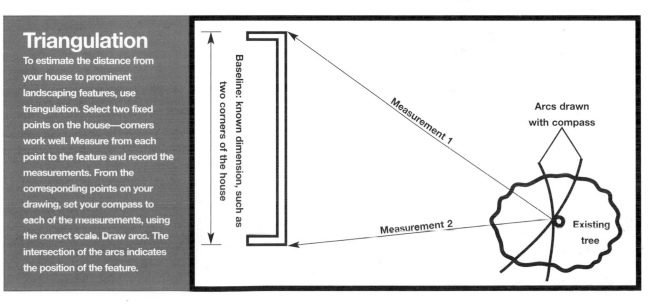

Triangulation

To estimate the distance from your house to prominent landscaping features, use triangulation. Select two fixed points on the house—corners work well. Measure from each point to the feature and record the measurements. From the corresponding points on your drawing, set your compass to each of the measurements, using the correct scale. Draw arcs. The intersection of the arcs indicates the position of the feature.

Baseline: known dimension, such as two corners of the house

Measurement 1

Measurement 2

Arcs drawn with compass

Existing tree

landscape. Depending on tree size, expect to pay between $200 and $1,500 to remove a tree, including cleaning up debris and taking out the stump.

In some instances, there may be undesirable views you'd like to block with a privacy fence or screen. Indicate these on your sketch, and plan accordingly (see Privacy Screens, pages 34–35). Often, a simple lattice screen is all that's necessary to block unwanted views and gain privacy.

Sketching in shade

Shade is a variable. That is, the position of shade changes throughout the day as the sun moves across the sky. The position of shade also changes over the course of a year. Usually, most people want to establish outdoor living areas in locations where afternoon and evening shade is available during the hottest months—on the east side of houses or large trees. Having a deck that wraps around two or more sides of your house provides flexibility that allows you to move in and out of sunny or shaded areas, depending on the temperature of the day.

Determine shade by observing shade patterns at different times of the outdoor living season—late spring, summer, and early fall. Trees, eaves, and two-story houses all cast significant shade. Take note of shade patterns at the times of day when you're most likely to use your deck for entertain-

ing and relaxing. On the other hand, if you're planning to wrap a deck around a swimming pool, you won't want shade in areas designated for lounging in the sun.

When you have identified the shade patterns of your yard, add them to your planning map. Draw in the shade patterns and include the time of day. Use different colored pencils to indicate morning and afternoon shade.

If the configuration of your property does not allow you to take advantage of naturally occurring shade patterns, plan for shade structures that offer relief from the sun (see Overheads, pages 37–38). Remember that shade structures do not necessarily provide shade directly underneath. Later in the day, when the sun begins to set but is still hot, the shade provided by an overhead arbor or pergola will shift toward the east. If you will be using your deck during those hours, plan a shade structure, or consider adding a vertical shade screen that blocks low-angled summer sunlight.

Mapping slope

Slope is the measure of the various contours of your property. How your property slopes and the direction of the slopes help determine the best shape for your deck. For the most part, decks can be built either to vault over the changes in terrain, or in multiple levels to follow the contours of the land.

Measuring Slope
Take measurements of the slope of your yard by extending a level string line from a fixed point on your house. Take measurements at regular intervals along the string—every 4 or 5 feet. Transfer the measurements to a scale elevation drawing.

line level

string line

Shade structures, such as this pergola, take the edge off intense summer sun, permitting access to the deck throughout the day. Make sure rafter spans are within the guidelines provided in the span tables on pages 62–64.

To get a clear idea of slope, create a sketch of your property when viewed from the side. Side views are called *elevations*. Your elevation should indicate the location of your house and how your yard falls and rises. Make your elevations to scale using graph paper. Don't be overly concerned about accuracy: At best, your elevation drawings will estimate the slope. Although not entirely accurate, these sketches will be valuable planning tools and an important means of communicating your ideas with an architect, builder, or other professionals involved in the construction of your project.

To create elevation drawings, stretch a string line from the base of your house foundation out a distance of about 20 feet. Two people make this task easier. Use a line level to make sure the string is level. Measure from the string to the ground every 5 feet, and record your findings on a sketch. If necessary, take another measurement, holding the string at the ground and extending it another 20 feet away from the house.

Planning Point— Building Around Trees

As you design your deck, you realize that a favorite tree is in the path of construction. What would you do? Fortunately, decks are adaptable structures. If you like, you can build your deck around the tree, letting it come up through the decking to give the finished design an unusual touch of character. A tree in the midst of your deck also provides shade. Some trees, such as cherries and flowering dogwoods, produce berries that may stain decking materials. Other varieties, such as certain species of birch, drip sap during the spring. If necessary, consult with a local plant specialist who can advise you about the wisdom of placing a deck directly beneath tree branches.

3. elements of design

LIKE MANY DO-IT-YOURSELF PROJECTS, the more thought and consideration that go into planning a deck, the better the results will be. Careful planning is essential to make sure construction goes smoothly and efficiently, stays on budget, and produces the deck of your dreams. Many enthusiastic homeowners or do-it-yourselfers, eager to see results, rush through planning and begin sawing wood before details are finalized.

It's better to take the time and experiment first with various ideas on paper.

Planning proceeds in stages. The first step is definitely fun—imagining all the things you'll want your new outdoor room to be. Will you entertain large groups of people at evening dinner parties under the stars or curl up with a good book in a private, shaded nook on a lazy afternoon—or both? What will your deck look like? Will it be a simple platform, a magnificent architectural statement, or an intimate, airy perch overlooking great views?

As your deck develops a personality, consider your options. Each component—the railings, stairs, even the decking itself—is an opportunity for self-expression and flair.

A thorough understanding of the possibilities is essential before you begin. Built-in planters, privacy screens, arbors, and hot tubs are interesting and useful possibilities for your deck project.

Considering your options and establishing specific goals are the keys to success.

A deck is a reflection of your lifestyle. If you frequently entertain family and friends, then you'll probably want a deck which will accommodate large groups of people, with room for seating and tables, easy access to your indoor kitchen, and an area for preparing food outdoors. If you prefer a quiet setting and privacy, a smaller deck, such as a second-level balcony off a master bedroom, might be exactly what you need. If you want both, consider a multiuse deck that is built on different levels or uses shade structures and railings to define public and private areas. As your design evolves, make sure it satisfies your goals.

Types of decks

Even though there are diverse and imaginative ways to design and construct decks, a deck typically takes one of three basic forms:

1. PLATFORM DECKS are the simplest type. They are usually built on level lots and attach to single-level dwellings. Typically, the platform deck is so low to the ground that railings are unnecessary. Most building codes require railings and balusters if the deck is 24 inches or more from the ground—check your local building codes before proceeding. On gently sloped lots, it is possible to build a series of platform decks that step down gradually to follow the contour of the land. Even though railings may not be required, they give vertical definition and mass to platform decks. Other enhancements include built-in planters or bench seating constructed around the perimeter.

Because platform decks are close to the ground, it is important that the materials used be resistant to moisture.

Structural materials for any deck should be pressure treated or rated for direct contact with the ground. For decking and other platform deck parts, make sure all materials receive two coats of protective sealer before they are installed so that undersides are well protected. In humid areas, install a vapor barrier of plastic sheeting over the building site beneath the deck prior to installation. Cover the vapor barrier with 2 or 3 inches of soil or a layer of gravel to conceal it.

2. RAISED DECKS are common because most houses sit on foundation walls that position the first-level floor several feet above grade. These decks require railing systems for safety and stairs that make the deck accessible to the yard. Designing aesthetically pleasing railing systems and locating

Following Architectural Clues

When planning a deck, work to preserve architectural harmony between your house and the new structure. Study your house for basic clues—its size and shape, the types of materials used, and the style and color of trim. The best designs follow commonsense rules of good design:

STRUCTURAL ELEMENTS such as posts and railings should blend well with the overall design of the house. A low platform deck, for example, complements the shape and scale of a

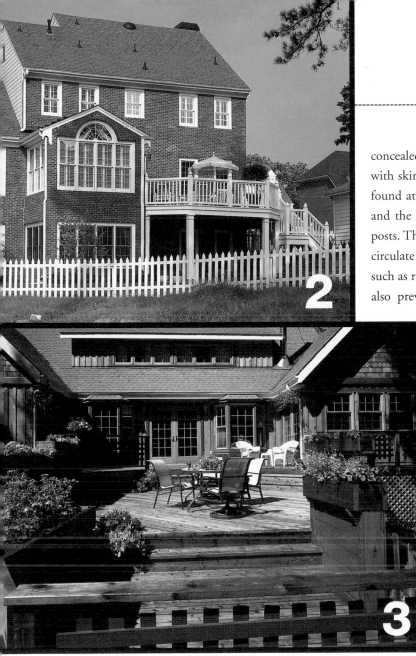

2

3

concealed with foundation plantings, such as shrubs, or with skirting. A popular skirting is panels of lath (the kind found at home centers) cut to fit between the deck surface and the ground. The cut panels are attached to perimeter posts. The lath hides the structural system yet permits air to circulate freely underneath the deck, discouraging problems such as rot or mold associated with excessive moisture. Lath also prevents certain large animals, such as raccoons or skunks, from taking up residence in the protected area under your deck. More elaborate skirting options include boards, solid panels, or masonry walls with vent holes to encourage air circulation. When designing a deck, be sure to include designs for skirting and decide how the skirting will be attached to the deck.

Some decks are designed to provide outdoor access to upper-level areas of a home. The structural posts and bracing required to support a two-story deck can be tall and present an aesthetic design challenge. Posts may be made thicker than codes require or faced with decorative boards to prevent them from appearing spindly. Partial skirting or decorative pieces spanning between exterior posts helps create a more balanced design.

stairs so that they establish sensible traffic patterns are keys to successful deck planning.

Raised decks have foundation posts that are exposed to view when the structure is complete. If the deck is less than one story above the ground, these structural members can be

3. MULTILEVEL DECKS are a series of decks connected by stairways or walkways. They are typically designed for yards with sloped lots so that the deck areas follow the contours of the land. Give a tall main deck access to the surrounding yard with a series of large landings and smaller

single-story, ranch-style home. Such a simple deck design would be out of place attached to a larger, more elaborate structure. A deck attached to an ornately detailed Victorian house should include some details from the original posts and railings. DON'T INTRODUCE too many new types of materials into the design. Resting your deck on brick-covered piers, for example, works only if the existing house already has brick elements. The same holds true for colors. Well-planned contrasting colors are fine, but it is often best to include tones

and hues that echo the original colors of the house. SCALE YOUR DESIGN to fit the house. Even if your budget is unrestrained and you want the most elaborate deck that includes every feature imaginable, the final design should be carefully proportioned so that it blends well with the main house. Sketching different possibilities on paper allows you to visualize changes and experiment with proportions. If you plan to hire a design professional, your sketches are a good way to communicate ideas.

FURNISHING TYPE	MINIMUM SQUARE FOOTAGE REQUIRED	IDEAL SQUARE FOOTAGE FOR COMFORT
36" round table and four chairs	A square or circle 9' across, a total of 80–90 square feet	A square or circle 12' across, a total of 140–150 square feet
48" round table and six chairs	A square or circle 10' across, a total of 100–110 square feet	A square or circle 13' across, a total of 160–180 square feet
barbeque grill on 2'x3' rolling cart	1' clearance at sides and back, 3' clearance in front, a total of 30 square feet	2' clearance at sides and back, 4' clearance in front, a total of 56 square feet
freestanding hammock with self-supporting stand	A rectangle 9' long and 6' wide,` a total of 54 square feet	A rectangle 9' long and 6' wide, plus 3' at each side for clearance, a total of 108 square feet
built-in bench seat 6' long	6' bench length, 17"-wide seat, 3' clearance in front of seat, a total of 27 square feet	5' clearance in front of seat, a total of 39 square feet

decks, each joined by a short run of stairs. This arrangement also prevents the lowest decks—those furthest from the house—from visually interfering with views from decks higher up.

A multilevel deck can take advantage of different mini-climates within your yard. Position one close to the house for entertaining, another amid shady trees, and a third for worshiping the sun.

Estimating deck size

How big should your deck be? The answer to that question depends on several factors, including keeping the deck design in proportion and scale with the main house, and planning a space large enough to accommodate several guests and outdoor furniture. Include space for specialty items, such as a barbecue grill and a hot tub.

To determine the total square footage, estimate the average number of guests you're likely to have for outdoor gatherings. Figure about 20 square feet per person; then add the space required for ancillary items, such as a barbecue cart.

As an example, suppose a 20×14-foot deck with a total of 280 square feet includes a barbecue cart. Using the chart *above,* subtract 30 square feet for the cart. The remainder is 250 square feet. The deck will comfortably handle about 12 persons standing at one time (250 divided by 20 = 12.5).

To calculate for seating, subtract the barbecue cart from the total of 280 to arrive at 250 square feet. If the goal is to include two 48-inch round tables, each with six chairs, figure a minimum of 110 square feet per table. That's another 220 square feet to subtract from the total. A 280-square-foot deck is able to seat 12 people comfortably at two large tables.

Connecting to interior spaces

Decks are typically considered outdoor rooms, but where they are positioned and how they are used may affect adjacent interior spaces. Redirected traffic patterns in and out of the house and new doorways can alter the furniture arrangements of interior rooms and increase costs. If a new deck is part of an overall remodeling, you'll want to ensure the new spaces flow easily from one to the other, and that all the changes meet your goals for comfort and livability. Mapping the location of interior rooms, as well as the proposed location for your new deck, helps visualize possible alterations.

All-purpose decks are most often accessed through kitchens and family rooms. These rooms tend to be less formal and make ideal, weather-resistant transition points to the outdoors for kids and pets. Features such as wear-resistant vinyl or tile flooring stand up to traffic well and are easy to clean. A door leading from a kitchen to a deck provides ready access for entertaining. If there is a standard 36-inch-wide exterior door in this location, consider changing it to a wider patio or French door to make comings and goings easier and to open interior rooms to views and light. Including all materials, plan to spend $2,000 to $3,000 for a contractor to install a 6-foot-wide patio door.

As you plan, consider traffic patterns leading from access doorways to deck stairs. Traffic patterns should be sensible and practical. Keep tables and eating areas well away from traffic. If possible, place grills and cooking equipment in out-of-the-way locations or in special niches created just for them. Allow enough legroom in front of built-in benches so that guests won't have to retract their legs every time someone walks past.

Marking utilities

Before planning begins, know the location of all underground utilities such as electrical power lines, television cable, water and gas supplies, and sewer mains. This is vital information for anyone needing to excavate any part of their yard. Notify all utility, cable television, and phone companies about your plans for building a deck and ask them to indicate the underground locations of wires, cables, pipes, and sewer lines. Most companies provide this service for free

Connecting to Interior Spaces
This well-planned deck project includes sliding patio doors that provide easy access to outdoor spaces. The area leading to the doors is free of furniture and other obstructions

or for a small fee. They'll mark locations with small stakes topped with colored flags or with brightly colored spray paint (that disappears within a few weeks). After utilities are marked, transfer the locations to your drawings so you'll have a permanent record.

Obtaining permits

Local building departments usually require you to obtain a building permit before you begin construction. If you don't, you may be liable for fines or be required to rebuild portions of your deck—at your expense.

Permits are issued when a member of the local building or planning department reviews your deck plans and evaluates them for safety and structural integrity. That's why good plans are essential. If your plans are not drawn by a professional architect, you can have them reviewed by a registered structural engineer before submitting them to a building department. This is particularly helpful if your deck is complex. Plan to spend $300 to $600 for a structural engineer to review your plans and make suggestions that will rectify problems.

Your plans also must meet local setback requirements. Setbacks determine the distance that new construction must be from property lines (for more information, see Size and Setbacks on page 15). In certain circumstances, you may be able to apply for a variance that allows you to build within a setback zone. Your application for variance must put forth compelling reasons for the variance, such as the construction of a wheelchair ramp.

Your building department also will be able to tell if your property includes any rights-of-way. Typical rights-of-way are corridors that allow utility companies or neighbors legal access through parts of your property. You will not be able to build in right-of-way areas.

Covenants and deeds

Increasingly, neighborhood development areas include restrictions on the kinds of structures that can be added to a property. These regulations, often called covenants, are intended to preserve the architectural character of the neighborhood and prevent the building of unusual or poorly designed ancillary structures in people's backyards. Usually, any new building must be preapproved by an architectural review committee. While most neighborhood review committees are comfortable with well-designed decks, complying with this step takes time. If possible, have your plans approved during the winter months, before construction begins in earnest.

You'll also want to carefully review your property deed. Some deeds restrict the location and design of ancillary structures.

Working with a design professional

The job of a professional designer is to create a space that meets your needs. Professional expertise and experience will provide fresh ideas, anticipate code restrictions, and deal with unusual concerns. If the cost of hiring a designer seems prohibitive, consider that professionals can help save on overall costs by contributing to the efficiency of the project by organizing and managing work flow and by helping to avoid expensive mistakes. Many pros are willing to work as consultants for an hourly fee.

Contacting a Pro

ARCHITECTS: For a listing in your area, look in the business listings of your phone directory or try the Internet search engine offered by the American Institute of Architects at www.earchitect.com/reference/home.asp
LANDSCAPE ARCHITECTS: Consult the Yellow Pages of your telephone directory under "Landscape Architects," or check with the American Society of Landscape Architects at 202-898-2444 or www.asla.org

LANDSCAPE CONTRACTORS: Look in the business listings of your telephone directory under "Landscape Contractors," or contact the Associated Landscape Contractors of America at 800-395-2522 or www.alca.org. Build/design teams: Check the phone directory for listings under "Deck Builders, Design & Maintenance," "Patio & Porch Builders, Design & Maintenance," and "Contractors—General." Watch for display ads within the listings for builders that specialize in decks.

When working with a professional, good communication is key. Start a clipping folder. Use it to keep articles and photographs clipped from magazines, newspapers, and pamphlets or printed from Internet sites that depict ideas and design elements that appeal to you. Add product brochures or advertisements that you can share with your designer. Keep sketches that express your ideas and share them with your designer. A good designer is interested in your lifestyle and should ask questions about how you live, your daily routines, and your project goals.

There are several kinds of design professionals available for help on a deck or patio project. Although they have specialized areas of expertise, most professionals are well-versed in all phases of design and can help you create a comprehensive plan.

ARCHITECTS work primarily with structure and reorganization of space. They are familiar with many types of building materials, finishes, and structural systems. For complex deck designs, architects are good choices. They will design your deck and make sure it is sensibly integrated with adjacent living areas, such as your kitchen or family room. Architects charge a percentage of the project's total cost, usually 10 to 15 percent. If hired on an hourly basis, they charge $50 to $125 per hour.

DESIGN / BUILD TEAMS that specialize in deck planning and construction typically are licensed building contractors with a flair for design. They likely do not have a registered architect on staff. However, they have hands-on experience and familiarity with the latest methods and materials—practical know-how that makes them well qualified to create plans, obtain all necessary approvals, and build efficiently. Because design/build teams offer complete project packages that include design, site preparation, and construction, their rates are usually less expensive than if the design and construction are contracted separately.

LANDSCAPE ARCHITECTS registered with the American Society of Landscape Architects (ASLA) are usually designers only—the plans they furnish must be given to a landscape contractor for installation. Occasionally, a professional landscape architect joins with a landscape contractor to provide full-service planning and installation.

The owners of this large, single-story house hired a landscape contractor to create a deck that blends with the overall backyard scheme. The result includes a host of features such as built-in seating, low-voltage lamps, easy access to the yard, and space for comfortable groupings of outdoor furniture.

An ASLA architect will charge $75 to $125 per hour to inspect and analyze the property, and then complete detailed drawings that include plantings and landscape features to help connect the new space to the outdoor environment. A landscape architect's plan may cost up to 15 percent of the finished project.

LANDSCAPE CONTRACTORS are skilled at installing various outdoor features such as decks, patios, walkways, retaining walls, plantings, and ancillary structures including pergolas and arbors. Many landscaping contractors are full-service business firms that employ landscape architects, designers, and installers. They will provide a full range of services including initial concepts, finalized plans, complete installation, and ongoing maintenance. If required by state law, a landscape contracting company should be licensed or certified, meaning they have passed examinations and have demonstrated experience, knowledge, and participation in ongoing programs of education.

Shade arbors, hot tubs, cooking centers, built-in lighting, and other special features add comfort and convenience to the outdoor living experience and give a deck character. Imaginative railings, grand stairways, decking patterns with stylistic flair, curved bump-outs, and dramatic cantilevers make your deck as unique as a signature. Consider all the options as you develop your plan, but the best place to start is with the key elements.

Decking patterns

Decking is most commonly put down lengthwise—usually running parallel to the longest edge of the deck. This type of installation is strong, installs quickly, and produces the least waste—only about 5 to 10 percent of the total decking material. For small or narrow decks, it's a commonsense method for installing decking.

To add visual interest, especially for large or intricate decks, install the decking in a pattern. Creative patterns are striking but take more time to install and produce more waste than basic patterns because of the many butt joints—seams created when the ends of two boards meet. You'll need to buy 10 to 15 percent more decking material than for a plain, lengthwise installation. Also, butt joints need extra framing support from below. Additional joists or blocking material must be installed. The supplemental framing mate-

Accessible Design

Constructing a deck so it is accessible to persons with limited mobility often means building a ramp that will accommodate a wheelchair. Your local building department should provide specifications for ramps. Typically, a ramp should not have more than 1 inch of rise for every foot of horizontal run. It should have handrails on both sides and be at least 42 inches wide between handrails to allow room for wheelchairs or other mobility aids. Long ramps should include a landing for every 3 feet of vertical rise so that users can pause or have a place to turn around. It's a good idea to provide a concrete slab at the bottom of the ramp for traction.

rials and the labor needed to install them add cost. To minimize the additional costs, use unique patterns only on part of the deck to define a single area or level.

Imaginative railings

The primary function of a railing system is safety. Building codes usually require railings on decks more than 24 inches above the ground. Railings also are a prominent design element and should reflect the style of the house. The railing on

Designer Railings

A WIRE GRID and a stylish handrail make a nearly transparent system that complies with building codes.

CUSTOM MILLWORK is expensive yet offers the incomparable beauty of fine period hand craftsmanship.

STAINLESS STEEL tubes set in painted wood posts create a sleek, contemporary look.

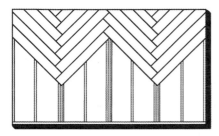

HERRINGBONE

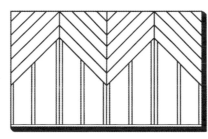

CHEVRON HERRINGBONE

PARQUET

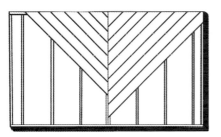

V-SHAPE

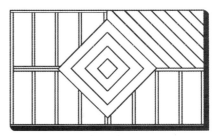

45-DEGREE SLANT

DIAMOND

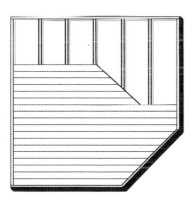

EDGE-TRIMMED

Decking Patterns

Give your deck kinetic beauty by installing decking in a creative pattern. The handsome redwood deck *at right* uses inset boards to visually divide the deck into several areas. Creative patterns require extra support framing—either additional joists, blocking, or both. Note in the diagrams *above* how extra framing members are used to support the cut ends of various decking patterns.

a deck attached to a classic older home, for example, might repeat the style and color of a cornice. A contemporary home might have a deck with a sleek, simple railing system. An imaginative railing may cost the same as a basic one and can turn your deck from plain to striking.

Railing systems include support posts. The posts may be an extension of the deck's structural system, or they may be bolted to the rim joists. Long posts can be used to support an overhead structure such as a pergola or an arbor. Wooden posts usually are 4×4s or 6×6s, depending on the design.

To ensure the railing system is strong, building codes place limits on how far apart railing posts can be; typically the dis-

tance is 4 to 6 feet. Horizontal pieces called rails run between the posts. Vertical members are called balusters. Balusters come in a variety of shapes. The simplest are square; the most decorative are turned balusters featuring delicate flutes, ridges, and grooves. These components can be arranged in many ways to form railings that are simple or highly decorative, as long as the final design conforms to building codes. Most codes require that balusters and other railing components be no more than 4 inches apart.

Standard railings available in home improvement centers are usually made of wood or galvanized steel coated with vinyl. These systems are designed to be durable and conform

Variations

Wooden railing systems use basic components that are easily rearranged to create interesting and imaginative designs. Top rails, for example, can be installed flat or sideways. Flat top rails are either butted into the posts or run across the top of each post. Both designs lend themselves to decorative finials. Some designs, shown *opposite,* eliminate posts altogether. Instead, all the balusters attach to the rim joists. One drawback of this arrangement is lack of a space under the balusters for cleaning leaves and debris off the deck surface.

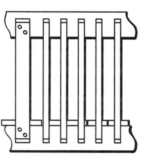

Balusters attached directly to rim joist—no bottom rail

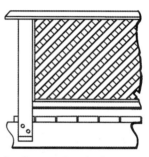

Lattice panels substituted for balusters

Top rail includes cap rail that runs over the tops of posts

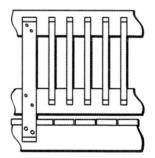

Rails installed flat with square balusters

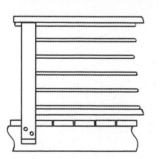

Steel tubes or pipe substituted for vertical baluster

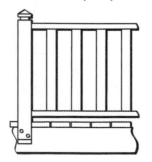

Wide-board balusters and 2×4 rails that butt posts

Square balusters and 2×4 rails that butt to posts

to codes but provide only limited options for styles of posts, railings, and balusters. Strong materials such as steel, copper tubing, and heavy-gauge wire also can be used if your construction methods meet the requirements of local building codes. Most of these materials are readily available at lumber yards and home improvement centers.

Prefabricated steel and aluminum railings mimic classic wrought-iron railings. They combine strength with low maintenance. Some prefabricated metal railings are available as complete systems, with posts designed for installation on decks. Others come as a section of rails and balusters only and are bolted to wooden posts.

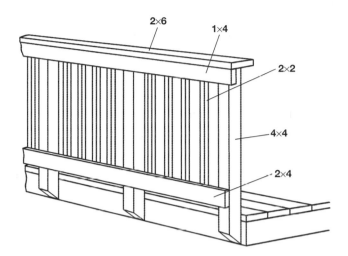

Alternate Railing Configurations

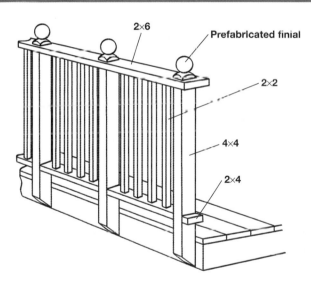

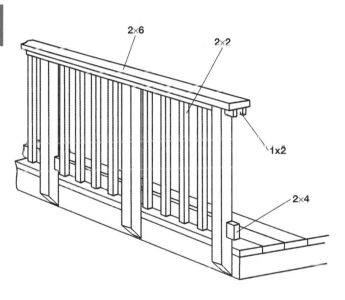

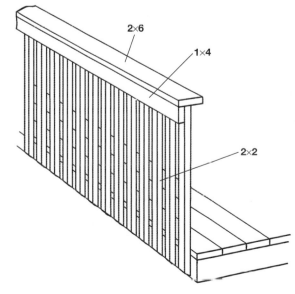

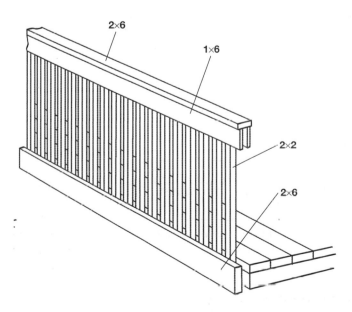

Stair Solutions

A graceful stairway provides access to a main deck from a second-level bedroom, *above*. The offset landing prevents the stairs from competing for space with the main deck. The 6-foot-wide lower stairway has room for potted plants. A prefabricated spiral stairway, *below*, is a space-saving way to connect an upper-level deck to the ground, especially in small yards.

Welcoming stairs

Stairs provide a transition between your home's interior and your yard. The best designs are expressive, inviting, and constructed with safety in mind. Locate a deck stairway to channel traffic away from main seating areas while allowing easy access to yards, patios, and garden pathways.

Building codes are important in the design of deck stairways. Typically, codes specify the maximum rise of a step to be 8 inches and the minimum width of a tread to be 9 inches. For comfort, the ideal stair height is 7 inches. Once you design your deck, calculate the number of steps needed and the true rise and run, using the height of the deck above grade as a starting point.

Although stairs must not be taller than specified by codes, they can be lower, as long as the total rise and run is no more than 19 inches. A 5-inch-high step, for example, should be accompanied by a tread 13 to 14 inches wide. Broad, shallow steps look good with long, low decks. However, you'll need the yard space to accommodate the long horizontal length of the stairway. Platform steps are a series of shallow decks and work well on gentle slopes where they can follow the contours of the land.

Stairs for tall decks, especially second-level decks, require careful consideration. The total run of the stairway can be long enough to project well into your yard. To compensate, try designing stairs that make one or two turns. Wrapping stairways around the deck helps to hide long posts and other structural members.

Stairways that change direction require landings—short platforms at least 3 feet by 3 feet. Increase the size of landings to create small decks, complete with built-in seating and planters that add visual texture.

Stair Tread Configurations

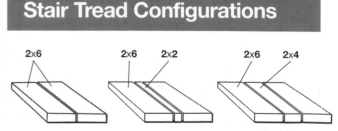

Stairs for decks usually have open risers. That is, there are no pieces of wood applied to the vertical, rear part of each stair. This prevents water, leaves, and other debris from accumulating at the intersection of the tread and the riser, resulting in moisture damage and rot.

Built-in benches

Planning built-in benches, planters, and privacy screens encourages you to get the most from your outdoor spaces by considering how you'll use your deck and how components are arranged. Typically constructed of the same materials as your deck, built-ins are a cost-effective way to provide seating and add functionality.

Built-in benches provide permanent seating without intruding on interior deck space. A built-in bench must be fastened directly to the deck's structural components. Typically the back supports for the bench extend through the deck floor and are bolted to the joists.

Bench seats should be 15 to 18 inches from the floor of the deck and usually are 15 inches deep. Benches built around the perimeter of a low deck can act as informal railings. However, if a deck is more than 24 inches from the ground, benches must conform to the building codes that

Bench Basics
Built-in bench seating is durable, low-cost, and adds definition to the edges of decks. The framing supports attach directly to joists with carriage bolts.

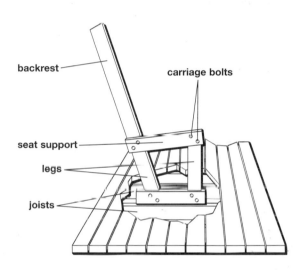

backrest

carriage bolts

seat support

legs

joists

Planning Point— Adding Style With Color
Give ordinary railing systems a dash of style with color. Wood can be left natural, stained, or painted. Even with regular applications of clear weather sealers, natural wood will eventually turn a soft, silvery gray. STAINED WOOD shows its grain pattern and is relatively easy to maintain because preparing the surface with scraping and sanding is unnecessary. Exterior stains for wood come in an ever-increasing variety of colors. PAINTED WOOD railings are dramatic and can be readily made to match or complement the color of your house. Paint railings only with top-quality exterior paints to minimize repainting. Cleaning and applying fresh coats of paint between balusters requires a steady hand and an abundance of patience. VINYL RAILINGS are made in a limited number of colors. Some types can be painted, but you'll need to check the manufacturer's recommendations. The big advantage of vinyl deck components is that they are virtually maintenance-free. If you paint them, you'll be committed to periodic maintenance.

planter box

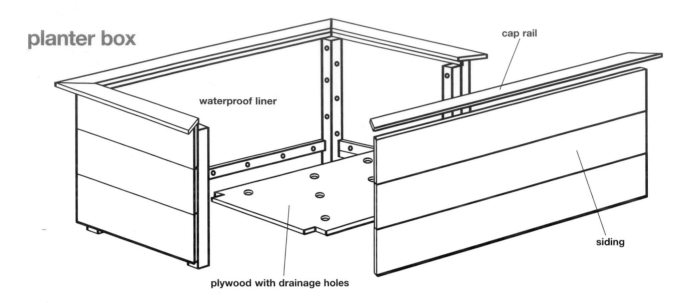

cap rail

waterproof liner

siding

plywood with drainage holes

apply to railings. Check with your local building codes to determine requirements for built-in benches. Built-in benches not used as railings can be built in any style.

Planters

Planters should harmonize with the overall style of a deck. On low decks, planters can be used to define the edges or perimeter of the deck. Plant material adds a sense of substance to otherwise plain deck structures. Do not use planters as a substitute for railings.

Make planters from moisture-resistant woods such as cedar, redwood, or pressure-treated lumber. For annual or perennial flowers, make planters 8 to 12 inches deep. For shrubs, make planters 18 to 24 inches deep. Drill drainage holes in the bottom of the planter, extending the holes completely through the decking material. Bore 1-inch holes every 12 inches throughout the floor of the planter.

To ensure that your planter has long life and to prevent soils from leaching out and staining nearby decking, line your planter with a waterproof membrane. Use plastic sheathing at least 3 millimeters thick or 15 lb. roofing felt, sometimes called tar paper. Start at the bottom and wrap the membrane up the sides. Overlap edges at least 4 inches. Cut out holes over the drainage holes. As an alternative, coat the interior of the planter with roofing tar.

Solid liners, such as fiberglass or galvanized steel, make the best liners. Make fiberglass liners using flexible fiberglass

cloth and paintable hardeners from a boat repair kit. Or, have a sheet metal shop prepare custom-made galvanized steel liners to fit exactly inside a planter. However, do not use galvanized steel with planters made of cedar. When both materials are wet and in contact with each other, a chemical reaction may take place, producing stains.

Privacy screens

Build a privacy screen to block unwanted views and to establish a sense of enclosure. Typical privacy screens are designed as open latticework or boards spaced several inches apart. This arrangement establishes privacy while permitting air

Screen Gem

A small but effective privacy screen is supported by extra-tall railing posts and is part of the original plan. The circle-top design is visually pleasant from both sides.

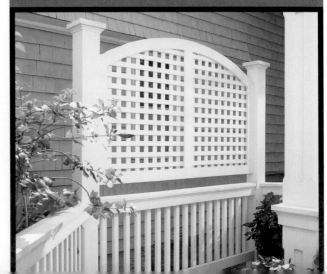

Privacy Screens

Host to an assortment of vining plants, this simple lattice privacy screen, *left,* is an attractive visual barrier between a deck and a close neighbor. Once they've leafed out, plants also help block sound transmission. Privacy screens are large, vertical surfaces and benefit from tasteful design. The examples *below* are made of standard dimensional lumber.

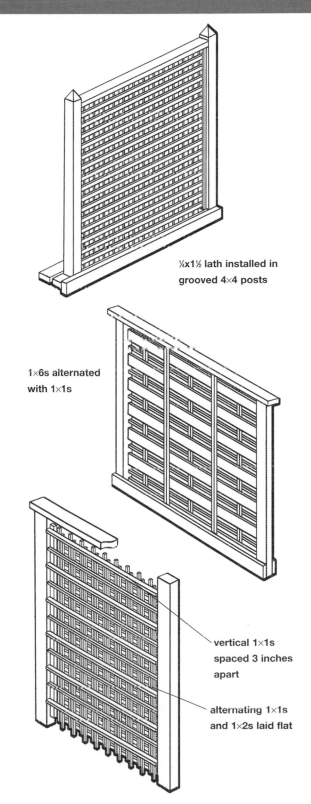

¼x1½ lath installed in grooved 4×4 posts

1×6s alternated with 1×1s

vertical 1×1s spaced 3 inches apart

alternating 1×1s and 1×2s laid flat

circulation and preserving the open feel of an outside structure. Buy premade plastic or pressure-treated wood lattice in 2×8- or 4×8-foot panels.

Privacy screens are freestanding fences or extensions of a railing system. Make them from the same material as other deck components so that they blend readily with the design. A privacy screen can be a modest wall. Sometimes, a well-placed piece of lattice is all that's needed to create privacy.

If your screen is situated between yourself and a close neighbor, remember how the screen will look from the other side. A well-planned privacy screen takes into account appearances from both sides. Building a trellis that supports a climbing plant such as a clematis or trumpet vine is a good-looking alternative. The trellis structure provides privacy during the early part of the outdoor season. By midsummer, it fills in with a leafy vine covered with blossoms.

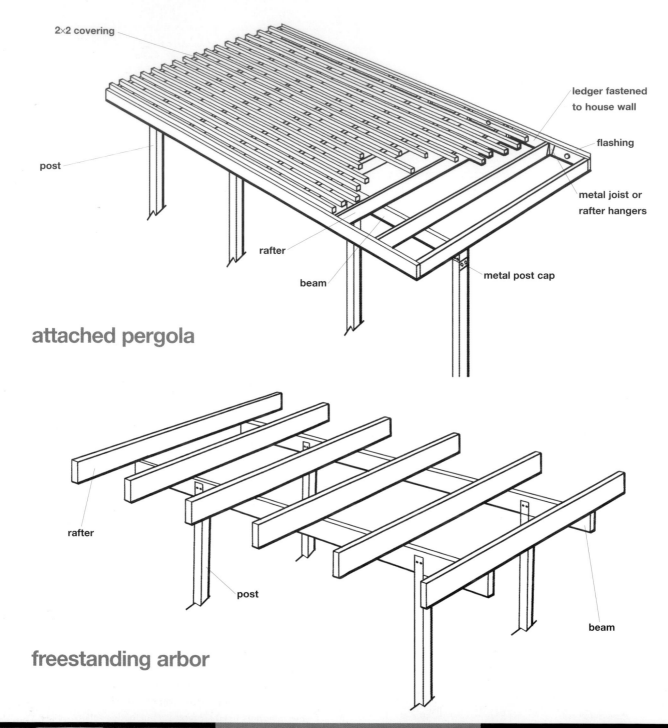

2×2 covering

ledger fastened
to house wall

flashing

post

metal joist or
rafter hangers

rafter

beam

metal post cap

attached pergola

rafter

post

beam

freestanding arbor

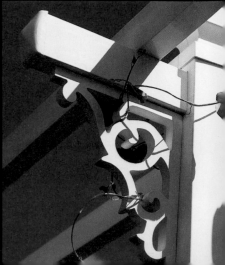

Overhead Beauty

A little imagination turns an arbor or pergola into an architectural statement. Combining 2×2s and flat 1×6s produces an arresting grid pattern, *left.* Fasten the pieces from above with 1-inch corrosion-resistant screws to hide the screw heads. Decorative brackets, *right,* fit in the intersections of posts and beams. They are good-looking and contribute rigidity to the structure. Prefabricated plastic and wooden brackets are available at home improvement stores, but look for quality designs from catalogs often advertised in shelter and home repair magazines.

Overheads

Overhead structures provide shade and define areas of a deck. The most common types are pergolas and arbors. A pergola is attached to a host structure, such as the main house. Pergolas feature a ledger board attached to the side of the house, with joists projecting out from the ledger. Traditionally, an arbor is freestanding.

An overhead has posts for support and a system of joists and cross members, or lath, to create a grid that forms an open roof. The tighter the grid pattern, the more shade the overhead provides. An interesting pattern for the grid enhances the visual appeal.

One way to support an overhead is to extend the posts of your railing system. Consider keeping the bottom of the overhead roof a bit lower than you would for an indoor ceiling. (A standard interior ceiling is 8 feet tall.) Plan for the bottom edges of the joists to be about 7½ feet from the decking platform.

Fasten an overhead securely to the deck substructure and use diagonal braces or brackets at the posts and beams so the structure remains rigid in the hardest winds. Bracing may be

Solid Support

The decorative framing between the posts of this pergola does triple duty—it reinforces the joint between post and beam, it supports the beam span, and it's good looking.

Outdoor Cooking Centers

If you like to cook, eat, and entertain outside on the deck, consider adding a fully equipped cooking center. With all amenities nearby, you won't have to run inside every few minutes to check the progress of steamed vegetables or other courses.

A cooking center is basically a short run of lower cabinets constructed to withstand outdoor climates. These may include sinks, gas or electric cooking appliances, and storage compartments for cooking utensils and cleaning supplies. Choose a cooking center made of materials identical or similar to the materials used to construct the deck or painted to match the overall scheme.

There are many cooktops, refrigerators, rotisseries, and other small appliances that are rated for use in outside environments. Hardy outdoor appliances feature stainless steel, anodized aluminum, or enameled bodies that withstand the rigors of weather and temperature changes. Check with your appliance dealer to ensure the unit you buy is rated for outdoor use.

Make cooking centers 34 to 36 inches high and at least 24 inches wide—the same width as a typical lower kitchen cabinet. Cabinets wider than 36 inches are awkward to reach across. Include at least 18 inches of countertop workspace on either side of a cooktop or sink.

Countertops must be impervious to weather. Solid countertops of weather-resistant redwood or cedar match the materials used for typical deck construction. Solid-surface countertops are durable but may expand and contract due to changes in temperature—make sure your professional fabricator has experience installing solid surface materials in exterior locations. Tile or stone is a good material if it is rated for exterior use. It should be set on a moisture-resistant base, such as cement tile backer installed over ¾-inch exterior-grade plywood. Don't use plastic laminate.

You can install a sink but take care to avoid frozen pipes. Insulate pipes and use valves and faucets rated for outdoor use. The best protection against freezing is common sense. When the outdoor cooking season is over, drain plumbing lines. If you want to entertain on a warm fall or spring day, use your indoor kitchen to supply water.

short pieces of lumber set at an angle and attached to both support posts and roof joists—sometimes called knee braces—or decorative brackets. Cut the ends of joists in decorative shapes for an especially stylish touch. Combine your overhead with a trellis or screen that adds privacy and a sense of enclosure.

Because an overhead is a basic structure with minimal intervening supports, the span of the joists should be calculated carefully. Although the joists of an overhead won't be counted on to carry a "live load" the way a floor must, undersized joists will sag over time. To prevent sagging, the joists must be large enough to support their own weight (see Span Tables, pages 62–63).

Decks around pools

Decks are great companions for swimming pools. They make comfortable surfaces for bare feet, and the weather-resistant nature of decking materials makes them durable surfaces for surrounding a pool. Some synthetic materials (see pages 50–51) include textured anti-slip surfaces ideal for potentially slippery areas. Cedar and redwood tend to be more splinter-free than pressure-treated wood, but these woods are more expensive. Because they are constantly exposed to moisture, even weather-resistant poolside decking materials require special care. Coat both sides of decking with a water sealant prior to installation, and plan to reseal the boards annually for top performance.

Adding a Spa or Hot Tub

A typical round hot tub is 6 feet in diameter and occupies 30 square feet. A rectangular tub takes up about 48 square feet. You'll want to plan additional space for sitting and unobstructed space at least 36 inches wide that allows you to walk around the tub easily—a total of 100 to 150 square feet of deck space. WHEN FULL OF WATER a hot tub may weigh 2 tons. A typical deck won't support that much weight, so include an independent foundation that is engineered by a qualified professional. A typical hot tub foundation is a solid concrete slab 4 to 6 inches thick reinforced with metal bar or reinforcing wire. IF YOU PLAN to set a tub on an existing deck, you'll need to restructure the supporting lumber and place additional footings underneath the tub. SOME BUILDING CODES require that tubs be protected by a fence with a childproof gate that restricts access to the tub area. If a fence with a gate is not possible, you may be able to substitute an approved tub cover with childproof latches.

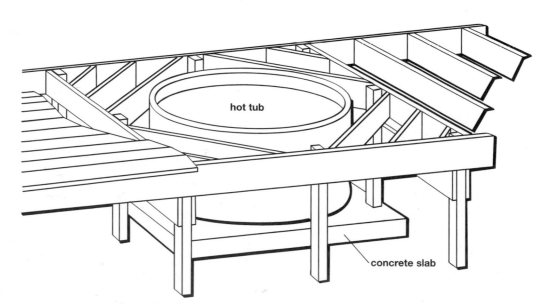

hot tub

concrete slab

A deck is an ideal way to provide access to an above-ground swimming pool. Add privacy screens, overhead shade structures, and cabanas for housing pool toys or for hanging up towels. Remember that most building codes require that pools be surrounded by childproof fences and gates. Check with your local building department so that any protective measures are incorporated in your final landscaping and deck-building plans.

You'll also need to plan for electrical and plumbing systems and for equipment such as water heaters and filters. If located beneath the deck, equipment should be accessible through a removable or hinged panel.

Outdoor lighting

A well-designed outdoor lighting system provides light that allows you to use your deck in comfort and safety during the evening. It should illuminate key points such as conversation areas, cooking centers, doors, walkways, pool surrounds, and stairs. Use outdoor lighting fixtures to highlight special features, such as plants or trees, and to provide security lighting around foundation plantings and fences.

The two most popular types of outdoor lighting are standard fixtures that use 120-volt household current and low-voltage lighting. Low-voltage lighting is popular because it is safe, inexpensive, and easy to install. It comes in an array of styles and configurations made for outdoor use. You'll find freestanding units and specialized units for fastening to posts, railings, and stair risers.

When planning a lighting scheme, keep the design flexible. Use several circuits, and include dimmer switches to vary the amount of light in individual areas. Place switches indoors. If you also want switches outdoors, install 3-way switches. To avoid annoying glare, hide the light bulb from direct view using shades, covers, or plantings. You can also direct the light to bounce off large reflective surfaces, such as walls, to reduce glare.

An outdoor lighting scheme usually is a combination of several lighting techniques. The most common types are:

DOWN LIGHTING is placed on poles, in trees, or on the sides of houses. It shines directly onto surfaces and is used for general illumination and safety.

PASSAGE LIGHTING is used to illuminate pathways and stairs. Typically, a series of small downlights are used to lead the way along a defined route.

UP LIGHTING is typically created by placing fixtures low to the ground and directed upward. Up lighting is used for dramatic effect and to highlight individual objects such as unusual trees or garden sculptures.

AREA LIGHTING illuminates larger surfaces such as lawns, patios, and decks. Area lighting usually employs several types of lighting to produce overall light that creates a pleasant atmosphere and enhances the setting.

Lighting with Style

Handsome outdoor fixtures, such as the Craftsman-era reproduction *above*, are attractive both day and night. An ingenious cubbyhole allows the fixture *below* to be set inside a railing. Wires run in channels cut in the sides of the posts.

4. materials

BUILDING A DECK IS PRACTICALLY A NATIONAL PASTIME. Lumber mills and manufacturers have responded to the ongoing demand for materials with a variety of products made specifically for deck construction. Some materials, such as redwood and cedar, are traditional favorites of deck builders. Others, such as plastic and synthetic components, are gaining reputations for quick installation and a long, maintenance-free life. Engineered, rust-proof fasteners, such as quick-driving screws and corrosion-resistant lumber connectors, provide strength and durability. Best of all, railings, posts, and decorative accessories are widely available, making it easier than ever to add style and character to the most basic deck structures. No matter what materials you choose, do-it-yourself deck-building projects are easier and more efficient than ever before.

Choosing deck materials is part of a planning strategy. Different materials affect the construction of the deck, its final appearance, and the total cost. Remember that a deck usually increases the value of your home—but only if it looks good when you're ready to sell. Learning about the uses for various materials allows you to make informed decisions and to achieve maximum value for your investment.

Understand the types of materials available and you'll make smart decisions in the design and construction of your deck.

parts of
a deck

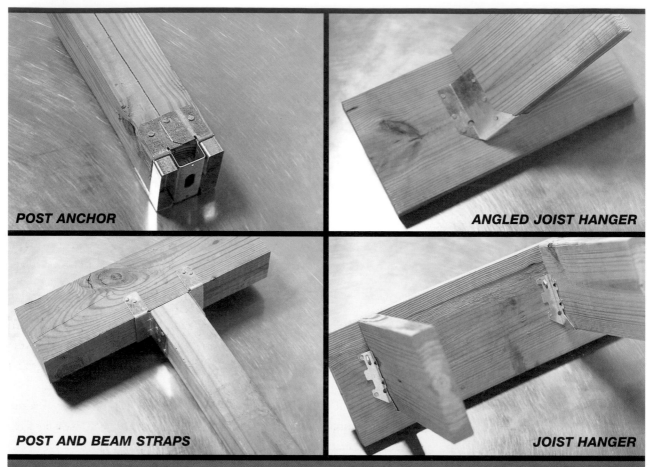

POST ANCHOR

ANGLED JOIST HANGER

POST AND BEAM STRAPS

JOIST HANGER

Lumber Connectors

Galvanized lumber connectors are at the heart of fast, efficient, and strong deck construction. Connectors are specially engineered to withstand climactic changes and occasional stress forces, such as heavy snow loads, high winds, and earthquakes. They are readily available at home improvement centers.

Knowing terms used in deck construction makes it easier to plan, order materials, and oversee any changes to plans that may occur during construction. An understanding of deck terminology also helps communicate effectively with designers, builders, building inspectors, and other professionals that may become involved in your project.

Basically, a deck has two types of components. The supporting members are called the *substructure*. Wood used to make the substructure must be strong, durable lumber. Pressure-treated wood combines high strength, moisture resistance, and reasonable cost. For the most part, the substructure is hidden from view beneath the deck. All other deck parts are *finish* components that are exposed to view.

Substructure

FOOTINGS are cubes or cylinders of poured concrete that extend into the ground. According to building codes, they must extend past the frost line so that freezing and thawing cycles won't disturb the position of the footings. In northern climates, a typical footing will be 36 to 42 inches deep. Footings support individual posts, and the location of the footings depends on the size and shape of the deck.

PIER BLOCKS are made of concrete and usually are about 8 inches on each side. Precast pier blocks are set on top of footings while the footing concrete is still wet. Pier blocks elevate the posts and keep them from coming in contact with the ground to prevent rot and moisture damage. Some pier blocks include galvanized metal lumber hardware to provide a secure connection to posts.

POSTS extend up from the footings and form the vertical supports for a deck. The thickness of the post depends on the configuration of the deck structure. Posts should be made of pressure-treated lumber to prevent rot and insect attack. Tall posts, such as those for second-story decks, need angled supports called *bracing* to provide stability.

BEAMS are large pieces of lumber used to support joists. Beams attach to the tops of posts and run at right angles to the joists. Beams can be made of solid wood or fabricated on site from two pieces of framing lumber. Like all structural components, beams made from pressure-treated lumber combine strength and durability.

JOISTS form a grid for supporting the decking material. Joists are 1½ inches thick, often called "two-by" or "nominal 2x" lumber. The joists that run around the perimeter of a deck are called *rim* joists. Typically, rim joists are doubled to provide firm, substantial support around the edges of the deck. Rim joists running parallel to the ledger and used to support one end of the interior joist system are *header* joists.

LEDGER BOARD is a joist mounted against the side of a house to provide support for one end of a deck. The ledger is bolted or screwed to the house and the space behind the ledger is sealed with caulk and covered with flashing to prevent water from penetrating to the interior of the house.

Finish Components

FASCIA BOARD is an optional treatment made from low-grade, pressure-treated lumber used to disguise rim joists. A typical fascia is a nominal 1-inch-thick board made from a good-looking wood such as redwood or cedar. An option is to use a nominal 2-inch, high-quality pine or cedar as the outer rim joist in place of fascia. This type of framing member contributes strength and an attractive appearance. The outer joist may then be stained or sealed to match other finish components. Fascia is often mitered at the corners for a clean, finished look.

DECKING installs over joists and forms the main walking surface of a deck. It is made of wood or synthetic materials especially designed to withstand weather and to resist splintering. Decking is usually installed flat and is fastened with galvanized nails, screws, or hidden fasteners called deck clips (for more information, see page 48). Decking boards are spaced ⅛ to ³⁄₁₆ of an inch apart to provide drainage and to allow for contraction and expansion of the wood.

STAIR AND RAILING SYSTEMS are safety features and a major component of design. They both have posts for support, horizontal rails, and vertical balusters set between the rails. Stairs include treads and risers.

BUILT-INS AND OVERHEADS are ancillary structures that provide shade, permit growing plants, provide additional seating, and help give a deck character.

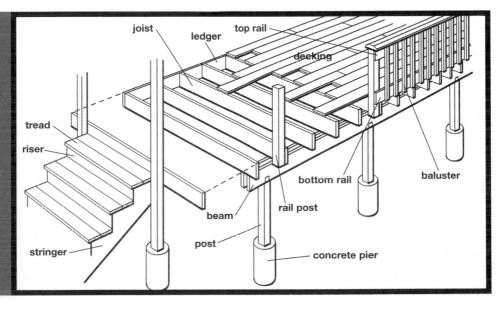

Parts of a Deck

A basic deck is a simple structure with a minimum of components and connections. Structural members—footings, posts, beams, joists, and ledgers—are strong pieces of lumber that support the deck. Finish components such as decking, railings, and stairs give a deck its visual appeal and provide safety features.

Use concrete to make footings to support posts and to make landing pads for stairs. Of all the tasks of deck building, working with concrete is one of the most strenuous and demanding. Fortunately, you should be able to pour all footings in about a day or two. Once the concrete work is complete, the physical labor gets easier.

Prepackaged concrete mix

Concrete comes in a number of forms. The most practical is dry, prepackaged concrete mix. It is available at home improvement centers and comes in 40-, 60-, or 80-pound bags. A 40-pound bag makes approximately one-third cubic foot (c.f.) of wet concrete; a 60-pound bag makes one-half c.f. These precise measurements make it easy to estimate the number of bags of concrete you'll need (see chart *below*).

Mix prepackaged concrete with water to form wet, ready-to-use concrete. Mix the ingredients in a wheelbarrow or rent an electric concrete mixer. A wheelbarrow is good for preparing small batches—no more than three 40 lb. bags at one time, or about the amount needed to fill an average-size footing hole. If you use a wheelbarrow, make sure it sits level on the ground—the considerable weight of the concrete and the vigorous action required to mix it will readily tip an unbalanced wheelbarrow. Pour the dry, prepackaged ingredients into the wheelbarrow, then add water from a garden hose in small amounts until the correct consistency is reached. Mix the ingredients thoroughly, using a garden hoe to rake the mixture back and forth.

If there are more than a dozen footing holes, consider renting an electric mixer. A rented mixer has a large mixing drum that is turned by an electric motor. This is a heavy, stable piece of equipment capable of mixing several cubic feet of concrete at once. Because it offers a continuous mixing action, the concrete batch stays pliable longer than if allowed to sit in a wheelbarrow. The drawbacks are that you have to visit a rental shop to get one, you have to pay a rental fee (typically $35–$75 a day), and you need a way to transport the mixer to your job site. Once at the job site, you probably need a helper to lift the mixer in and out of your vehicle. After the preliminaries, however, an electric concrete mixer is a real back-saver.

Concrete options

Another way to make concrete is to buy Portland cement, sand, and aggregate in bulk form and mix your own. If you are preparing large amounts of concrete, this may be a way to save some money, but the prepackaged preparations are much more convenient and take the guesswork out of measuring each ingredient.

You can also buy wet, premade concrete from a ready-mix concrete dealer. These dealers will provide a trailer that can be hitched to your vehicle for hauling the concrete. A trailer typically holds a cubic yard of concrete (27 cubic feet). While having a ready supply of professionally mixed, wet concrete at your disposal sounds like a good idea, consider this carefully. You need a wheelbarrow to transport the concrete from the trailer (that's usually parked in a driveway) to the job site (that's often in the back yard). Also, you want to work fast to prevent the unused concrete from hardening before you can pour it all into the footing holes because concrete more than 90 minutes old is unusable. Some concrete dealers charge additional fees if the trailer needs to be cleaned.

Estimating Concrete

To estimate the amount of concrete needed, use the formula for finding the volume of a cylinder. In this formula, the height refers to the height of the hole, expressed in inches. The radius is one half the diameter of the hole—cardboard tube footing forms in 8- or 10-inch diameters make obtaining the radius simple. The formula uses the handy geometrical multiplier pi, expressed mathematically as 3.14. Therefore, volume = height x (3.14 x r^2). If this is too much math, use the quick-reference chart, *right*.

Hole hgt. in inches	Tube dia. in inches	Cu. ft. of concrete	No. of 40lb. bags needed	No. of 60lb. bags needed
24	8	.70	2	1.5
24	10	1	3	2
36	8	1	3	2
36	10	1.7	5	3.5
42	8	1.2	4	3
42	10	2	6	4

Working with concrete

Concrete begins to harden shortly after it's mixed. Pour each batch immediately. As soon as a footing is complete, add necessary hardware such as post anchors and j-bolts (see pages 54–55). After all the footings are poured, wait 48 hours for the uncured or "green" concrete to set thoroughly before continuing work. Subjecting green footings to any stresses, such as dropped timbers or hammer blows, risks cracking or chipping the footings.

Proper consistency

Knowing when concrete is ready to pour is easy. First, make sure all dry ingredients are mixed into the batch completely. Carefully "comb" through the mixture with a garden hoe to look for pockets of dry ingredients and blend them into the batch. Properly mixed concrete is thick but pliable. It cuts readily with the edge of a trowel but won't stick to the trowel blade. When you run the flat part of the blade over the mixture, the result should be a smooth, uniform surface. If the concrete is too dry, it will be stiff and crumbly; add more water. If it's too wet, it will be soupy and unworkable with a trowel; add more dry ingredients to thicken the batch. When the batch is ready, use it at once before it begins to harden. Between batches, wash off excess concrete from tools to prevent the mixture from hardening.

pressure-treated wood

Pressure-treated wood is saturated with chemicals that resist moisture, decay, and attack from insects. It is made from readily available woods, such as fir or pine, that combine strength with low-cost. Pressure-treated wood is ideal for outdoor use.

Pressure-treated wood features a pale green color that generally fades to dark gray over time. The color comes from chromated copper arsenate (CCA) used to treat the wood. CCA is classified as a pesticide and makes the wood unusable as a source of food for wood-eating insects and the types of fungi that cause rot. Occasionally, CCA wood comes from the factory stained brown to disguise the green color.

The term "pressure-treated" comes from the process that adds the chemicals to the wood. After it is milled to its final size and dried to about 20 percent moisture content, the lumber is placed in large, airtight steel chambers. Liquid preservatives are introduced into the chamber using intense air pressure that forces the chemicals into the wood fibers. Lumber manufacturers have standards that determine how far the preservative chemicals must penetrate into the wood to be effective. For wood less than 1-inch thick, penetration is complete. In thicker woods, however, the center of the lumber usually remains untreated. For this reason it is important to apply a preservative or sealer to the ends of freshly cut pressure-treated boards.

Pressure-treated lumber is readily available at home improvement centers and lumber yards. It is rated by the

Pressure-Treated Ratings

Most pressure-treated lumber is clearly marked with a label indicating the amount of chemical in the wood. This 2×4 is rated for direct contact with the ground.

amount of chemical allowed to penetrate the wood. You can find the rating on the lumber grade stamp on each piece of lumber:

.25 LB. PER CUBIC FOOT is the least amount of chemical used to treat the wood. This type is intended for above ground use only.

.40 LB. PER CUBIC FOOT is rated for direct contact with the ground. This is the most common type of pressure-treatment.

.60 LB. PER CUBIC FOOT is required for building below-grade wood foundations and is recommended for deck support posts. However, it is usually not required by building codes and may be available only by special order.

Pressure-treated wood is used to make most deck parts, including lumber for substructure and finish components such as railings, posts, finials, and decking. Contrary to popular belief, pressure-treated wood is not maintenance free. If it is used for finish components, it must be coated at least every two years with a clear sealer or stain to prevent excessive checking and splintering.

Despite the strength of pressure-treated lumber, the medium-grade woods used to produce it usually contain knots, chips, and other defects, making it less attractive than finish-grade

How Safe is Pressure-Treated Wood?

Pressure-treated wood is saturated with chromated copper arsenate (CCA) to make it resistant to rot and decay. Reputedly, it is safe to handle, is not dangerous to plants, and will not leach into groundwater. However, observe commonsense precautions when working with pressure-treated wood. Wear a dust mask and eye protection while cutting it. To prevent releasing toxins into the air, never burn pressure-treated wood. Dispose of the scraps by putting them in the garbage. Wash your hands after handling the material.

4×4 is usually used for posts

4×6 for posts and beams

2×4 for general construction

4×6 rated for direct contact with the ground

2×6 for joists and general construction

2×10 for joists, ledgers, and beams

woods, such as redwood or cedar. Also, some species of wood used for pressure-treated material, such as fir, have a greater tendency to split and crack over time. Although these minor defects cause no loss of strength, most deck builders prefer to use pressure-treated wood exclusively for structural members such as posts, beams, and joists. Because these components are mostly hidden from view, the appearance of the material is not a concern. The structural members can then be covered with decking, railings, and overhead structures made from more attractive materials.

Most of your deck will be a large, flat surface—the decking. Because decking is such a prominent feature, it should be attractive, durable, smooth, and free of defects such as cracks and splinters. Traditionally, decking is made from wood. Wood decking is easy to work with, is readily available, and comes in a range of prices to fit any budget.

The most popular wood decking is radius-edged decking (RED). RED is made specifically for decks. It features soft, rounded edges that limit splintering and are comfortable underfoot. RED usually is made from high grades of wood and features few knots and other defects.

RED is called "five-quarter" material because it has a thickness of about 1¼ inches. This thickness means the boards have great strength when installed over joists that are 16 inches on-center. RED is available in nominal 6-inch widths (with an actual width of 5½ inches). This width is ideal for decking—narrower boards require excessive labor to install; wider boards tend to crack and split excessively after exposure to the elements.

Before RED became popular, wood decking primarily was made from nominal 1-inch lumber (referred to as 1× or "one-by") that is actually ¾-inch thick. Standard 2-inch lumber (also called 2x or "two-by") is 1½ inches thick. Both these lumber sizes are widely used for general construction but have drawbacks as decking material. They have squared edges that tend to splinter and split. Also, certain species of one-by material may be close to its span limits when placed over joists 16 inches on-center. As a result, the deck may feel springy. Two-by material is more costly, heavy, and difficult to work with.

Several species of wood decking offer attractive grain patterns and colors. However, almost all woods turn silvery gray after months of exposure to the elements. Preserving the

Tropical Woods and Rain Forests

Beautiful tropical woods such as ipé are increasingly available throughout North America. Their use, however, raises the question of possible rain forest destruction. If you are concerned, it's best to look for wood that is certified to have come from sustainable tree plantations. Check the Certified Forest Products Council in Beaverton, Oregon (www.certifiedwood.org) or SmartWood (www.smartwood.org) for more information.

original color of attractive woods requires a yearly maintenance schedule of cleaning and applying sealers or stains (for more information, see Finishing Decks, pages 138–141).

REDWOOD is naturally resistant to rot and decay. For best performance it should be treated with clear sealers once a year. It is a soft wood with a distinctive reddish hue and features a tight, uniform grain pattern that is exceptionally good looking. Lower grades of redwood have creamy-colored streaks—the sapwood. Sapwood is vulnerable to decay. To ensure longevity, limit the amount of sapwood in your redwood deck. Although redwood is also an excellent paint-grade wood, the cost of redwood suggests it should be used in its natural state for best effect. Unfortunately, redwood is increasingly rare and generally not available east of the Rocky Mountain states.

CEDAR is a lightweight wood that is naturally resistant to rot and decay. It is reddish or tan and features streaks of cream and brown with occasional knots. It cuts and shapes easily. Cedar is plentiful and grows as an indigenous species throughout North America, ensuring its availability at local

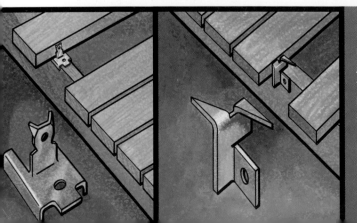

Deck Clips

Deck clips are used to attach decking to joists so that the fasteners remain hidden from view. Decking installed with clips presents a continuous, unblemished surface. Most have a tab for fastening the clip to framing and a pointed spike used to secure the decking. They also provide correct spacing between boards.

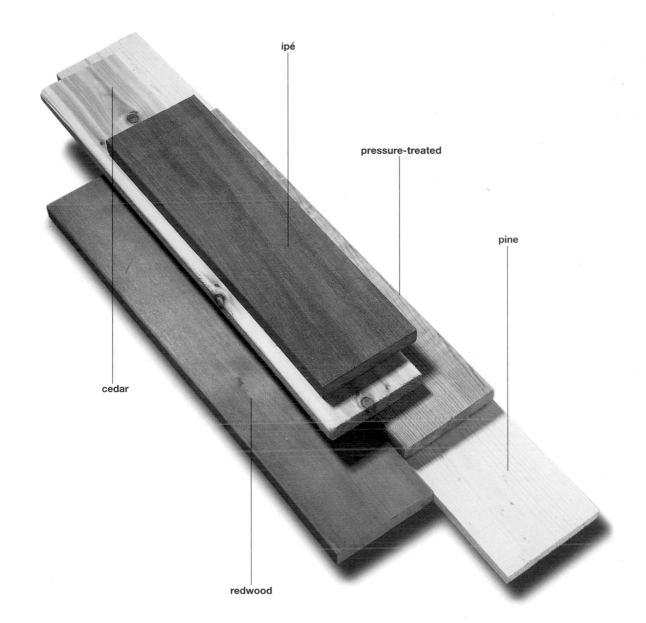

ipé

pressure-treated

pine

cedar

redwood

lumber yards and home improvement centers. It is more expensive than pressure-treated varieties of wood.

UNTREATED PINE is not resistant to rot and decay and should be coated with a clear sealer, stained, or painted prior to installation. It is a soft, lightweight wood with an even grain pattern that cuts and shapes easily. Untreated pine is not available as radius-edged decking (RED) and comes in nominal 1- or 2-inch thickness.

PRESSURE-TREATED WOOD is widely used as decking material. It is strong and the cost is low compared to other decking materials. It comes in either a green or brown color that some find unattractive. However, it can be stained or painted. Pressure-treated RED has few knots and features rounded edges to prevent splintering.

SOUTH AMERICAN IPÉ and other tropical hardwoods marketed as deck materials are increasingly popular, despite a hefty price tag. These woods are dense, extremely durable, and highly resistant to weather and insect attack. They are stronger than other decking materials of the same dimension, which means milling to ¾ thickness is not necessary. A nominal 1-inch board will perform better than thicker domestic woods. Ipé has a rich, lustrous, dark reddish color.

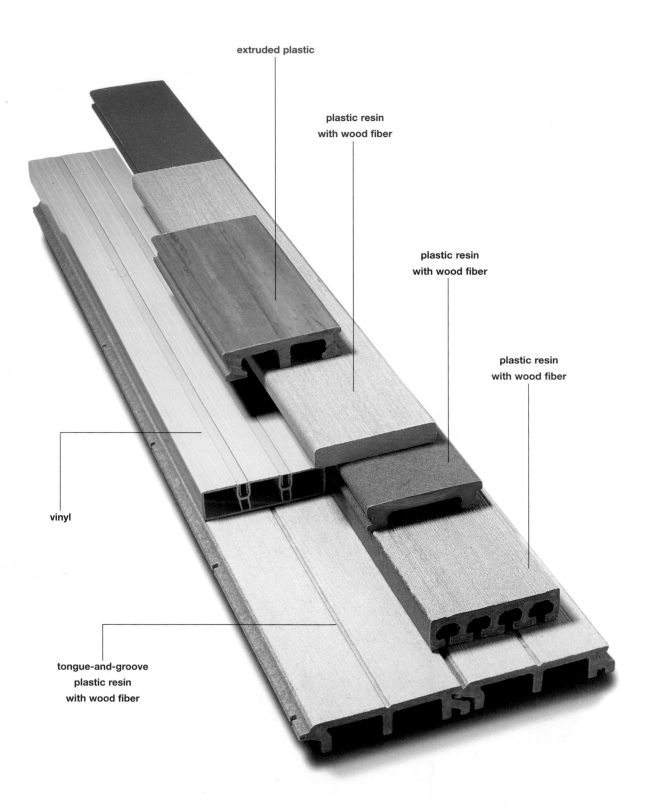

extruded plastic

plastic resin
with wood fiber

plastic resin
with wood fiber

plastic resin
with wood fiber

vinyl

tongue-and-groove
plastic resin
with wood fiber

Synthetic decking material is increasingly popular. Planks made from synthetics are uniform in size and color, won't chip, splinter, or warp, are completely waterproof, and are virtually maintenance-free. To anyone who labors with a yearly ritual of swabbing a wood deck with protective sealer, maintenance-free decking can sound very attractive. One drawback is price—synthetic decking is about twice as expensive as regular grades of pressure-treated or cedar decking. Also, synthetic planks must be used strictly for decking, never for structural components. For synthetic planks, most manufacturers recommend a maximum joist spacing of 16 inches on-center.

Today's marketplace is crowded with many types of synthetic decking materials from a variety of manufacturers. Viewing cross-sections of individual pieces reveals an array of structural designs—some pieces are honeycombed with separate chambers; some are hollow; others are solid. Each varies in the way it is to be installed. Some are fastened with traditional screws or nails; others require special hidden clips that attach to the joists and hold the planks in position. A few are made with interlocking edges or tongue-and-groove fittings. Check the specifications and manufacturer's recommendations for the type you are considering.

New types and combinations of materials are produced every year, but the two main types include:

WOOD/PLASTIC COMPOSITES are made from a mixture of wood fibers and plastic resins. The result is a dense, heavy board that has some flexibility, and it can be cut, shaped, and nailed like natural wood. Composites mimic the grain patterns and colors of real wood. The top surface features a special slip-resistant texture. Manufacturers often make a major contribution to recycling efforts by using 50 to 100 percent post-consumer wood products and plastics to produce composite decking. Some manufacturers use chips of aromatic cedar so that the decking smells like real wood.

VINYL AND PLASTIC DECKING is made from polyvinyl chloride (PVC) or recycled plastics. It is lightweight, strong, weatherproof, and maintenance-free. Its appearance is quite different from wood, and the smooth surface produced during manufacturing must be etched to provide slip resistance. It is primarily made in three colors—white, tan, or gray.

Synthetic decking is available in two thickness, ¾ and a nominal 2-inch material that is 1½ inches thick. Almost all synthetics are made a nominal 6 inches wide. Color choices are limited, although some types accept oil-based stains. Left exposed to the elements, most synthetics will fade over time, but the color change is uniform throughout the deck.

Prices for synthetics range near the middle of the decking marketplace. At $2 to $4 per linear foot of 1×6 or 2×6 material, they are cheaper than redwood or ipé but more expensive than cedar and pressure-treated pine or fir.

Hidden Fasteners

Several types of synthetic decking are engineered for unique installations. The vinyl decking shown here includes narrow channels with sliding covers. At *left,* a worker installs the decking by driving screws inside the channels to the joists below. After securely fastening each synthetic wood plank, you can slide the channel covers into place, *right,* hiding both the channel and the screw head. Removable end caps keep the channels in place yet allow the channel covers to slide back in the event the decking needs replacement.

Prefabricated posts, post caps, railings, stairs, and skirting provide great flexibility for adding style to deck design. Premade parts are manufactured in all typical decking materials—redwood, cedar, pressure-treated pine and fir, plastic, wood/plastic composites, and vinyl. Most are readily available at home improvement centers and lumber yards. Before finalizing a design, visit your local home improvement center or lumber yard to see what's available. For more choices, ask a sales representative for a catalog.

REDWOOD AND CEDAR PARTS are precisely machined from high-grade woods to produce smooth, blemish-free surfaces with crisp details. They must be carefully treated with clear sealers, stains, or paints before installation. These parts usually are not available at neighborhood home improvement centers. Instead, you must ask for them at lumber yards or look for advertisements in home/shelter magazines. Expect to pay a premium price for top-quality redwood or cedar parts.

PLASTIC AND VINYL PARTS are widely available. You can choose from various post, hand rail, and baluster styles and create modular sections of railings for deck sides and stairs. They are weatherproof and maintenance-free. By themselves, most of these materials do not meet standards of safety for railings. As a result, the posts and hand rails include cores of galvanized steel strong enough to pass building codes. The steel itself is bolted or screwed to joists to give the system the necessary strength.

WOOD/PLASTIC COMPOSITES are durable and maintenance-free. Most install using techniques similar to those used to install wood deck parts—check the manufacturer's recommendations. Composite railings and posts are often hollow, making them lightweight and easy to work with. Their hollow bodies makes them ideal for adding wires for stereo speakers and low-voltage outdoor lighting. The wood/plastic composites cut with regular power tools. Because of their partial wood content, they weather to a silvery gray in three or four months of exposure to weather.

PRESSURE-TREATED WOOD PARTS also are widely available. There are usually only a few styles to choose from, but the parts themselves are strong, long-lasting, and inexpensive. However, pressure-treated wood often is lower grades of fir or pine that have a tendency to twist and warp when exposed to weather cycles. When choosing parts made from pressure-treated wood, take the time to select individual pieces carefully. Choose only parts that are straight and free of defects including knots, chips, and cracks. If you are staining or painting deck railings or other components, do so prior to installation. Let parts dry thoroughly for two weeks in a protected environment, such as a garage, prior to finishing. That way, each piece receives a protective coating on every surface. Plan to reapply stain or paint every two years.

STEEL OR ANODIZED ALUMINUM is used primarily to make railings that mimic wrought iron. This type of system can be used with either wood or metal posts. The result is a strong and durable railing with an unusual design twist. Before committing to this type of railing, check with your local building department about using metal railings on your deck.

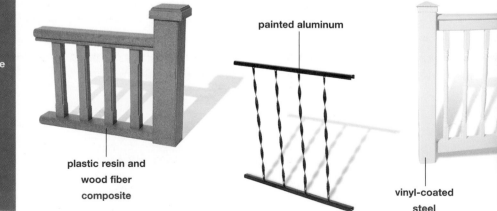

Modular Railings

Premade railing systems combine design flair and convenience. Manufacturers usually offer several choices of colors and styles of rails, balusters, and posts that can be combined a variety of ways.

plastic resin and wood fiber composite

painted aluminum

vinyl-coated steel

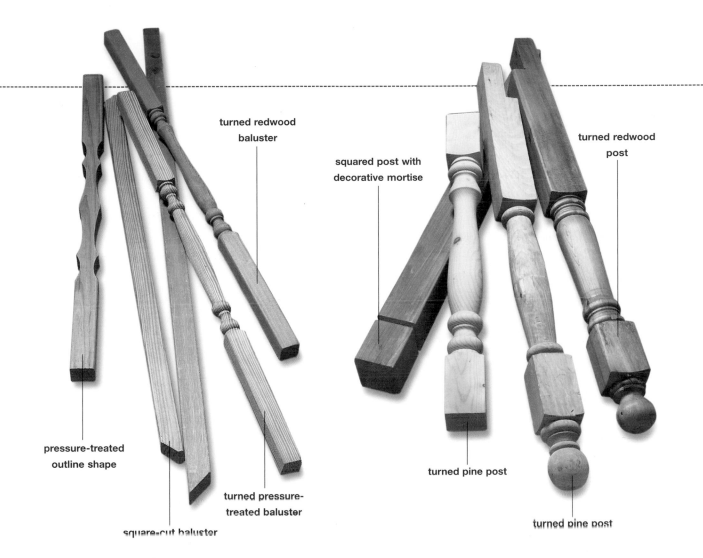

turned redwood baluster

squared post with decorative mortise

turned redwood post

pressure-treated outline shape

turned pine post

turned pressure-treated baluster

square-cut baluster

turned pine post

Posts and balusters

Railing parts come in every style imaginable and are made from different materials. The simplest types—and least expensive—are square-cut posts and balusters. Railings made from square-cut pieces blend readily with many architectural house styles. Turned balusters and posts are more refined and harmonize with Victorian and neoclassical designs. Some types of balusters feature outline shapes cut only on opposite sides. While inexpensive, these balusters produce a lively pattern.

Finials and caps

Even a plain railing system can receive the royal treatment when posts are topped with decorative finials and caps. Finials come in many shapes designed to fit standard 4×4 and 6×6 posts. Decorative caps cover post tops and provide the added benefit of protecting vulnerable end grain from the elements. Some finials include lag screws—a hole is drilled into the top of the post and the finial is screwed into position. Run a small bead of silicone caulk around the bottom edge of the finial before installation to prevent water from seeping underneath and causing damage.

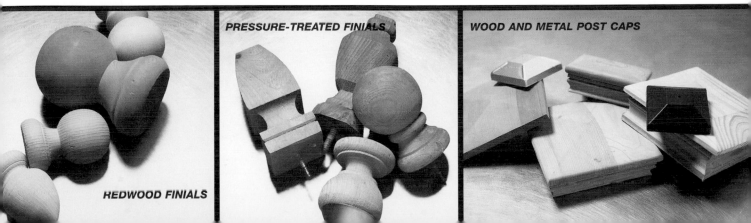

REDWOOD FINIALS

PRESSURE-TREATED FINIALS

WOOD AND METAL POST CAPS

Constructing your deck requires the use of many different kinds of fasteners. Because decks are exposed to outdoor environments, choose hot-dipped galvanized or another type of corrosion-resistant fastener rated to withstand exterior use. Stainless steel fasteners are expensive but afford the best protection against corrosion and staining. They are recommended for building decks in marine climates. Follow these general guidelines for using fasteners:

• When driving screws or nails within 1 inch of the end of a board, predrill to prevent splitting.

• Don't nail into the end grain if you can avoid doing so; end grain does not hold nails well.

• After predrilling holes for bolts, saturate the inside of the hole with sealer or preservative.

• When installing decking, make sure nail or screw heads are driven below the surface of the wood.

Attaching to concrete

EXPANSION SHIELDS AND LAG BOLTS are some of the most common heavy-duty concrete fasteners. The shield is a soft casing made of lead alloy that comes in various diameters. To use the shield, drill a hole into the concrete using a properly sized masonry bit. Then tap the shield into place. Pass a lag bolt through a hole in the workpiece (typically a piece of lumber) and insert it into the shield. Turning the lag bolt causes the shield to expand and wedge against the hole, securing the workpiece.

J-BOLTS are designed to be inserted into wet concrete. They have a special hooked end that ensures they won't pull out once the concrete is set. Typically, j-bolts are used to fasten post anchors to footings. After the footings are poured, insert the j-bolts so that the threaded end remains above the concrete. A post anchor attaches to the j-bolt.

CONCRETE NAILS are especially hard and are made to penetrate concrete while withstanding repeated blows from heavy hammers. They are effective fasteners, but they are not recommended for supporting structural members, such as attaching a ledger to a concrete foundation. Sinking a concrete nail in hardened concrete takes skill and accuracy—one errant hammer blow will bend the nail.

Fastening lumber

LAG BOLTS have threaded shafts similar to screws, but their heads are hexagonal so the bolt can be turned with a wrench or ratcheting socket set. They provide excellent holding power. Because the shaft of a lag bolt is large, predrilling is necessary. Use a drill bit that is no more than three-quarters the diameter of the bolt. For a ½-inch bolt, use a ⁵⁄₁₆-inch drill bit. Slip a galvanized washer under the bolt head to prevent crushing the workpiece when tightening the bolt.

CARRIAGE BOLTS come in many diameters and lengths and are designed to pass completely through all workpieces. A nut turned onto the end of the bolt draws the workpieces tightly together. Drill a hole that is ¹⁄₁₆ inch larger than the diameter of the carriage bolt you are using. The head of a carriage bolt includes a special square collar designed to be drawn into the wood and prevent the shaft of the bolt from rotating during tightening. No washer is necessary at the head of the bolt; use one behind the nut. After they are installed, check carriage bolts periodically to make sure they remain tight.

POWER-DRIVEN SCREWS are used with electric screwdrivers and drills fitted with either square-drive or Phillips-head screw-driving tips. They are convenient to use, have considerable holding power, are reversible, and have taken the place of nails for many carpentry jobs. Their

GALVANIZED LAG BOLTS

LAG SHIELDS

CARRIAGE BOLTS

specially shaped heads are designed to be self-countersinking. Clamp workpieces together to prevent traveling, the tendency of one board to ride up on the spiral screw shank and pull away from the other board.

NAILS have been around for thousands of years and do an excellent job of securing workpieces together. They are inexpensive and require only a hammer for driving. Common and box nails have wide heads for superior holding power. Finishing and siding nails have narrow heads that are difficult to detect when driven below the surface of the wood. Joist nails are used for attaching metal lumber connectors and are designed to resist splitting when used at the ends of joists.

Securing decking

POWER-DRIVEN SCREWS are the most popular method of securing decking to joists. You can countersink the heads below the surface of the wood and reverse the screws in the event a board needs replacing. Hardware stores and home improvement centers are well-stocked with various kinds of corrosion-resistant, power-driven screws made especially for decks. Some come in colors to match different woods or stains. For ¾ decking material, choose screws that are 2¼ inches long. For nominal 2-inch decking, use 3½-inch-long screws.

NAILS are an inexpensive way to secure decking, but there is some risk that during installation errant hammer blows (there's bound to be some) will dent and mar the decking surface. Also, the tendency of wood deck boards to shrink and expand during different seasons may loosen ordinary common or box nails, exposing the heads. For secure holding power, use spiral-, twist-, or ring-shank galvanized nails. Use 8d (2½ inch) nails for ¾ decking and 12d (3¼ inch) or 16d (3½ inch) nails for nominal 2-inch-thick material.

J-BOLTS

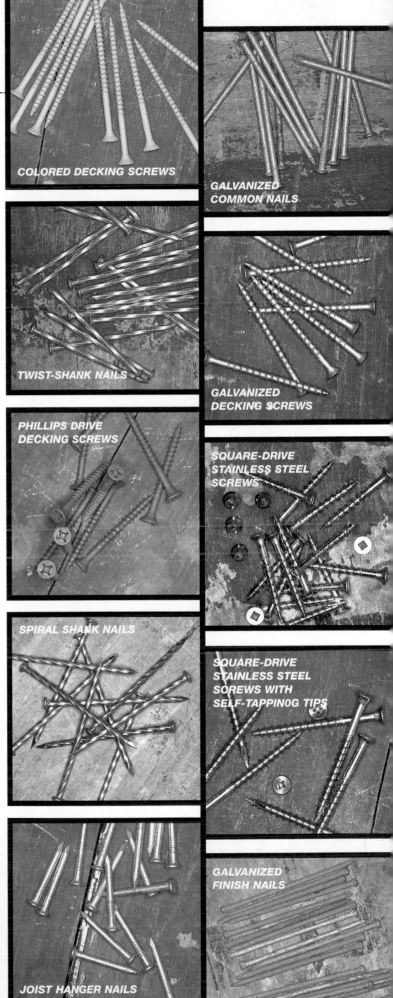

COLORED DECKING SCREWS

GALVANIZED COMMON NAILS

TWIST-SHANK NAILS

GALVANIZED DECKING SCREWS

PHILLIPS DRIVE DECKING SCREWS

SQUARE-DRIVE STAINLESS STEEL SCREWS

SPIRAL SHANK NAILS

SQUARE-DRIVE STAINLESS STEEL SCREWS WITH SELF-TAPPINOG TIPS

JOIST HANGER NAILS

GALVANIZED FINISH NAILS

5. finalizing plans

SOME OF THE MOST USEFUL TOOLS for constructing a deck are the drawings and sketches produced during the planning stage. Getting ideas on paper helps you organize your thoughts and determine how the deck will be used. You can also spot and work out any potential problems before construction begins.

Strive for accuracy and usefulness as you sketch plans rather than concerning yourself with artistic flair. Draw in a style comfortable for you, from simple "bubble diagrams" to full construction drawings. If creating detailed drawings is beyond your skill level, you may need to hire a designer or architect for the final drawings. The more detailed your sketches, however, the more thoroughly you'll understand the construction process. If you use professional builders for any portion of the construction, detailed sketches will help you communicate effectively and efficiently.

After the drawings are completed, use your plans to do materials estimates. With your list of materials, go to home improvement centers and lumber suppliers for cost estimates; these provide a clear picture of budget requirements. Many suppliers offer this service at little or no cost. Be sure to inquire about discounts available for buying large quantities of materials from a single supplier.

Turn ideas into reality with plan sketches that let you work out construction details, estimate materials, and develop a budget.

Drawing plans proceeds in stages. Initial sketches show the size of your deck, where it attaches to the house, and how it fits with other features on the property, such as outbuildings and gardens. Detailed drawings, created using the basic drafting techniques described in this chapter, take into account all local building codes and will enable either you, your contractor, or a professional designer to estimate materials, develop an accurate budget, and establish a timeline for completing the work.

Use drawings to obtain a building permit from your local building and zoning commission. If your plans are not very detailed or you want to ensure they are sound, hire an architect to refine them or have them reviewed by a licensed structural engineer familiar with residential construction (see Working With a Design Professional, page 26).

Bubble diagrams

Detailed drawings are of two basic types: *Plan views* show the site and structure from directly above. *Elevations* are views from the side. Your first drawings, however, can be less formal. The most basic planning tool is a simple plan view

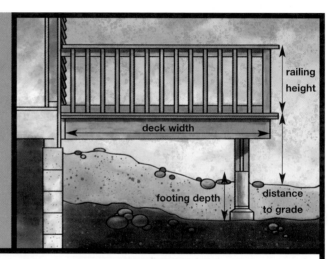

ELEVATION drawings show the deck from the side, *right.* A complete set of elevations shows all sides. Elevations are helpful for designing railing systems, planning stairs, designing cantilevers, and choosing skirting.

PLAN VIEW drawings, *below,* show the deck structure from above. This view is helpful for planning the arrangement of the overall space, determining the relationship between the deck and interior spaces, designing the substructure, arranging deck furniture, and estimating materials.

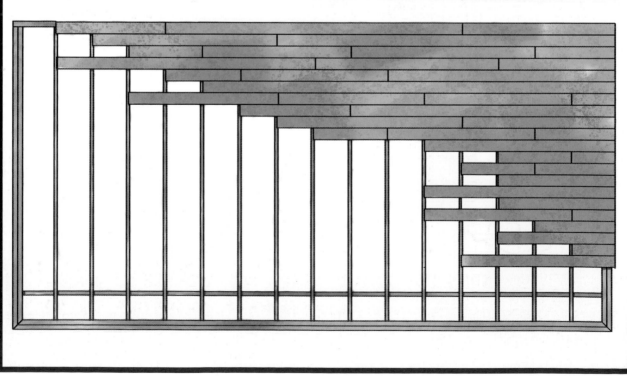

Planning to Code

Knowing basic building codes ensures your deck will be safe and that your plans won't meet opposition from your local building department. Most codes concerning the construction of decks apply to steps, stairways, and guardrails. When it comes to installing framing lumber, using galvanized metal framing connectors almost always ensures your construction methods conform to code.

BUILDING CODES vary from one area of the country to the next. Before you commit to a design element, you should check your local building codes. The following guidelines are generally accepted standards of many codes:

OPEN SIDES OF STEPS, stairways, landings, and decks more than 24 inches above grade must be protected by a guardrail.

SPACING BETWEEN THE RAILINGS (balusters) must be less than 4 inches (a 4-inch diameter ball cannot pass through any opening).

HEIGHT OF THE GUARDRAIL must be at least 36 inches.

THE TRIANGULAR AREA formed by the tread, the riser, and the bottom of the guardrail cannot be larger than 6 inches (a 6-inch diameter ball cannot pass through).

FOR STAIRWAYS, the following guidelines are generally accepted standards used for many local building codes:

THE STAIRWAY MUST BE at least 36 inches wide.

STEPS SHOULD HAVE a maximum rise of 8 inches and a minimum run of 9 inches.

THE TALLEST RISER should not exceed the shortest by more than 1 inch.

STAIRWAYS WITH 4 OR MORE RISERS must have a handrail.

THE TOP OF THE HANDRAIL should be between 34 and 38 inches above the nose of the tread.

THE HANDRAIL SHOULD BE SMOOTH and no more than 2 inches thick.

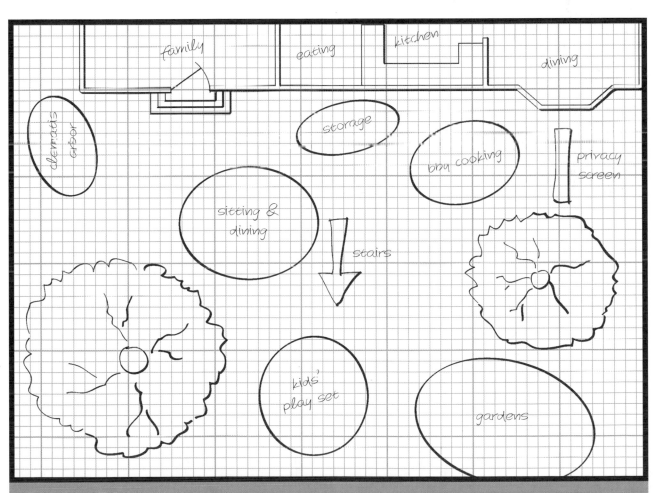

Bubble Diagrams

Use colored pencils to make bubble diagrams that are filled with ideas. Don't worry about making anything too perfect—an eraser makes changes easy. Include ideas that reflect your lifestyle, such as plenty of seating for entertaining guests, access to the kitchen, or areas throughout the yard that make up your outdoor environment.

called a *bubble diagram*. This is an easy, fun way to begin planning a deck, and a preliminary step in creating the final detailed drawings.

Start with the basic plan-view property map described in Chapter 2. Make plenty of photocopies of this view so you can experiment with ideas and make changes. Then, draw circles or "bubbles" to indicate each activity and need in the place you anticipate it will take place throughout the yard. Include main dining areas, locations for stairs and walkways, pergolas and arbors, bench seating, hot tubs, patios, and bar and cooking stations. See how the circles intersect and crowd each other, competing for space. Continue creating fresh drawings, refining and prioritizing your ideas. Let your most important ideas dominate the scheme.

Scale drawings

Use your final bubble drawing as the basis for more refined sketches. Although absolute precision isn't required yet, use the drawing tools described on page 14 to help draw neat, straight lines. If you are experimenting with angled portions of your deck, try basic 45-degree angles. They keep calculations simple, and building them is not difficult. Start by creating a scale drawing in plan view of your house and the area where you'll build your deck. Draw a simple outline of the deck, indicating stairways. Outlines give a close approxima-

tion of space requirements, traffic flows, and the connection of your deck to other outdoor areas, such as gardens and patios. With this plan view, experiment with the elements of a deck: the overall shape, stair location, placement of built-in benches and planters, level changes, seating arrangements, and the location of hot tubs, arbors, or other ancillary structures. The larger the scale of this drawing, the more precisely you'll be able to refine ideas.

Add measurements for the main areas of the deck. When this drawing is complete, make several photocopies. That way, you can compare different design ideas for the finer points, such as decking patterns, without having to erase the basic outline and start over.

Once the basic shape is defined, you're ready to tackle framing diagrams. Use the Span Tables on pages 62–63 to establish the dimensions, lengths, and quantities of the various framing members.

Planning curves

Curves are some of the most visually pleasing and intriguing features of deck design. As you might expect, curves require some special construction techniques; those are described later in this book (pages 109–111).

The essential feature of curved decking is a curved rim joist made from many thin pieces of wood that are individ-

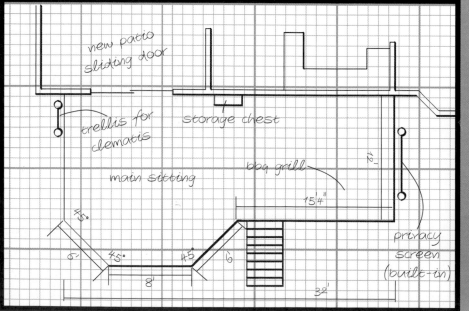

Use graph paper and an architect's ruler (see page 14) to produce a scale drawing of the outline of the deck. Start with an accurate scale drawing of the house, and include basic interior features. Add the deck, indicating the location of stairways and ancillary structures such as privacy screens, trellises, and pergolas.

ually bent and fastened into position. Once constructed, a curved rim joist acts like any perimeter joist—it is a strong structural member that helps support the weight of the deck. Interior joists and railing posts can be attached directly to it.

Because of the intricate construction requirements of these curved sections, it is essential that you contact your building department about approval for curved rim joists. Curved decks are increasingly common and most building departments are familiar with them. However, some departments may have developed their own requirements for building curved joist systems that should be strictly followed. Remember that building a curved rim joist is only part of the overall design. You also must build a curved handrail that will require additional time and expense.

To plan a curve, you'll need a compass and one of your initial plan view drawings. The distance from the metal (fixed)

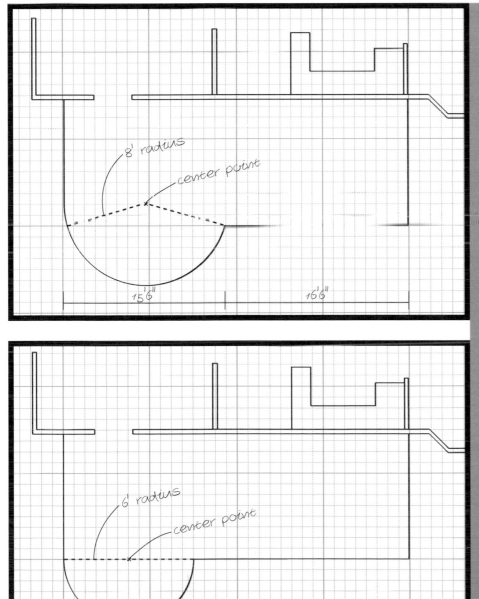

Planning Curves

A curved portion of deck adds distinct character. The curve you design for your deck is a portion of a circle called an arc. You can vary the size and shape of the arc two ways. Altering the length of the radius—the distance from the center of the circle to its edge—changes the size of the circle. A longer radius produces a large circle for making shallow, gentle arcs. A shorter radius makes a more pronounced curve.

You also can vary the location of the center point of the circle. The further away the center point is from the edge of the deck, the smaller the arc will be.

Use a compass and a plan view of the deck to create curves in proportion to the overall design. The construction techniques for curves appear on pages 109–111.

Curved Character
Giving this modest redwood deck a gently curved corner adds lots of style in a minimum amount of space.

point of the compass to the drawing point is the radius of a circle. Use your scale to make this a number that's easy to work with—an even 8 or 10 feet, for example. The portion of the circle that you draw is called the arc.

Experiment with different radii. The larger the radius, the shallower and more gentle the arc of the curve. Shallow arcs are easier to build but occupy more space across the edge of the deck. Choosing the right radius is also affected by personal preference; find an arc that you find pleasing. When you're satisfied that the curve is appropriate to the size and style of your deck, indicate the ends of the arc carefully. When building the curve, you'll use these measurements to determine the center point of your circle. Knowing the cen-

ter point allows you to scribe the ends of the joists for cutting in a circular pattern (for more information, see Building Curves, pages 109-111).

Span tables

First, check with your lumber supplier about what kinds of wood you'll be using. The most common type of lumber used for substructures is pressure-treated Douglas fir or Southern yellow pine. Both are exceptionally strong woods that are easy to work with. In some areas of the country, other types of wood are more readily available and less expensive. Once you've determined what wood you'll be using, check the Wood Strength Chart (below) and note which group it belongs to. Use this group designation when referring to the span tables.

The measurements referred to in the tables indicate the distances that the materials will safely span. The measurements are taken "on-center" or o.c.—from the center of one supporting member to the center of the next.

WOOD STRENGTH CHART
Based on #2 or better grade
GROUP A (strongest): cypress, Douglas fir, western hemlock, western larch, Southern yellow pine, ipé (decking material only)
GROUP B: Western red cedar, white fir, eastern hemlock, lodgepole pine, Norway pine, ponderosa pine, sugar pine, northern white pine, redwood (clear, all-heart), eastern spruce, Sitka spruce
GROUP C (least strong): Northern white cedar, southern white cedar, balsam, redwood (construction heart)

Planning Point—Refining Plans
Don't expect your deck drawings to work out the first time. Typically, a deck plan takes several tries because a variety of interdependent elements must work together to produce satisfactory results. As an example, suppose your initial scale drawing calls for a deck that's 16 feet wide and 22 feet long. You decide you'd like to use a modular railing system that comes in 5-foot-long sections and attaches to posts 3½ inches wide. If you figure 3 sections of railing and 4 posts to enclose one side of your deck, the total length of the railing will be 16 feet 2 inches—2 inches longer than planned. Do you modify the railing to fit the deck, or do you elongate the deck to accommodate the railing? These are some of the questions that careful

drawings will solve. Remember that one of the most important tools of the designer is the eraser. Good design often includes some trial-and-error.

Use a plan view to help complete elevation drawings. Elevations are good ways to work out the details of your railing and stair designs. Elevations are especially important if your deck includes a tall structure such as an arbor or pergola.

When designing, take time to think through all the details. Factor in all elements and recalculate as necessary. Being off an inch might seem like a small mistake, but it can make all the difference between a deck that is constructed efficiently and one that is an endless number of midstream corrections and hasty fix-its.

Decking spans

This is the maximum allowable distance between joists for the most common types of decking material. Boards wider than a nominal 6 inches may develop excessive cupping and checking and are not recommended.

	Group A	Group B	Group C
Untreated 1×6 boards	16"	14"	12"
Pressure-treated 1×6	16"	16"	—
¾" radius-edge decking	16"	16"	16"
Synthetic decking			
—refer to manufacturer's specs—			
Pressure-treated 2×6	24"	24"	24"

Joist spans

This is the maximum allowable distance for joists spanning between beams or between a ledger and a beam. Note that when joists are spaced closer together, they are able to carry more weight and will span longer distances.

Joists spaced 12" o.c.	Group A	Group B	Group C
2×6	10'6"	10'	9'
2×8	14'	12'6"	11'
2×10	17'6"	15'6"	13'6"
2×12	21'	19'	17'6"

Joists spaced 16" o.c.	Group A	Group B	Group C
2×6	9'6"	8'6"	7'6"
2×8	12'6"	11'	10'
2×10	16'	14"	13'
2×12	19'	18'6"	16'

Joists spaced 24" o.c.	Group A	Group B	Group C
2×6	8'6"	7'	6'6"
2×8	11'	9'6"	8'6"
2×10	14'	12'6"	11'
2×12	16'6"	16'	13'6"

Beam spans

This chart shows the maximum allowable distance between support posts for beams of various sizes. When calculating beam spans, you must take into account several variables—the distance between beams (or between a beam and a ledger) and the size of the beam. The farther apart the beams are from each other, the greater the load each must carry. Increasing the load requires either more posts to support the beam you've selected, or larger beams. The final decision often balances common sense with aesthetics (see Beam Configuration on the next page). Fewer beams means having to dig fewer holes for foundation footings. However, you won't want to specify a beam so massive that it's difficult to move and looks awkward and out of scale with other parts of your deck.

A solid beam is preferred. It is also possible to construct an acceptable beam from two pieces of lumber placed side by side and nailed together. The tables below give specifications

GROUP A	If the distance between beams (joist span) is:				
	4'	6'	8'	10'	12'
Beam size	then the max. recommended post spacing is:				
4×6	6'	6'			
(2) 2×8	8'	7'	6'		
4×8	10'	8'	7'	6'	
(2) 2×10	11'	9'	8'	7'	6'
4×10	12'	10'	9'	8'	7'
(2) 2×12	12'	10'	9'	8'	
4×12	12'	11'	10'	9'	

GROUP B	If the distance between beams (joist span) is:				
	4'	6'	8'	10'	12'
Beam size	then the max. recommended post spacing is:				
4×6	6'				
(2) 2×8	7'	6'			
4×8	9'	7'	6'		
(2) 2×10	10'	8'	7'	6'	6"
4×10	11'	9'	8'	7'	6'
(2) 2×12	12'	10'	8'	7'	7'
4×12	12'	10'	9'	8'	

GROUP C	If the distance between beams (joist span) is:				
	4'	6'	8'	10'	12'
Beam size	then the max. recommended post spacing is:				
4×6	6'				
(2) 2×8	7'				
4×8	8'	6'			
(2) 2×10	9'	7'	6'	6'	
4×10	10'	8'	7'	6'	6'
(2) 2×12	11'	9'	7'	7'	6'
4×12	12'	10'	9'	8'	

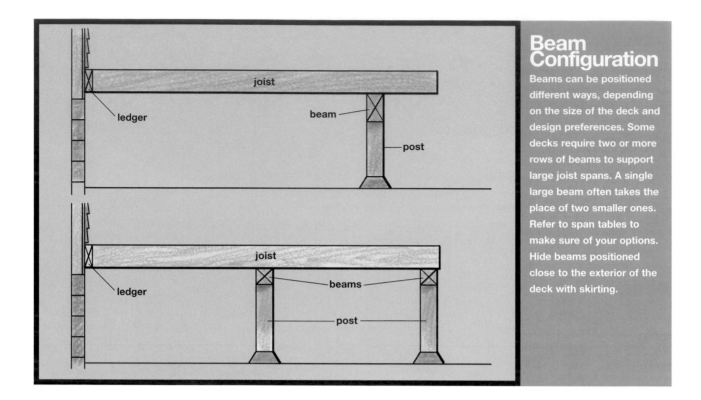

Beam Configuration

Beams can be positioned different ways, depending on the size of the deck and design preferences. Some decks require two or more rows of beams to support large joist spans. A single large beam often takes the place of two smaller ones. Refer to span tables to make sure of your options. Hide beams positioned close to the exterior of the deck with skirting.

for several fabricated beam sizes. If you will be fabricating beams, they must conform to your local building codes (see Fabricating a Beam, page 102).

Post size

The most common post sizes are 4×4, 4×6, and 6×6. Calculate the necessary size by determining the area of the deck the post is required to support (load area) and the height of the post. Find the load area by multiplying the beam spacing by the post spacing. Posts positioned at the perimeter of the deck typically carry only half the load as interior posts. Measure the height of the post from the footing to the point where the post is attached to the beam. To ensure stability, building codes usually require larger (thicker) posts and bracing for decks more than 5 feet above grade. Check with your building department (for more information, see Bracing, page 103).

For aesthetic reasons, keep posts uniform in size. Determine which post carries the heaviest load (usually an interior post in the middle of the deck), calculate the necessary size of that post, and make all posts the same size. For aesthetic reasons, deck designers often specify 6×6 posts even if smaller posts are sufficient. That's because larger posts generally look better and visually give a deck the appearance of stability. To some, 4×4 posts look too spindly.

GROUP A	If the load area (beam spacing × post spacing, in square feet) is equal to or less than:											
	36	48	60	72	84	96	108	120	132	144	156	168
Post size	then the max. recommended post height is:											
4x4	10'	10'	9'	8'	7'	7'	6'	6'	5'	5'	5'	
4x6	14'	12'	11'	10'	9'	9'	8'	8'	7'	7'	7'	6'
6x6	17'	17'	17'	17'	17'	16'	15'	14'	13'	12'	11'	9'

GROUP B,C	If the load area (beam spacing × post spacing, in sq. feet) is equal to or less than:											
	36	48	60	72	84	96	108	120	132	144	156	168
Post size	then the maximum recommended post height is:											
4x4	10'	9'	7'	7'	6'	5'						
4x6	13'	11'	10'	9'	8'	7'	7'	6'	5'	5'		
6x6	17'	17'	17'	15'	9'							

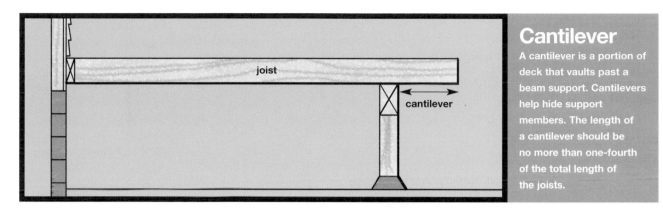

joist

cantilever

Cantilever

A cantilever is a portion of deck that vaults past a beam support. Cantilevers help hide support members. The length of a cantilever should be no more than one-fourth of the total length of the joists.

Cantilever

A cantilever is an unsupported portion of the joist system that projects past a beam. The length of a cantilever should be no more than one-fourth of the total length of the longest joist in the cantilever.

Designing a cantilever is an important aesthetic consideration because it places the substructure behind the front edge of the deck so it is hidden from view. Also, plan cantilevers when designing around trees. With a cantilever, you can install decking material close to the tree trunk but keep posts and footings at a distance to reduce the chances for causing damage to the root structure.

Planning substructure

The next step in refining your plans is working out the details of the substructure. Draw a plan view of the structural system and indicate the location of the ledger, foundation footings, posts, beams, and joists. Next, design the stairs and the railing system, adding those to both the plan and the elevation drawings. When creating planning drawings, follow this sequence:

DRAW THE LEDGER where it is positioned against the house (or the structure to which it is attached). The ledger is a valuable fixed reference point both for creating plans and during the construction phase.

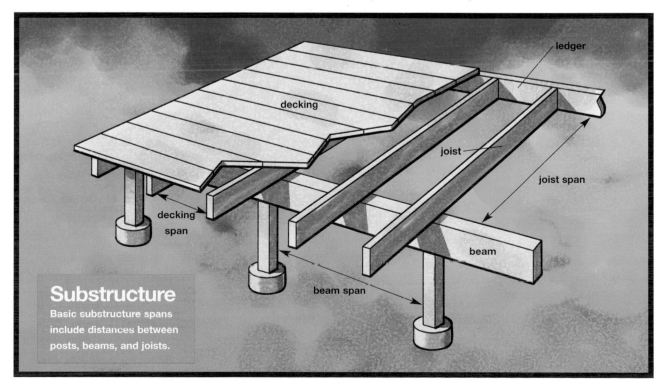

decking

ledger

joist

joist span

decking span

beam span

beam

Substructure

Basic substructure spans include distances between posts, beams, and joists.

Loads & Codes

Most building codes require decks to support a minimum of 40 pounds per square foot (psf) live load, plus 10 pounds psf dead load, for a total of 50 pounds psf. A live load is the weight that is applied at random—including people walking on the deck, moveable furniture, or the weight of a heavy snowfall. Dead load refers to the weight of the construction material itself. The span limits presented in the accompanying tables will safely handle 50 pounds psf loads.

Understanding span limits for dead loads is especially important when constructing arbors and pergolas. For these structures, the overhead joists must be able to support themselves over time without sagging.

Place heavy objects, such as a large planter, on areas of the deck designed to withstand extreme loads. Consult an architect or structural engineer. Hot tubs or spas should not be supported by decking. Instead, place them on their own foundations and build the deck around them.

DRAW THE PERIMETER JOISTS, also called rim joists. In the plan view, you'll see only the top edge, so you won't have to figure the width of the rim joists just yet. Using the construction techniques described in this book, the rim joists are doubled or "sistered"—two side-by-side joists are bolted or screwed together down their entire length. This method creates an exceptionally strong, rigid outer edge for the framing system—ideal for attaching rail-

ing posts. The inner rim joist should be pressure-treated wood. The outer rim joist also can be pressure-treated wood, or, if you prefer, use untreated fir, pine, or cedar for a more pleasing appearance. These woods can be coated with a clear sealer and left natural or stained other color combinations as part of the overall look of the deck. All three woods accept exterior stains well and yield richer colors than painted or stained pressure-treated wood.

CONSTRUCTION DRAWINGS show the location of all footings and framing members. Include notes indicating lumber sizes and the location of stairs. Use graph paper to keep the scale accurate. Plan view drawings give the best overall view of substructure framing. For a view of the railing system, and to work out spatial relationships between balusters and posts, use elevation drawings.

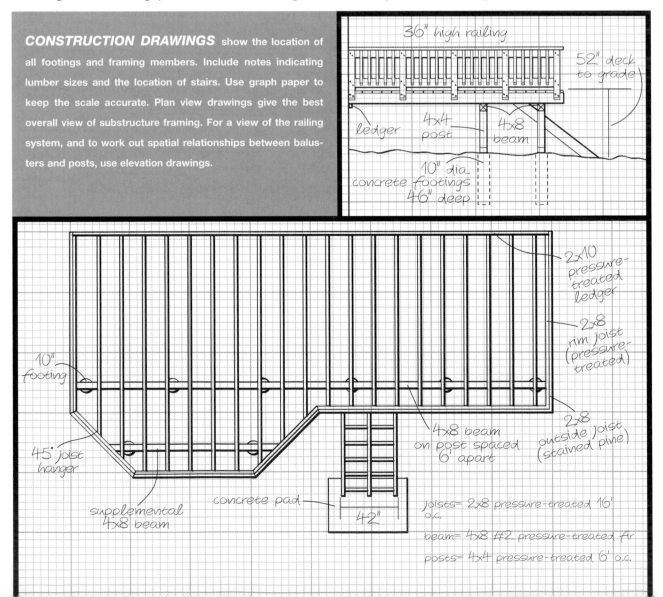

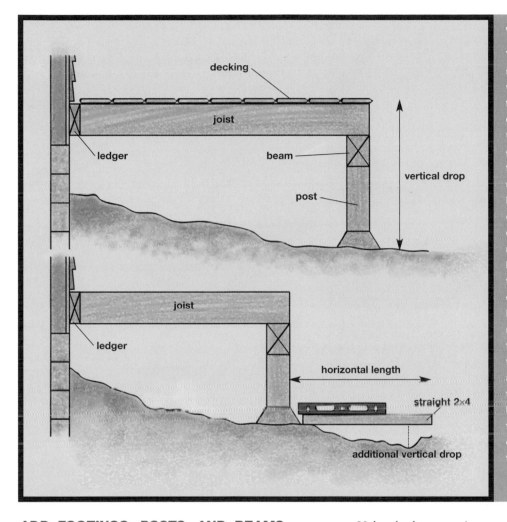

decking

joist

ledger

beam

post

vertical drop

joist

ledger

horizontal length

straight 2×4

additional vertical drop

Vertical Drop

The first step in designing stairs is calculating vertical drop—the distance from the top of the decking surface (including the decking boards) to the ground. Use this number to determine how many steps in the stairway (see Preliminary Calculations on page 68). After determining the horizontal run of the stairway, use a level and a straight board to determine if any slope exists in the building site. Hold the board level, measure out horizontally the estimated distance of the stair run, and measure any additional distance from the bottom of the board to the ground. Add this distance to the original number used for the vertical drop.

ADD FOOTINGS, POSTS, AND BEAMS to your drawing. Use the charts on pages 62–64 to calculate all lumber spans—the maximum distance between two supports that a piece of material can bridge and still maintain the strength necessary to support loads of at least 50 pounds psf (see Loads & Codes, on the opposite page). Calculating spans begins with the decking—the top-most component. The type of decking you use and its span capabilities determines the spacing of the joists. When planning to use synthetic decking material, refer to the manufacturer's recommendations for spans and usage (for more information about decking, see pages 48–51). Remember that all the structural components of a deck work together. Reducing the thickness or load-bearing capacity of one part of the structure means other components must be wider or thicker to compensate.

Unless budget restraints or aesthetic considerations give you a compelling reason to do so, avoid designing the structural system so that the lumber is installed to the limits of its capacity. If you do, your deck may be springy or bouncy underfoot, making it feel unstable.

Planning stairs

Stairs are a challenging aspect of building a deck. Creating steps that are level, evenly spaced, and attractive often tests the skills of an experienced designer or builder. The key is patience, attention to detail, and careful review of your calculations as you proceed. Work out dimensions thoroughly on paper. Once complete, a well-designed and constructed stairway will be a source of satisfaction.

Stair plans begin with a deck elevation that shows the height of the decking above the surrounding grade—the vertical drop. Note that the vertical drop includes the thickness of the decking material. From this measurement calculate the number of steps in your stairway, the length of each tread, and the place where the stairway lands.

As you proceed, recalculate several times. During site preparation and actual construction, for example, the distance from the top of the decking to the surrounding grade may change, so it's a good idea to recheck your calculations for accuracy before building stairs. Do this final check after building the main deck and installing the decking. Because building codes require that the height of all steps vary by no more than ⅜ inch, accuracy is important.

Preliminary calculations

At the stair location, measure the vertical drop from the top of the decking to the surrounding grade. Divide that number by 7 and round off the result to the nearest whole number. The result is the number of steps in the stairway. To determine the rise of each step, divide the vertical drop by the number of steps.

To figure the total length of the stairway, you'll need to design a stair tread. A typical tread features two 1×6s side-by-side. The total width should be about 11 inches. Add a gap of ⅛ inch between the boards for a total of 11⅛ inches. Your tread design may vary, as long as it conforms to local building code.

Determine the complete horizontal length of the stairway—from the edge of the deck to the landing—by multiplying the tread width by the number of treads. If the top step is not flush with the decking surface, the number of treads will be 1 less than the number of steps.

Stair Possibilities

Above: The treads and risers of a stairway are in relationship to each other—the lower the riser, the longer the tread must be. Generally, codes place limits on the maximum height of the riser. *Below:* Open stringers are notched and show the shape of the stair from the side; closed risers are made from solid boards.

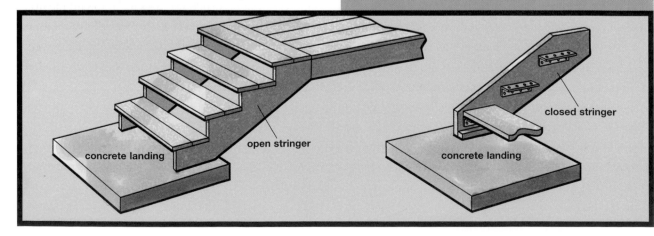

concrete landing

open stringer

closed stringer

concrete landing

EXAMPLE:

1. A deck has a vertical drop of 47 inches. Dividing 47 by 7 equals 6.71. Rounding off to the nearest whole number yields 7—the total number of steps in the stairway.

2. Dividing the vertical drop by the number of steps yields 6.71. The rise of each step will be 6.71 inches. For convenience, round this number to the closest common fraction in increments of $\frac{1}{16}$ inch. In this case, 6¾ inches. There are 7 steps, each with a vertical rise of 6¾ inches.

3. The tread width is 11⅛ inches. There are 6 treads (1 less than the number of steps). The total horizontal length of the stairway is 11⅛ × 6, or 66¾ inches.

Ensuring accuracy

Unless your yard is as flat and level as a gymnasium floor, you need to recalculate your stairs because most yards have some slope. The point where the stairs actually reach the grade of the yard is likely to be different than the vertical drop you initially measured.

To make more accurate measurements, use the horizontal length of your stairs as a good—but rough—estimate. Set a level on the edge of a straight board. Place one end of the board on the ground at the point where you took your original vertical drop measurement. Use a level to make sure the board is level; then measure out horizontally a distance equal to the horizontal length of the stairway. At this point, measure from the bottom of the board to the ground. If there a difference of an inch or more, add this distance to the original vertical drop and recalculate your stairway.

Common questions

Designing a set of stairs usually leads to a number of questions. Some of the most common queries are:

Q. How many stringers do I need?

A. The number of stringers is determined by the span capabilities of the tread material. Because treads usually are made from the same materials as the decking, refer to the span requirements for decking listed on page 63. With nominal 1-inch tread material, a 48-inch-wide stairway requires 4 stringers. A possible exception is a 36-inch-wide stairway with ⁵/4 decking—a fairly typical stairway design. The

⁵/4 material is stronger than nominal 1-inch material and has better span capabilities. If you want to plan a 36-inch wide stairway using ⁵/4 material, three stringers should be sufficient. However, check with your local building department before finalizing the design of the stairs.

Q. How far can stair stringers span without support?

A. Stairways built with 2×12 stringers can span up to 12 feet measured vertically. This is usually sufficient to reach from a second-level deck to the ground. However, plan carefully before committing to a long, unbroken stretch of stairway. Adding a landing or turning the stairway usually looks much better and is easier to use.

Q. How are railings attached to stringers?

A. Railings are attached with the same methods used for attaching to the perimeter rim joists of the main deck. In this book, the railing posts are bolted to the sides of the stair stringers. Building codes usually require that the handrail be no lower than 32 to 36 inches above the nose (the very front) of the stair tread. Check your local codes for the exact height.

Q. How do I turn a stairway?

A. One way to turn stairs is building a landing. A landing is actually a small deck, so it must meet all requirements for lumber spans, post footings, and railings specified by building codes. Landings must be at least 36 inches square.

Another way is to turn the stairway. Turning a stairway requires cutting the stringer into sections. If you do that, each splice location must be supported by a post and footing. Turns also have tread shape and size requirements and the minimum size of the treads in the turn. At the turn location, treads will be wedge-shape—smaller toward the inside of the turn and larger at the outside. Typically, codes require the inside width of the tread to be at least 6 inches. At a distance measured 1 foot from the inside edge of the tread, the tread must be at least 9 inches wide.

Changing levels

Rather than having one large deck on a single level, you can create separate spaces by changing the level of the deck one or more times. This is a good choice for decks that access the house at a height significantly higher than the ground.

Multilevel decks also can create separate activity zones—a cooking zone, a sitting/dining zone, and a play zone. Multilevel decks are essentially separate decks attached to each other. The technique for building these decks is not complicated—fasten the ledger board of the lower deck to the posts or perimeter rim joist of the upper deck. Attach joists of the lower deck to the ledger using joist hangers. For larger spaces between deck levels, build two independent decks with a bridge of stairs to connect them.

The distance from the upper decking to the lower decking (the vertical drop) should be designed in increments that make sensible steps. A distance of 6½ to 7 inches is good for a single step. For greater vertical drops, make the distance in similar increments. Then plan stairs—complete with treads and stringers—to bridge the difference. Check with your building department to see if your level change requires stair railings.

To design a level change with a single step, make sure the substructure of the upper deck has the posts, beam, and rim joists all flush to the outside of the deck. This arrangement makes it easy to attach the ledger of the lower deck. The size of the shared posts should be calculated from the total load of both decks. Depending on the span between posts, you may need a ledger that is wider than your joists to support the weight of the lower deck. Discuss the size of this ledger with your local building department.

Landings

Break up long runs of stairs with a landing. Landings are convenient places to pause when climbing long flights of stairs, creating a visual break for lengthy stairways as well. Landings are simple decks and include footings, posts, joists, decking, and railings.

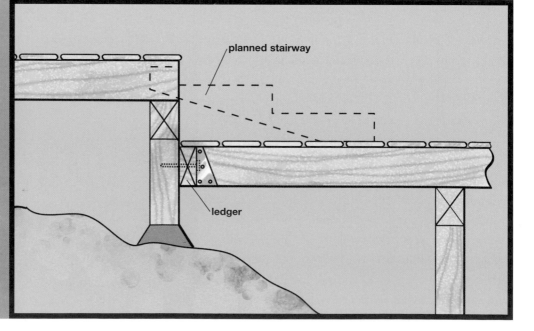

Changing Levels

Change levels by building two decks—one attached to the other. The posts, beams, and rim joists of the upper deck carry the ledger of the lower deck. A simple level change should have a drop of about 7 inches—the distance of a typical step. Greater distances require building a stairway.

planned stairway

ledger

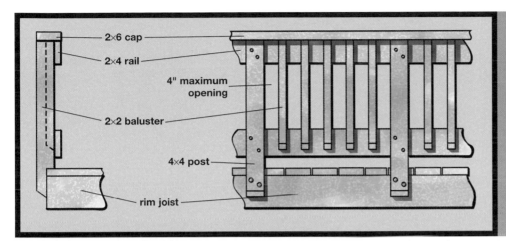

- 2×6 cap
- 2×4 rail
- 4" maximum opening
- 2×2 baluster
- 4×4 post
- rim joist

Basic Railing Designs

A simple railing includes notched posts attached to the rim joists, upper and lower rails running between posts, a cap rail installed flat, and balusters installed between the rails. Make rail joints at posts.

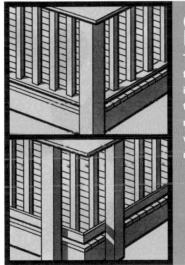

Corner Posts

Two common designs for the corners of railing include a post notched to fit the corner of the rim joists and two posts with balusters and rails meeting at the corner.

Planning railings

Railings are prominent features that influence a deck's character and style. They are simple structures, but you can make them as complex and interesting as time and budget allow. The basic, cost-effective railing system presented in this book can be readily modified into new designs. Try to reflect key architectural features of your house in the railing system, such as handrails or stair risers painted to match house trim, so that the finished deck blends with the overall scheme of your house.

Design railings with safety in mind. Know your local code requirements before beginning a plan. Most codes require railings on decks that are more than 24 inches above grade. However, use common sense. If you have small children or anticipate frequent visits from friends or relatives with chil-

dren, you might want to include railings even on the lower portions of the deck.

Railings also should be at least 36 inches high and designed so that there are no spaces in the railing system big enough to allow a 4-inch-diameter ball to pass—a feature that prevents small children from crawling between the railing members. As another commonsense safety feature, design railings with vertical balusters. A series of horizontal rails—even properly spaced according to codes—may entice curious children to climb them like a ladder.

Use detail drawings to work out any problem areas. Corners are one part of the railing system requiring special attention during design. Imagine how all members of the railing will meet and turn. Work out railing designs in both plan views and elevations until you're confident that your ideas are practical. For more ideas on railing corners, see Building Railings on pages 123–129.

Planning Point

Built-in benches and planters cannot take the place of railings. If you want to include built-ins along the perimeter of your deck, their design must conform to building codes for railings. Usually, that means the top of the back of a bench seat must be at least 36 inches above the seat. Because a seat is typically 15 to 17 inches high, the top of the back of the bench will be over 50 inches high!

6. tools & techniques

THE OLD SAYING, "THE RIGHT TOOL FOR THE RIGHT JOB," holds true today. Whether you are digging a hole or installing a finely made handrail, proper tools help to make the job safe and efficient.

Building a deck requires tools from four basic groups: safety equipment, measuring and marking, site work and foundation preparation, and general construction. You may already own many of the tools needed. If you must purchase new tools, choose durable, high-quality ones that will last through this job and be at the ready for future projects.

Tools for building a deck generally are simple and inexpensive. The few expensive specialty tools mentioned in this book can be obtained from rental centers.

Tools are a joy to own and use, and always keep safety first. Observe all manufacturer's recommendations for tool use and care. Keep tools clean and in good repair. Don't use tools that are dull or damaged—have them sharpened or fixed immediately, or replace them. Properly store when not in use. Don't leave tools where children have access to them. Keep power cords neatly stored until needed. When you disconnect a tool from a power cord, disconnect the cord as well.

The most important tool you have is your common sense. Don't work with tools when you are tired or upset. If you are unsure of your abilities, seek the help of a professional builder who can teach you correct techniques or do the job for you.

The most important tool a builder has is good old-fashioned common sense.

Preparing the construction site, digging footing holes, and mixing concrete require several simple tools—a shovel, a hoe, a wheelbarrow, and a posthole digger. If you are buying these tools for your deck project, you'll find many uses for them over the years.

Even though these tools are rugged, take care to prevent rust from forming on them. Don't leave them outside. Even in fair weather, morning dew can form on metal parts, causing rust. After use, clean tools with a stiff wire brush. Rinse them thoroughly with water and dry them in the sun or with

Site Tools
Tools needed for working the construction site, digging holes, and mixing concrete are simple and inexpensive. Look for tools that are guaranteed for many years or come with lifetime warranties.

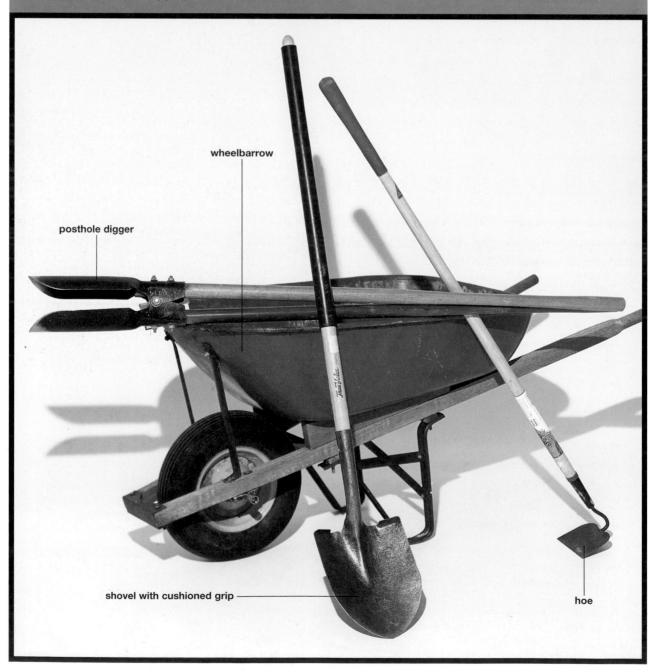

posthole digger

wheelbarrow

shovel with cushioned grip

hoe

a rag. Once the tools are dry, rub some lightweight machine oil on the metal parts to prevent rust and keep tools in top condition. If rust forms, generally it can be removed with a little machine oil and a stiff wire brush.

SHOVELS are used for digging holes, moving dirt, and general site work. Choose a good-quality shovel that will last for many years. Choose a pointed shovel with a wood or fiberglass handle. For extra comfort, select a model with a cushioned grip.

HOES are used primarily for leveling soil and gravel, and for mixing batches of concrete. Use a hoe to combine concrete mix with water. After each batch is prepared, clean the hoe with spray from a garden hose to remove any concrete clinging to the blade or shaft. If you wait until the end of the day to clean off concrete, it will harden and you may not be able to remove it.

WHEELBARROWS come in different sizes; for a deck project choose a heavy-duty model with a large, inflatable tire. Narrow tires can get stuck in the soft, exposed soil around the construction site. Use wheelbarrows as mixing tubs when preparing batches of concrete and for hauling materials from one place to another. When cleaning up at the end of the work day, put hand tools in a wheelbarrow and move them to a protected area, such as a garage.

POSTHOLE DIGGERS, also called clamshell diggers, are used to dig narrow, deep holes for the footings of a deck. They bite into all kinds of soils, and the rounded blades can be used to precisely shape a hole. Although digging a hole by hand may seem daunting, with a little practice you'll discover the work proceeds fairly quickly. In moderately difficult soils—those with occasional rocks and patches of sticky clay—expect to dig a 42-inch-deep, 10-inch-diameter hole in about half an hour. When you finish, thoroughly clean the blades. If they seem dull, sharpen them with a metal file.

ELECTRIC CONCRETE MIXERS feature large barrels that typically hold about 2 cubic feet of wet concrete. They take all the hard work out of preparing the mix. Again, two people are needed to move the mixer in and out of a vehicle. A mixer rents for $25 to $50 per day.

Rental Tools

For big deck-building jobs—those featuring a dozen or more footing holes—consider renting a power auger for digging the holes and a power mixer for preparing concrete. Both large pieces of equipment are available from rental stores.

GASOLINE-POWERED AUGERS come with 6-, 8-, 10-, and 12-inch-diameter augers—choose the right size for the design of the foundation. Augers are heavy and awkward to handle—even if it's rated as a "one-person" machine, you'll probably need two people to heft the tool in and out of a truck. Expect to pay $50 to $100 per day for a power auger.

One of the best ways to have your project proceed smoothly and efficiently is to take accurate measurements and establish precise layouts. When foundation footings line up, corners are square, and lumber is cut exactly to length, the building process is much easier and safer. High-quality measuring tools help to ensure reliable results.

MASON'S STRING is made of nylon that can be stretched taut to establish a level line over distances of up to 30 feet. Use mason's string to lay out the perimeter of the deck and to indicate the center of footings.

CHALK LINE AND REEL uses colored, powdered chalk to mark long, straight lines. The reel holds the line and chalk. As the line is played out, it picks up a coating of chalk. The line is stretched taut between two points; then a worker raises a portion of the line a few inches, releasing it so that it snaps against the work surface. As it does, the line leaves a clear, thin marking of chalk.

LINE LEVELS attach to mason's string and indicate if the string is level. Line level readings should be considered a good approximation, not an exact indication of level.

TORPEDO LEVELS are small—about 6 inches long—and are helpful for determining the position of short objects, such as the tops of concrete blocks.

CARPENTER'S LEVELS come in 2-foot, 4-foot, and 6-foot lengths. The longer the level, the more precise the indication will be. However, longer levels can be awkward and unwieldy in tight spaces. A practical combination for the average homeowner is a 2-foot and a 4-foot level.

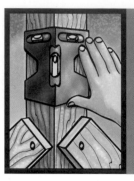

Corner Level

90-degree corner levels are designed to wrap around the corners of upright pieces of lumber. Because they indicate level in two directions simultaneously, they are handy for checking whether posts are plumb.

WATER LEVELS allow precise marking of level over large distances of 50 feet or more. The mechanism is simple—a clear tube filled with water and run between two points. The level of the water at one end is exactly the level of the water in the other. Some water levels include an electronic sensing device that provides an audio signal to indicate when a precise measurement is reached.

PLUMB BOBS are weighted strings that use gravity to indicate vertical level or plumb. Because the bob end swings free, it's difficult to take precise measurements of plumb over distances longer than 8 feet. Avoid using a plumb bob on windy days. If you must, try to block the wind temporarily with a piece of plywood or other large windbreak.

TAPE MEASURES come in various lengths. If you have only one, it should be a 25-foot tape with a 1-inch-wide blade. This handy tape handles small and large measuring chores. A 50-foot or 100-foot tape is quite helpful when making yard measurements and laying out large decks. Smaller tapes, such as a 12-footer with a ¾-inch-wide blade, are handy for carrying in a pocket.

COMBINATION SQUARES include a stiff, adjustable, 12-inch-long blade for marking and measuring, and a triangular head that indicates exact 90-degree or 45-degree angles. In addition to marking lumber for cutting, this essential tool has many uses, such as squaring up the blades of power tools, checking angles, and marking small distances with precision.

SPEED SQUARES perform many of the chores of combination squares. However, all sides of the speed square are fixed into position so the tool can never come out of adjustment. The blades are thick—about ³⁄₁₆ inch—so the tool can serve as a precision guide for power saws.

Water Level

These handy devices use basic physics—that water seeks its own level—for remarkably precise results. When the tube is filled with water to a certain mark on one end, the water on the opposite end is exactly the same.

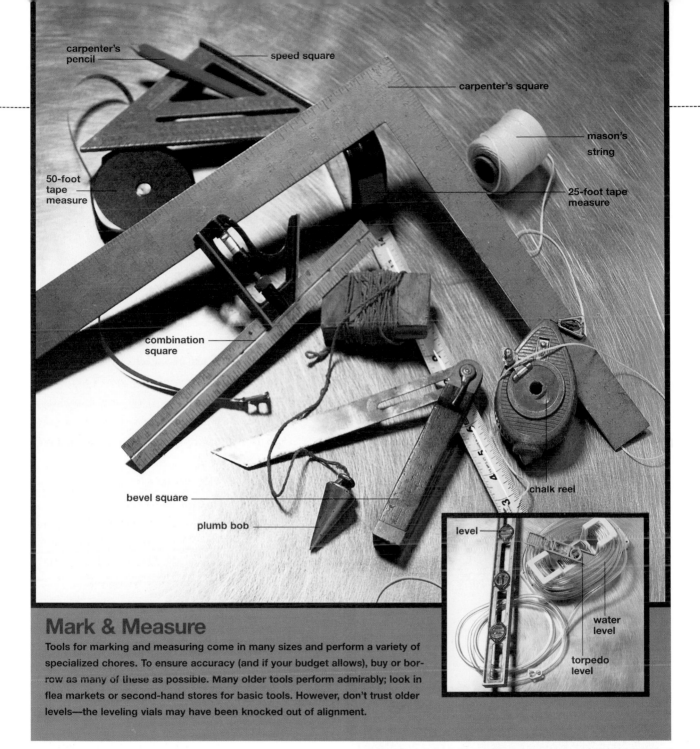

carpenter's pencil — — speed square

— carpenter's square

— mason's string

50-foot tape measure —

— 25-foot tape measure

combination square

bevel square —

plumb bob —

chalk reel

level

water level

torpedo level

Mark & Measure

Tools for marking and measuring come in many sizes and perform a variety of specialized chores. To ensure accuracy (and if your budget allows), buy or borrow as many of these as possible. Many older tools perform admirably; look in flea markets or second-hand stores for basic tools. However, don't trust older levels—the leveling vials may have been knocked out of alignment.

CARPENTER'S SQUARES are used for marking 90-degree angles and for layout chores, such as determining the rise and run of a stair stringer. The large blade of the typical framing square is 24 inches long and prone to being damaged. To prevent damage, framing squares should be handled carefully and stored when not in use.

BEVEL SQUARES include an adjustable blade that locks in any position for marking and transferring various angles.

CARPENTER'S PENCILS are thick and flat for marking along a ruler or similar tool. The pencil lead is especially chunky so that the point won't break easily.

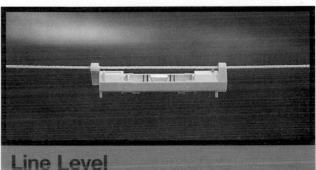

Line Level

A line level clips onto mason's string to indicate if the string is level. These small plastic or steel levels are handy for general work but don't provide perfect accuracy.

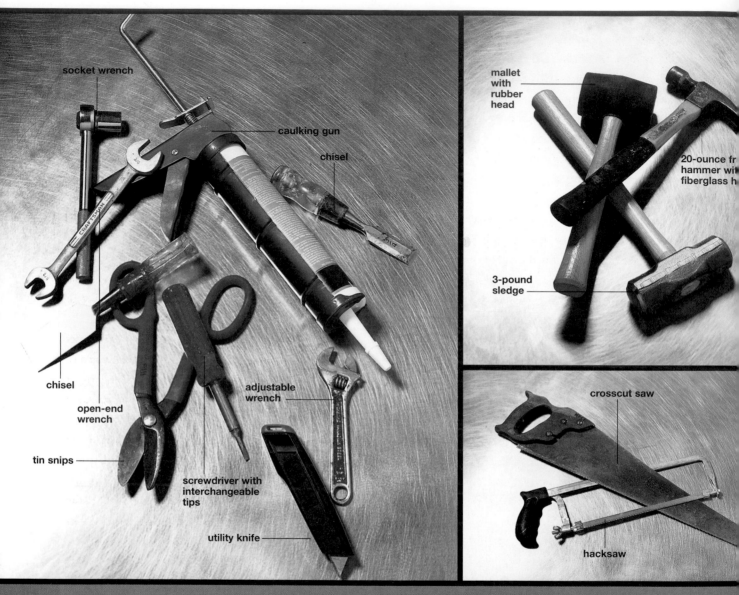

socket wrench

caulking gun

chisel

chisel

open-end
wrench

tin snips

screwdriver with
interchangeable
tips

adjustable
wrench

utility knife

mallet
with
rubber
head

20-ounce fr
hammer wit
fiberglass h

3-pound
sledge

crosscut saw

hacksaw

Hand Tools

Hand tools are simple, reliable, and easy to use. With care, hand tools should last a generation or longer. Lubricate hinges, pins, and other moving parts at regular intervals with lightweight machine oil. If blades become dull, have them sharpened or replaced immediately—dull tools are a safety hazard.

Construction tools include a broad range of hand tools, clamps, and power tools. Most are simple and relatively inexpensive. Well-made hand tools are often good substitutes for power tools although the work may take longer and require more muscle. When purchasing tools, buy the best tools you can afford. If you're not sure which model to select from a number of similar tools, ask a sales representative for infor-

mation and advice. Also, look for guarantees; longer guarantees are often an indication of a tool's reliability.

Hand tools

HAMMERS come in various sizes. A 16-ounce hammer is good for 8d and smaller nails. For deck-framing work, select a 20-ounce framing hammer. Some framing hammers have

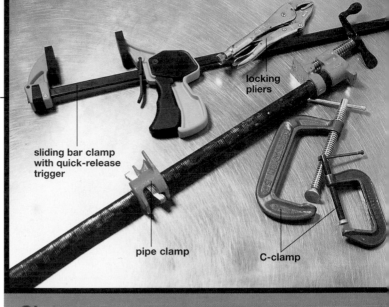

locking
pliers

sliding bar clamp
with quick-release
trigger

pipe clamp

C-clamp

Clamps

Clamps come in many sizes and styles. To prepare for a deck-building project, have a variety of clamps on hand. Buy clamps in pairs and use two clamps for most holding tasks.

cross-hatch patterns on the striking face to prevent the head from slipping when striking nails. Use a smooth-face hammer for driving large finish nails. Hammer handles are made of wood, steel, or fiberglass. Wood absorbs the jarring shock of repeated blows but cannot be used for pulling nails. Steel is tough but transfers force and may tire your arm. Fiberglass is a good combination of durability and shock absorption.

SLEDGE HAMMERS are used for driving stakes into the ground and for knocking large pieces of lumber into position. A sledge with a 2- or 3-pound head is a handy size. Use a sledge hammer only on unfinished materials—it could easily damage delicate parts or fine woods of finish materials. For these, use a heavy mallet with a rubber head.

HANDSAWS have largely been replaced by the many types of power saws currently available. However, a good-quality 8-point crosscut saw is useful for making quick, accurate cuts, for sawing off the ends of posts, and for cutting trim. Use a handsaw to finish large cuts that a typical circular saw can't complete, such as cutting through a 6×6 post. A hacksaw is designed to cut metal using hardened blades with small, sharp teeth.

CHISELS have a sharp cutting edge for trimming excess wood, smoothing rough edges of lumber, and making

notches. For safety, keep chisels sharp so that you won't have to force the tool. Never use a chisel for prying materials or turning screws.

CAULKING GUNS dispense caulk from the tubes it comes in. If excess caulk gets on the gun, remove it before it hardens. When you've finished caulking, always push the release trigger at the rear of the tool to relieve pressure inside the tube and stop the caulk from continuing to ooze out the tip.

WRENCHES are used to turn nuts and bolt heads. Fixed wrenches have jaws that are machined to precise sizes; you'll need an entire set for different-size nuts and bolts. An adjustable wrench has a moveable jaw that can be set to the correct size. Buy an 8-inch wrench for small nuts and bolts and a 10- or 12-inch wrench for larger work.

RATCHETING SOCKET WRENCHES come as sets with various size sockets to fit almost any nut or bolt head. The ratcheting mechanism allows plenty of leverage and one-handed operation. Ratcheting socket wrenches are the fastest way to turn nuts and bolts.

UTILITY KNIVES have sharp, razor-edged blades for almost any cutting task. The knife body is designed to fit comfortably in the hand. The blades can be retracted into the body of the tool when not in use.

Clamps

Clamps are some of the handiest tools on any job. Clamps hold workpieces steady while cutting, sanding, shaping, and installing fasteners. Clamps draw pieces together and hold

Cutting 6×6s

Some large pieces of lumber, such as 6×6s, can't be cut using only a circular saw because the blade on a standard 7¼-inch circular saw does not go deep enough. To cut a 6×6, mark it for cutting on every side, using a square to keep the marks aligned. Set the blade of a circular saw to its maximum cutting depth. Make sure the saw is unplugged, and check the blade for square. Use the circular saw to cut all around the lumber. Finish the cut with a hand saw or a reciprocating saw equipped with a wood-cutting blade.

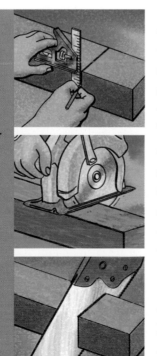

them in position for driving nails, screws, and drilling holes. Use a clamp as an extra pair of hands to hold large pieces of wood for measuring and marking. For maximum holding power and safety, use at least two clamps for each task.

Clamps come in many shapes, sizes, and styles. Each offers advantages and performs different tasks. A deck builder should have an assortment of clamps from which to choose.

Clamping puts direct pressure on the workpiece. Prevent dents in finish materials and softwoods, such as cedar or redwood, by inserting a protective shim or other material between the jaws and the workpiece. Some clamps come with protective rubber coverings on the jaws.

C-CLAMPS feature bodies shaped like the letter C. They have threaded rods that turn to apply or release pressure. The body is made of steel or aluminum. Because they are so rigid and strong, these all-purpose clamps can apply considerable pressure. They come in various sizes—both in the size of the jaw opening and the depth of the throat, the distance from the threaded rod to the back of the tool.

PIPE CLAMPS are unique—you purchase the jaws separate from the pipe. The jaws are designed to fit standard ½- or ¾-inch-diameter black iron plumbing pipe. The pipe is sold precut, with the ends threaded, in lengths as short as 12 inches to as long as 6 feet. Pipe clamps are inexpensive, strong, and versatile. Purchase several lengths of pipe and a few sets of jaws to create clamps of different sizes.

BAR CLAMPS are similar to pipe clamps, but they are made as complete units with a rigid bar that keeps the jaws in alignment. Bar clamps are stronger than pipe clamps because the shape of the solid bar is designed to resist flexing. They are also more expensive.

SLIDING SPEED CLAMPS feature a thumb-operated latch that allows one jaw to slide so it can be quickly closed on the workpiece. When squeezed, a pistol-type trigger applies clamping pressure. A speed clamp can be operated by one hand, leaving the other hand free to steady the workpiece or to hold a tool.

LOCKING PLIERS have incredible power. The adjustable jaws are designed to hold hard-to-grip objects, such as worn nuts, pipe, and irregular surfaces. They can be used like small clamps, but take care not to crush wood

Clamping
Secure workpieces with at least two clamps. Space the clamps as far as possible from each other for maximum holding power.

fibers or delicate parts by putting a shim between the jaws and the workpiece. Locking pliers come in a variety of sizes. A 10-inch model is an all-purpose size.

Power tools

Power tools make quick work of many carpentry tasks. They are either corded or cordless models. Corded tools must be plugged into an electrical outlet. They are powerful and operate with a constant, reliable source of electricity. Cordless models are battery-operated. Their advantage is portability and convenience. The heavy-duty batteries used by cordless tools must be periodically recharged. With moderate use, a battery will last 2 to 3 hours between charges.

DRILLS are used to bore holes and drive screws during all phases of a deck-building project. Look for power drills with variable speeds, keyless chucks, and electric brakes. A ⅜-inch chuck is standard, but a ½-inch chuck permits the use of large-size bits. An electric brake stops the motor from turning the instant you release the trigger—a good safety feature. Most name-brand drills are rugged and reliable, so select a model that feels comfortable and well balanced.

For cordless drills, choose a 12-volt or 14.4-volt model. These drills balance power with moderate weight. Bigger drills, such as 18- and 24-volt models, offer more power but may be too heavy to use comfortably. Buy a second battery so that one can be charged while the other is in use.

HAMMER DRILLS are designed to bore into concrete and brick. The motor includes a special hammering action that drives the drill bit into tough materials as it rotates. These drills require two-handed operation and feature two handles. Most hammer drills can be switched between hammer mode and regular mode for normal drilling. Use only carbide-tipped masonry bits for drilling in concrete or brick.

CIRCULAR SAWS are used for cutting lumber. The most common circular saw has a 7¼-inch-diameter blade. Smaller models with 5½- or 6 inch blades are increasingly popular,

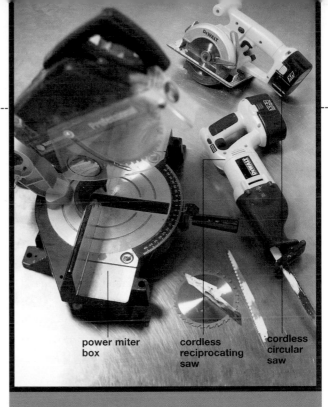

power miter box

cordless reciprocating saw

cordless circular saw

Power Tools

Corded power tools are powerful, rugged, and affordable. Cordless tools are the ultimate in convenience but use batteries that require recharging at regular intervals.

cordless drill

hammer drill

cordless drill

wood bore

spade bit

masonry bit

especially as cordless, battery-powered models, but they do not have the cutting depth for thick lumber and may bog down quickly. They are better suited for light-duty cutting, such as sawing decking boards. Use a carbide-tipped combination blade with 24 teeth—carbide blades remain sharp much longer than ordinary steel blades.

POWER MITER SAWS, sometimes called chop saws, have a bed and a fence that align square to each other for accurate positioning. The blade swivels to cut a variety of angles. In relationship to the flat bed of the tool, the blade stays fixed at 90-degrees for making accurate, square cuts. Most power miters come with positive stops that can be engaged so that the blade will snap exactly into position to make 90- and 45-degree cuts. The most common models feature a 10-inch-diameter blade and will cut stock 5 inches wide and 4 inches thick. For best results, equip your saw with a carbide-tipped combination blade with 40 to 60 teeth, These blades are available at home improvement centers and cost about $50.

A close relative of the power miter saw is the combination miter saw. This tool features a blade that both swivels and tilts. It is designed to cut compound joints, such as those found on a piece of handrail that changes direction to follow a stairway. These saws are expensive and usually are purchased by professional carpenters.

RECIPROCATING SAWS are tough workhorses designed to cut almost anything. Saw manufacturers make blades for efficient cutting of wood, metal, plastic, and other materials. Use a reciprocating saw for cutting concrete forms, post tops, metal flashing, and nail-embedded lumber. Especially long, flexible blades are good for reaching into awkward areas that can't be reached otherwise.

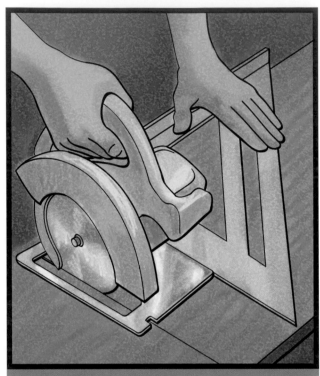

MAKE ACCURATE SQUARE CUTS by running the foot of a circular saw along the blade of a speed square. Hold the flat leg of the square against the workpiece.

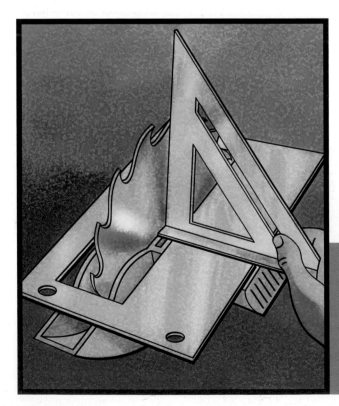

Speed Square
ALIGN THE BLADE OF A CIRCULAR SAW using a speed square. Make sure the saw is unplugged. Then rest the flat leg of the square across the foot of the saw. Sight between the upright leg and the blade to make sure the blade is square to the foot.

Safety equipment

Make safety a priority. Use safety equipment for all tasks and protect yourself before beginning to work. Keep the job site clean and free of debris by making a habit of cleaning up at the end of every work day.

Work within your range—don't stretch or reach beyond what's comfortable for you. When cutting or shaping wood or other materials, securely clamp and position the workpiece at a reasonable height.

One of the most important safety features is clothing. Wear durable but comfortable clothes for outdoor construction work. Long pants are preferable to shorts in all seasons. Don't roll up shirtsleeves—they may come loose and snag a workpiece or catch on a tool. Button down long sleeves or switch to short sleeves. Don't wear jewelry, and be sure to tie back long hair. Keep loose items, such as pencils, notebooks, or calculators, out of pockets. Stash them where they can be easily retrieved if needed. Basic safety equipment includes:

WORK GLOVES of canvas or leather keep hands from getting cuts and splinters. They are indispensable when handling rocks, lumber, debris, and for preventing blisters when using large hand tools such as shovels. However, don't wear work gloves when operating power tools—they may prevent you from having a safe grip.

SAFETY GOGGLES should always be worn when using power tools or striking tools, such as a hammer. If you wear prescription glasses wear safety goggles and glasses made to fit around your glasses and prevent objects from entering the sides. A safety shield covers the entire face with clear plastic and affords unrestricted vision when using a table saw or other large pieces of equipment.

DUST MASKS prevent small airborne particles and dust from entering the lungs. Wear a dust mask when handling concrete and sand, when cutting any material, and when cleaning up at the end of the day. Dust masks do not protect against toxic fumes. Use a respirator with removable filters to protect from these fumes.

POWER CORDS should be rated for exterior use. Select only 3-prong cords rated for 12 amps or better. Use only enough cord to reach the tool you are using. Don't string together more than two 25-foot cords. When not in use, coil up cords in an out-of-the-way location. Always disconnect power cords when not in use.

GROUND-FAULT CIRCUIT INTERRUPTER (GFCI) RECEPTACLES shut off electrical power instantly when they sense a tiny change in current. Always use GFCI receptacles for outdoor work. Never use power tools in wet or damp conditions. If a tool gets wet, dry it thoroughly before use.

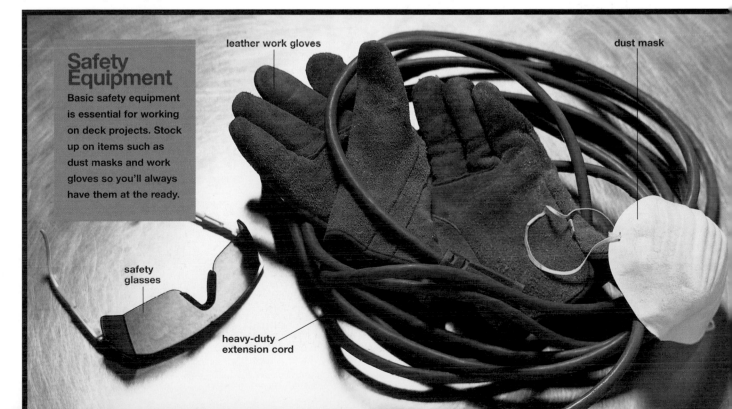

Safety Equipment

Basic safety equipment is essential for working on deck projects. Stock up on items such as dust masks and work gloves so you'll always have them at the ready.

leather work gloves

dust mask

safety glasses

heavy-duty extension cord

7. building substructure

DECK BUILDING MAY LOOK STRAIGHTFORWARD, but in reality, it's an elegantly complicated affair. Construction methods vary depending on the types of materials available in a particular region, the kinds of tools brought to the job, and the particular techniques that a worker feels most comfortable using. Nevertheless, the primary goal of any deck-building project is to create a strong, long-lasting, and good-looking structure. The construction methods described in here are selected for their simplicity, reliability, and safety. Throughout each chapter, alternative techniques are presented to give the reader an idea of possible design variations and how to achieve them.

Substructure includes the foundation and the support members of the deck—concrete footings, posts, beams, ledgers, and joists. They're referred to as the substructure because they basically are underneath the deck surface. Many substructure components are big, heavy pieces of wood. When setting posts, beams, and joists, enlist the aid of a companion to assist in lifting and steadying large structural members.

Pace your work. Thoroughly study each portion of the project, then proceed carefully until the task is complete. That way, you'll be sure not to miss any steps or make mistakes that require time and money to fix.

Keep safety first. If you're unsure about how to proceed, seek experienced help to guide you. Don't ever undertake a task that you don't fully understand.

Tackle one job at a time and see each task through to completion to ensure that construction proceeds safely and efficiently.

Ledger basics

The ledger attaches directly to a house (or another solid structure) and supports one edge of a deck. It is installed first—before the building site is prepared and footings are poured because the ledger provides a convenient, fixed reference point for the steps of layout and construction that follow.

A typical ledger is made from a piece of pressure-treated 2×8, 2×10, or 2×12 lumber. The ledger can be the same width or wider than the joists, but not narrower. Once securely fastened to a structure, a properly installed ledger is exceptionally strong and easily bears the weight of a deck.

To fasten the ledger, bolt it to a solid backing, such as a concrete block or solid concrete foundation wall, or to the rim or band joist that runs on top of the foundation wall behind the siding. Do not attach a ledger to brick only. Brick is a veneer covering. For a firm connection, drill holes completely through the brick and attach the ledger to the supporting substrate—either

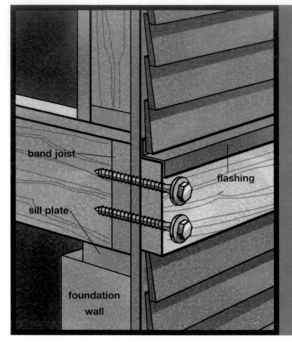

band joist

sill plate

foundation wall

flashing

Securing the Ledger

Bolt ledgers to solid backing, such as the band joist that runs around the perimeter of the house. Flashing covers the top of the ledger.

concrete block, solid concrete, a band joist, or wall studs. Do not attach a ledger to siding, stucco, or wall sheathing only—these are not strong enough to support the weight of a deck. If the deck design calls for the ledger to attach to the house where a band joist is not available, such as between floors, secure it to wall studs. Fasten it to every stud within the span of the ledger.

When positioning a ledger outside a door, allow for the thickness of the decking material. Keep the height of the finished deck 1 to 2 inches below the height of the interior floor to prevent rain water or melting snow from entering the house.

Once the ledger is in place, use silicone caulk to seal the seam between the house and the ledger, or cover the top

Caution Flag! Ledger Length

Although your deck plans should include the exact position of the ledger, remember that the width of the finished deck—measured across the face of the house to which it's attached—is different from the length of the ledger. That's because the outer rim joists slide past the end of the ledger as shown in the illustrations below. When removing siding material to install the ledger, make sure the ledger is 3 inches shorter than the cutout—1½ inches on each end. If you plan to add decorative 1× fascia, calculate an additional 1½ inches to account for a layer of ¾-inch finish material covering the rim joists.

house

ledger

house

ledger

outer rim joist

house

ledger

inner rim joist

inner rim joist

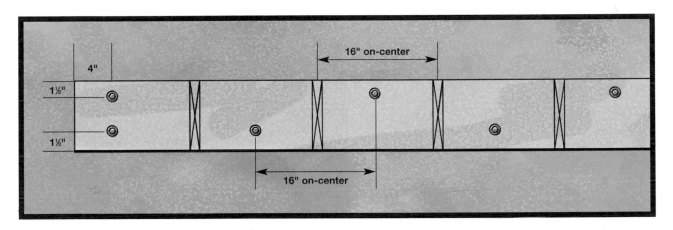

16" on-center

4"

1½"

1½"

16" on-center

16" on-center

of the seam with galvanized metal flashing. Otherwise, moisture will seep behind the ledger and damage both the deck and the house.

Lay out the ledger by marking the location of all joists. Use a combination square or speed square to indicate both sides of each joist. Then mark the location of the bolts that fasten the ledger to the house. Use pairs of bolts within 6 inches of the ends of the ledger and single bolts spaced every 16 inches along the length of the ledger, alternating along the top and bottom edges. Marking all joists first avoids conflicts with the bolt hole locations. Drill clearance holes for the bolts. Use lag or carriage bolts at least ⅜ inch in

diameter. Carriage bolts provide superior holding power. To use them, you must have access to the inside of the

band joists from a basement or crawl space to install the washers and nuts. Measure carefully so bolt locations in the ledger match openings between the interior floor joists. Temporarily remove insulation placed against the band joist. Replace the insulation after the bolts are secure.

Vinyl, aluminum, wood, and masonite siding

Ledgers should not be attached directly to siding made of vinyl, aluminum, wood, or masonite. First, remove the portion of the siding where the ledger is positioned. Then secure the ledger to the foundation wall, the band joist, or the walls studs.

1 BRACE THE LEDGER in position against the siding. Make sure it is

level. Mark the outline of the ledger, using a pencil or felt-tipped marker with a narrow point. Leave room at the ends for the rim joists and fascia. Remove the ledger.

2 CUT OUT the marked portion of siding, using a circular saw. Set the blade depth to cut only the thickness of the siding—not the sheathing under the siding. Cutting metal can make quite a racket—wear ear protection. Note: Once cut, metal and vinyl siding might hang in place because the bottom edge of each piece is nailed to the sheathing. The nails are hidden behind an interlocking seam. To unlock the seam, use a specialty tool called a zip tool—a simple, inexpensive tool available at hardware stores and home improvement centers.

5 SECURE THE LEDGER. Use lag screws long enough to penetrate at least 1½ inches into the band joist or wall studs. Carriage bolts must be long enough to accommodate washers and nuts. Make sure the flashing fits snugly along the top edge of the ledger. Seal the seams between the ledger, siding, and flashing, using silicone caulk. Be sure to caulk the bottom edge of the ledger.

3 INSERT GALVANIZED metal flashing, called Z-flashing, behind the siding along the upper edge of the cutout. The flashing should extend at least two inches behind the siding. If one piece of flashing isn't long enough to do the job, splice two or more together. Overlap ends at least 6 inches and seal the seam with silicone caulk. Do not nail the flashing in place; pressure exerted by the siding should keep the flashing in place until the ledger is installed. If nails behind the siding prevent the flashing from being inserted, use tin snips to cut notches in the flashing.

4 POSITION THE LEDGER and hold it temporarily in place with nails through each end of the ledger into the band joist or wall studs. Drill pilot holes for the lag screws or clearance holes for carriage bolts.

Concrete & concrete block foundation walls

Fasten a ledger to a foundation wall made of concrete or concrete block by using masonry anchors or lag shields and bolts. Begin by temporarily bracing the ledger in position, and check that the ledger is level.

1 DRILL PILOT HOLES through the ledger into the face of the concrete, using a ⅜- or ½-inch

masonry bit. Exert firm pressure when drilling through wood with a masonry bit. This method lines up the holes in the ledger with the masonry anchors installed in the concrete. When all the holes are complete, remove the ledger. Drill clearance holes for the lag bolts through the ledger.

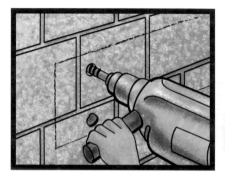

2 USE A HAMMER DRILL and a masonry bit to drill seat holes in the concrete according to the specifications provided by the manufacturer of the lag shields.

3 TAP THE LAG SHIELDS into the holes until they are flush with the masonry. Secure the ledger to the foundation wall by inserting lag bolts through the ledger into the lag shields—have a helper support an end of the ledger to make this task easier. Caulk the seam between the ledger and the foundation wall.

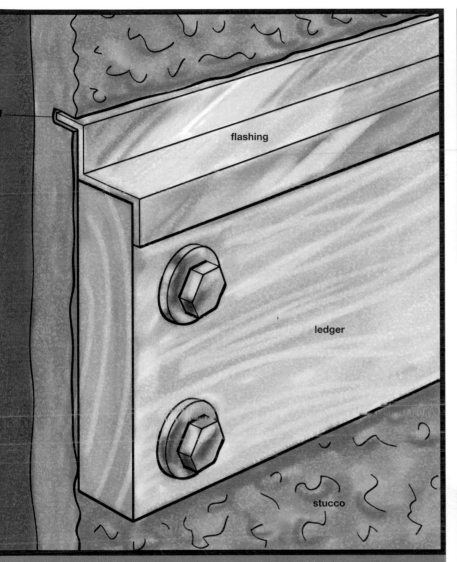

kerf

flashing

ledger

stucco

Ledgers Against Stucco

To seal flashing against moisture, bend the top edge of the flashing and insert it into a saw kerf cut in the stucco. Seal this connection with silicone caulk.

1 POSITION THE LEDGER and drill clearance holes completely through the ledger and the stucco. Fasten the ledger in place, using lag or carriage bolts. Seal all seams between the ledger and the stucco with silicone caulk. Place the modified galvanized metal flashing on top of the ledger. Mark the location of the flashing lip.

2 CUT A ¼-INCH-deep kerf, or slit, in the stucco, using a circular saw equipped with a carbide-tipped blade. Use a saw guide or the edge of the ledger to ensure the cut is straight. Insert the lip of the modified flashing into the saw kerf. Seal this connection with silicone caulk.

Stucco

A ledger can be installed directly against stucco, but the fasteners must penetrate completely through the stucco into a band joist or wall studs. Begin by using a rasp or sander to remove any large bumps in the stucco that will prevent the ledger from lying flat.

Protect against moisture damage by installing galvanized metal flashing. On stucco, the technique requires the upper edge of the flashing—about ¼ inch—to be bent at a right angle so it can be inserted into a saw kerf cut into the stucco. Seal this connection with silicone caulk. Bending the upper edge of the flashing is a job best left to a professional sheet metal shop.

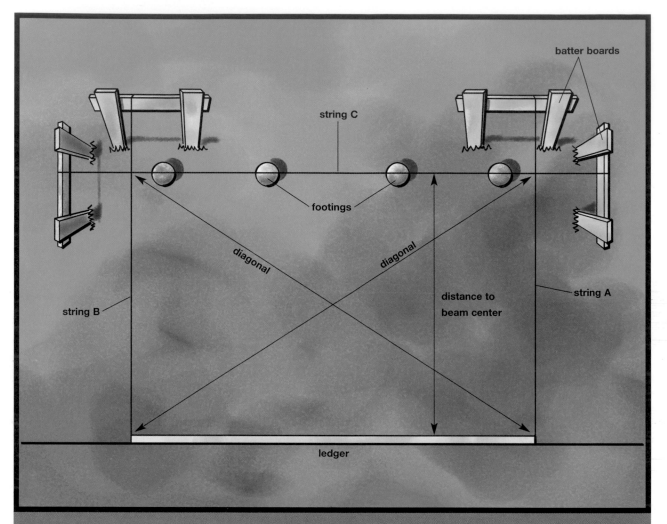

batter boards

string C

footings

diagonal

diagonal

distance to beam center

string A

string B

ledger

Overview of String Layout

From the ledger, stretch a mason's line to indicate an edge of the deck—remember that the string indicates the inside edge of the inner rim joist. Begin at one corner of the ledger and pull String A to a set of batter boards placed several feet beyond the location of the footings. Check that this line is square to the ledger. Pull a second line—String B—from the other ledger corner, checking that the string is square to the ledger. Measure out along each string to the center of the support beam and also the center of the footings. Mark Strings A and B at this distance. Run a third string—String C—perpendicular to the other two. Measure along String C to indicate the location of each footing. Drop a plumb bob to the ground from String C to mark the footing locations.

Laying out the footings begins by making a basic outline of the deck on the construction site using mason's strings supported by sets of batter boards. Take your time to establish that the strings are square to the ledger, ensuring that the layout is as accurate as possible. A precise layout makes the remainder of the deck construction easier.

Laying out deck footings has three basic phases—an initial phase to set up batter boards and position the mason's strings, an adjustment phase to ensure that corners are square and strings are level, and a final phase where the foundation footings are marked on the ground. Mason's string is designed to be stretched tightly so that it stays straight and won't sag over distances up to 30 feet. With mason's string, you can accurately transfer measurements from design drawings to the construction site. Remember that the string grid must be level. If it isn't, the resulting layout may be inaccurate.

Measure along the grid to mark the locations of the footings. Use a plumb bob to transfer the locations of the footings from the string to the ground.

Attach the mason's string to batter boards—simple, temporary frames made from 2×2, 2×4, or 1×4 lumber. Batter boards are made from two stakes driven into the ground and a crosspiece that runs between those stakes. The stakes must be firmly planted so the tension of a taut mason's string won't move them. Shape the ends of the stakes into points to make driving them in the ground easier and sink them at least 12 inches into the ground. Fasten the crosspiece to the stakes with screws—using screws allows you to remove a screw to adjust the height of the cross-piece if necessary. When driving the stakes, alternate hammering on each stake to keep even pressure on the joints.

Ensure accurate measurements by using a line level on the mason's string. Clip the line level onto the mason's string within 2 feet of a batter board so the weight of the level won't cause the line to sag.

Laying out the string grid

Start with a plan view drawing of the substructure. Note the distance from the ledger to the support beams. This distance establishes the location of the

mason's string that indicates the center of the beam.

For tall decks, such as a second-story deck, transfer the ledger board location to a place closer to the ground. To do so, drive a set of batter boards directly

under each corner of the ledger. Drop a plumb bob from each corner to the batter boards. Mark the location on the top of each batter board crosspiece. Use these reference marks for establishing the string grid.

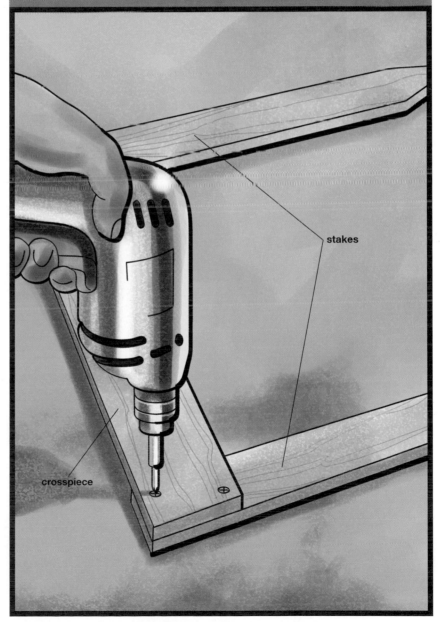

Making Batter Boards
Make sets of batter boards by attaching a crosspiece to two stakes. The stakes must be long enough so that when the stakes are driven about 12 inches into the ground, the top of the crosspiece will be level with the top of the ledger.

stakes

crosspiece

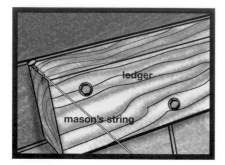

mason's string
ledger

3 ft.
5 ft.
4 ft.

the string is square to the ledger. Secure this string (String A) to a set of batter boards driven into the ground at a point 3 to 5 feet beyond the location of the footings. Loop the string several times around the crosspiece to secure it temporarily.

1 DRIVE A 6d NAIL at a 45-degree angle into the upper corner of the ledger, leaving ¼ inch of the shank exposed. This corner marks the upper surface of the ledger and joists and the inner edge of the rim joists. Tie a loop in one end of a mason's string and loop it around the nail head. The string should touch the ledger corner.

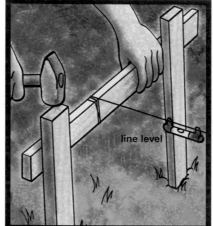

line level

batter board

2 PULL A MASON'S STRING out from the ledger. Have a helper use a framing square to estimate that

3 CLIP A LINE LEVEL on String A within 2 feet of the batter board. If the crosspiece is too high, tap the batter board stakes until the bubble indicates level. If it is too low, remove a screw from the crosspiece and raise an end slightly. Repeat with the other crosspiece end until the bubble indicates level. Refasten the crosspiece to the stakes with the screws.

4 FIX STRING A at a right angle to the ledger using the "3-4-5 square." The 3-4-5 square uses a simple geometric formula ($a^2 + b^2 = c^2$) to establish a precise right angle. To use the formula, measure along the ledger from the corner and mark it at 3 feet. Measure along the mason's string and mark the string at 4 feet, using a piece of masking tape folded over the string for marking. If the string is at a precise right angle to the ledger, the distance between the marks will be 5 feet. (When measuring between the marks, read the measurements from the same tape edge at both marks.) If the distance between the marks is not

Making Half-Hitches

A series of two or more half-hitches is a good way to secure a mason's string because it is reliable yet easy to undo when adjustments are necessary. Simple pressure keeps the string from slipping. The tighter the string, the more secure the hitches will be. To make half-hitches, pull a mason's string over the top of a batter board. Make a simple loop around a nail and check that the free end of the string passes behind the string coming from the top of the batter board. Hold the free end in one hand. With the other hand, reach over the top of the batter board and draw the mason's string toward you. Pull on the free end to take up slack. When the string is taut and straight, slip a second half-hitch over the head of the nail and tug until hitches are snug. Add a third half-hitch for insurance. To loosen the hitches, pull on the mason's string to release some of the tension. Loosen the hitches until they open up.

exactly 5 feet, adjust the string as needed. Mark the top of the batter board to keep the correct string location. Drive a nail behind the batter board and secure String A to the nail, using half-hitches. Note: To keep from bouncing the batter board around while hammering, use a "dead weight" to absorb the shock of the blows. Place the head of a 2-pound hammer behind the crosspiece of the batter board, directly opposite the nail location.

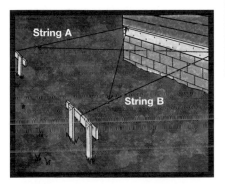

5 REPEAT THE PROCEDURE for a second string (String B) pulled from the other corner of the ledger. Check that String B is level, square, and secure. Establish the center of the footings (also the center of the support beam) by measuring out from the ledger the proper distance along both strings. Mark the strings with masking tape. Check that the strings are parallel by measuring the diagonal distance from each corner of the ledger to the masking tape mark on the opposite string. If the strings are parallel, the two diagonal measurements will be equal. If adjustments are necessary, drive another nail behind the batter board. Loosen the

half-hitches and retie the line to the second nail. Erase the mark on the top of the batter board and draw new marks.

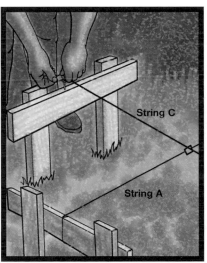

6 PLACE BATTER BOARDS opposite the marks that indicate the beam location, 3 to 5 feet outside of the parallel strings. These batter boards are 90 degrees to the original pair. Have a helper stretch a third string (String C) between this new set of batter boards, perpendicular to Strings A and B. Adjust the batter boards so that String C is level. It should be ⅛ to ¼ inch above Strings A and B.

7 MEASURE THE DISTANCE to the center of each footing and mark String C with masking tape. Check your marks by measuring from the opposite string. Hold a plumb bob so that its string barely grazes String C. Lower the plumb bob until the tip is about ¼-inch from the ground. Make sure the bob is steady; then transfer the footing location to the ground, using a short stake as a marker.

Repeat the procedure until all the footing locations are marked.

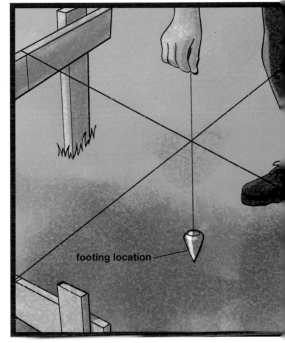

Inspections

Expect two or three visits from a local building inspector during the course of construction. The inspector will examine the structure to ensure it is being built safely and is in compliance with local codes. Communicate with your inspector to determine at what stages he or she expects to visit the site. Plan to be on hand so that you can answer questions.

Don't be intimidated by the idea of an inspection. Most building inspectors are knowledgeable and helpful. Their main concern is safety, and most are willing to talk about your specific plans and methods of construction to ensure that your deck project is built soundly and is completed on schedule.

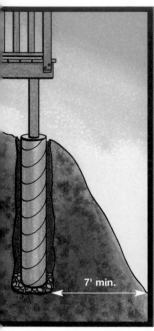

Footings on Slope

Building codes may have special requirements for decks built on steep slopes. To ensure the footing is embedded in the soil, codes may require that the bottom of the footing be no closer than 7 feet to the outside surface of the slope, measured horizontally.

7' min.

Footing basics

Concrete footings provide a solid foundation that supports the deck. They must be large enough to carry the weight of the deck and deep enough to prevent seasonal movement of the soil—called frost heave—from disturbing the footings. The size and depth of the footing depends on your local building codes—frost lines and footing requirements vary with regional climates. On steeply sloped lots, codes may prohibit the bottom of the footing from being located within 7 feet of the surface, measured horizontally. Usually, the depth and placement of footings must be checked by a building inspector before work proceeds. Ask your local building or planning commission about codes and schedule an inspection. Check with utility companies to keep from digging holes and placing footings too close to underground lines, cables, and pipes.

A typical footing is a cylinder of poured concrete. Use a posthole digger or power auger to make round holes; then insert cardboard footing tubes into the holes to form the footings. Footing tubes are designed to be left in the ground—over time, the cardboard gradually deteriorates into the surrounding soil. Footing tubes make it easy to estimate the amount of concrete needed for each hole. Once the concrete is poured, footing tubes prevent moisture in the concrete from wicking into the soil too quickly and weakening the concrete (for more information, see Concrete on pages 44–45).

Some regions do not have frost lines. If your local codes allow, you can construct simple square or block footings that are 18 inches on each side and 1 foot deep. Set preformed concrete pier blocks in the wet concrete to elevate posts above ground level.

Making footings

Digging holes by hand is hard work, but you should be able to dig four to eight 42-inch-deep holes in a day, using

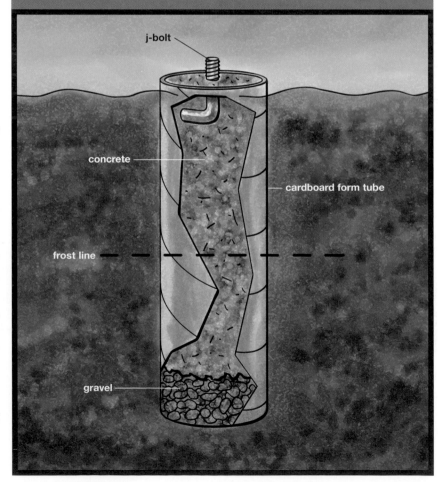

Footing Cross Section

A typical footing is a cylinder of poured concrete. It extends into the ground past frost lines. Cardboard footing tubes make it easy to form footings.

j-bolt

concrete

frost line

cardboard form tube

gravel

a posthole digger. Wear work gloves to prevent blisters. A rented power auger shortens the work load; however, it is a large, heavy tool that's awkward to use. Plan to have a helper to assist in lifting a power auger in and out of a vehicle. Once on the site, be careful not to bump into batter boards and stakes that mark footing locations.

If you encounter an obstruction, such as a rock or tree root, don't be dismayed. Most rocks can be pried out, using a crowbar. Cut and remove tree roots. If you are digging at least 15 to 20 feet away from the trunk, cutting the root will not damage the tree. Use a handsaw or reciprocating saw to cut the root.

Before starting to dig, clearly mark the string positions on the crosspieces of the batter boards, then remove the strings. Leave batter boards in position in case you accidentally dislodge a stake for a footing. Reposition a mason's string and remeasure the distance to the hole to re-mark the location.

1 REMOVE A MARKING STAKE and dig a hole at each footing loca-

tion, using a posthole digger or a power auger. Dig one hole before removing the marker for the next hole. Place a piece of scrap plywood at least 3-foot square next to each hole and put the dirt on it to make it easier to transfer the dirt to a garden or fill location. Use a plumb bob to check that the hole is straight up-and-down.

2 PUT GRAVEL IN THE BOTTOM of footing holes to a depth of 3–4 inches. Pack the gravel tightly, using a 2×4 or 4×4.

3 CUT THE CARDBOARD FOOTING tube to length. The tube should be 1 to 2 inches longer than the length of the hole so that the top of the form protrudes above the ground. Slide the tube into the hole. If the hole is tight, remove the tube and shave the sides of the hole to fit. If the form is loose in the hole, backfill around

the form. Use a level to ensure that the top of the form is level.

4 MIX CONCRETE according to the directions on the bag. Pour wet concrete immediately. Have a spot established for dumping small batches of unused concrete. Don't put small batches in the next hole—it will begin to cure before the next batch is ready. It won't combine with freshly mixed concrete, weakening the footing. Eliminate air pockets by reaming the wet concrete with a piece of 1×2 or 2×2 scrap lumber long enough to reach the bottom of the footing. Use a two-handed grip. Push the stick into the concrete and vigorously churn up and down to settle the mixture.

5 SCREED OFF excess concrete using a short piece of 2×4. Pull the 2×4 toward you with a side-to-side motion, holding the 2×4 firmly against the edges of the tube form.

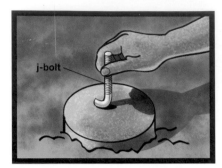

j-bolt

6 PUSH A J-BOLT into the center of each footing, adjusting the bolt so that ½-inch of the threads is visible. Do not allow concrete to get onto the exposed threads. If the bolt sinks or sags, you may have to hold it in place a minute or two until the concrete begins to cure. Use a square to ensure the bolt is square to the top surface of the footing. Allow footings to cure for 48 hours.

Footings for no-frost regions

In areas of the country that do not have frost-line depth requirements for footings, pour a block footing. A typical block footing is 18 inches on each side and 1 foot deep. Frame the footings from ¾-inch plywood or nominal 2×12 lumber. Coat the inside of the forms with used engine oil to make them easier to remove.

1 REMOVE A MARKING STAKE and dig a hole at each footing location, using a posthole digger or shovel. Dig one hole before removing the marker for the next hole. Make sure the hole is wide enough to accommodate the footing forms. Make each

Block Footings

In regions that do not have frost-line requirements, use block footings. Form up square block footings using 2×12 lumber. Set footings on a compacted bed of gravel.

hole 14 to 16 inches deep. Fill the bottom of the hole with several inches of compacted gravel.

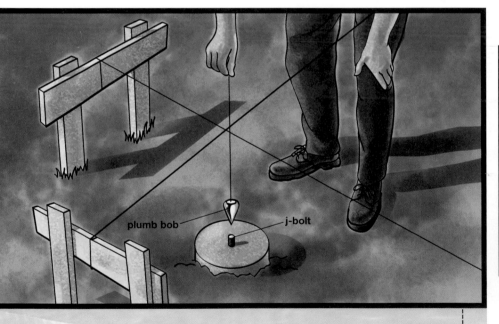

plumb bob   j-bolt

Caution Flag! Aligning J-bolts
Digging holes is not an exact art; the center of the footing hole may not end up precisely where it was marked. Post anchors allow for small variations because they are adjustable. However, it's a good idea to reposition the mason's strings before beginning to pour footings. Then use a plumb bob to determine the location of the j-bolt on top of the freshly poured concrete. A drawback is having the mason's strings set over the footings—you'll have to work carefully not to disrupt the strings.

2 PLACE THE FORMS into the holes. Drive two 1×2 or 2×2 stakes along each side of the form. Drive the tops of the stakes below the tops of the forms so that the forms can be screeded. Level the forms using a level. Drive screws through the stakes into the forms to hold the

Setting Pier Blocks

Pier blocks with notched tops are convenient for building low platform decks that do not have posts and require only beams. Set the outside piers and use a long, straight piece of lumber to make sure all the notches are in alignment.

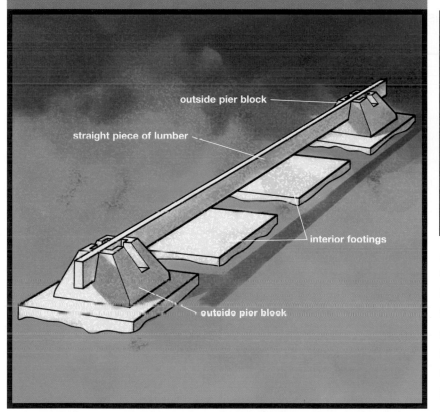

outside pier block

straight piece of lumber

interior footings

outside pier block

set the pier blocks in the water for several minutes. Wet pier blocks bond to footing concrete much better than dry ones.

2 SET THE PIER BLOCKS on freshly poured concrete, making sure the pier settles about ¾ inch below the surface of the concrete. Use a slight twisting movement to settle the pier block. Level the pier with a level, tapping the edges with a rubber mallet to adjust it. If you are using the grooves of the pier block to receive a beam to build a low, platform-style deck, set the outermost pier blocks first. Dry-fit the beam or a long straight piece of lumber to align the grooves. Set the interior blocks one at a time, checking for alignment with the piece of lumber.

forms in place. The screws should not protrude into the interior of the form. If they do, removing the forms will be extremely difficult.

3 MIX AND POUR CONCRETE according to the directions on the concrete bag. Use a piece of 2×4 to screed excess concrete off the tops of the footings. Pull the 2×4 toward you with a side-to-side motion. Place a j-bolt in the center of each footing, exposing ¾ inch of the threads. Allow the concrete to set for 48 hours before removing the forms. Backfill around the footings with dirt, and tamp the dirt to compact it.

Concrete pier blocks

Use precast concrete pier blocks with block footings to build low, platform-style decks where posts are unnecessary. The notches in the top of the pier are designed to hold 4× lumber and are ideal for supporting 4× beams. Make the block footings at least 2 inches wider than the pier block on each side.

1 SOAK THE BOTTOMS of the pier blocks in water prior to use. Use a trough or a basin, if you have one. Otherwise, fill a wheelbarrow with water to a depth of 4 to 5 inches and

Pouring a landing

A landing is a small concrete slab used to support the base of a stairway. Pour the slab while you are pouring footings and are set up for concrete work.

Plan to make the slab 3 to 4 inches thick—slabs don't have to extend beyond frost lines. However, check with your local building department for the requirements in your area. You may be required to reinforce the slab with wire mesh. Even if your codes do not have this requirement, it's a good idea to add the mesh anyway—it helps to prevent the slab from cracking. Buy #10 wire mesh at your local home improvement or hardware store.

Landings

A landing is a small concrete slab used to support the end of stair stringers. The bottom ends of the stringers should rest toward the back portion of the slab.

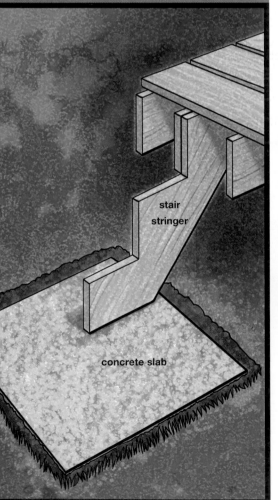

stair stringer

concrete slab

Position the landing at the end of the stairway, using your plan drawings to calculate the correct distance. The ends of the stair stringers should rest toward the back one-third of the slab. Allow a generous portion of the landing—at least 2 feet—in front of the stair stringers. If the landing is larger, you won't have to worry about exact calculations—a few inches won't make a great deal of difference. For a 3-foot-wide stairway, plan a 4×4-foot landing.

1 **EXCAVATE FOR THE LANDING to a depth of 6 to 8 inches. Be sure to include the added width of the 2×4 forms around the edges. Fill the excavation with gravel to a depth of 3 to 4 inches and tamp the gravel with a 4×4 to pack it tightly.**

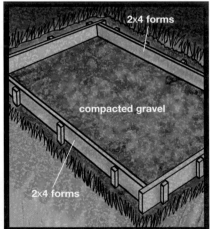

2×4 forms

compacted gravel

2×4 forms

2 **INSTALL 2×4 FORM FRAMING around the perimeter of the excavation. Nail the corners of the frame. Coat the inside of the forms with used engine oil to make removing them easier. Secure the frame with 1×2 or 2×2 stakes driven every 2 feet around the outside edges and**

within 4 inches of the corners. Drive the heads of the stakes below the top edge of the forms so the concrete can be screeded. Level the forms. Secure the forms to the stakes with screws driven from the outside of the forms. Make sure the screw tips do not penetrate the interior of the forms. Cut #10 wire mesh to fit inside the forms and install it over the gravel. Elevate the mesh with 1½-inch diameter stones placed at the wire intersections.

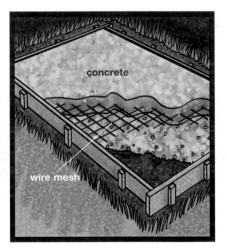

concrete

wire mesh

3 **FILL THE FORM with concrete. Use a straight 6- or 8-foot-long 2×4 to level the concrete and to screed off the excess. If desired, use a flat hand float to smooth out scratch marks in the top surface of the concrete. Do not make the surface too smooth—a slick surface could be hazardous in wet or freezing weather. Cover the concrete with plastic sheeting to prevent the top of the slab from drying out too quickly. Let the concrete cure 48 hours before removing the plastic sheeting and the forms.**

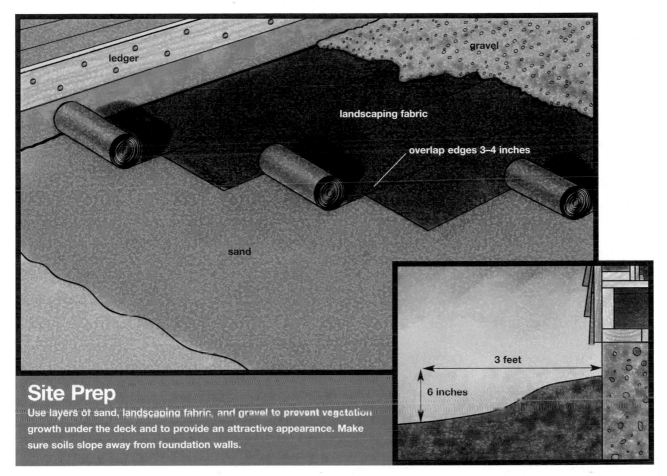

ledger

gravel

landscaping fabric

overlap edges 3–4 inches

sand

3 feet

6 inches

Site Prep
Use layers of sand, landscaping fabric, and gravel to prevent vegetation growth under the deck and to provide an attractive appearance. Make sure soils slope away from foundation walls.

Many types of weeds and other vegetation will grow in adverse conditions, even in the sunless space beneath a deck. Prevent vegetation from growing by grooming the site with sand, gravel, and landscaping fabric. Landscaping fabric is a barrier designed to allow water to flow through but to block the sun and inhibit vegetation growth. Grooming with sand and gravel gives the area beneath a deck a neat, clean appearance. After the footings are poured—and while the concrete is curing—is a good time to do this work.

First, remove all mason's strings and batter boards. Use a hoe to remove any rooted vegetation within the outline of the deck. Use a steel rake and a hoe to smooth the site and break up any large clumps of dirt. The soil near foundation walls should have plenty of slope to direct water away from the foundation. Water that soaks into the soil near foundation walls may freeze during colder weather, expanding and cracking the foundation walls. To help move water away from the foundation, the soil should slope at a rate of 6 vertical inches for 3 horizontal feet measured from the wall.

Spread sand over the site to a depth of 1 to 2 inches. Smooth the sand with the back of a steel rake. Unroll landscaping fabric over the sand, parallel to the house. Begin at the lowest part of the site (furthest away from the house) and overlap seams 3 to 4 inches. Use a utility knife to cut holes in the fabric so it fits around the tops of the footings. Cover the fabric with gravel to hold it in place and create a neat appearance.

Caution Flag!
Rent a Mixer
A typical landing slab measuring 4 feet on each side and 4 inches thick requires about 5.5 cubic feet of concrete—about a dozen 60-pound bags of dry pre-mix concrete. For a job this size, consider renting an electric mixer. You'll speed up the work and won't risk having the early batches start to harden before all the concrete is poured.

Posts support the weight of the deck. For peak efficiency and to make the substructure as rigid as possible, the posts must be plumb. Posts must also be aligned to support beams. Adjustable post anchors allow the posts to be moved about ½ inch in any direction to ensure proper alignment. Post anchors are designed to elevate the posts slightly above the concrete footings to prevent moisture from entering the end grain of the post. Even the end grain of pressure-treated material is susceptible to damage from moisture.

After posts are set, hold them upright and plumb by using temporary braces. The next step is to cut off the tops of the posts to the proper height. This requires careful calculation—be sure to account for the height of the support beams and joists before trimming the posts to length.

To make quick, square cuts on standing posts, use a circular saw. Two passes with a circular saw will cut 4×4s and 4×6s. For 6×6s, however, you'll need to make four passes—one on each side of the post. Even then, part of the center of the post will remain uncut. Finish the cut with a handsaw or reciprocating saw.

Installing posts

To set posts, you need 1×4s for braces and 2×2 stakes about 1 foot long. Shape one end of each stake to a point to make driving them into the ground easier. When setting the braces, make sure the upper ends of the braces won't interfere with setting the beam into position.

1 INSTALL POST ANCHORS on the footings. Slip the anchors over the exposed ends of the j-bolts. Secure the anchors with galvanized washers and nuts. Tighten the nuts with a ratchet wrench but leave some play so that the anchor can be moved by hand if necessary. For a final tightening, use a flat box-end wrench that fits the nut exactly. Post anchors have openings in the bottom to allow the use of a box-end wrench for a final tightening.

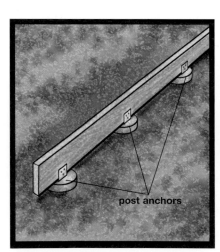

2 ALIGN THE POST ANCHORS by setting a straight beam in the post anchor flanges. Make sure the

beam is square to the ledger by measuring from the ends of the ledger to the beam. Adjust the beam if necessary. Tighten all post anchors, using a box-end wrench. Remove the beam.

3 CHECK THE ENDS OF POSTS for square. Trim them if necessary—a power miter box makes reliably square cuts. Coat the bottom ends with preservative or sealer. Install posts one at a time by placing the bottom end in a post anchor and securing it with a single galvanized 6d box nail or 1¼-inch joist nail.

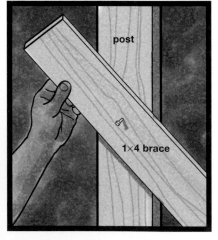

4 BRACE THE POST with 1×4s. Make the braces long enough to reach from the ground to the top one-third of the post at about a 45-degree angle. Secure one brace flat against one side of the post with a single screw. Secure a second brace on an adjacent side of the post.

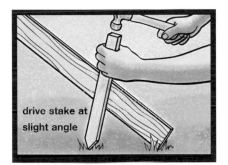

5 **DRIVE STAKES** alongside each brace, tilting the stake back slightly to increase its holding power.

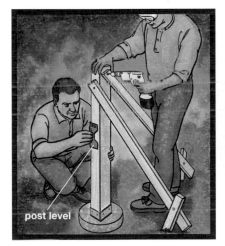

6 **USE A POST LEVEL** to plumb the posts. Post levels are designed to level two sides of a post simultaneously. If you don't have a post level, an ordinary level will do. Plumb one side of the post at a time. When the level reads plumb, secure each post to the brace with two screws. Drive another screw through the bottom of the brace into the stake. Note: Using two screws at each connection is important—a single screw allows the connection to pivot. When the

posts are plumb, secure them to the post anchors by driving galvanized nails through the anchor flanges into the posts.

Cutting posts to length

To cut posts to proper height, use the ledger as a starting point. Transfer the top of the ledger to the post, using a level. Subtract the vertical height of the installed beam and joists, measured vertically. Check your drawings to make sure the design of your substructure includes beams resting on post tops and joists resting on beams.

1 **TRANSFER THE HEIGHT** of the top edge of the ledger to the post, using a water level. If you don't have a water level, set a long straight 2×4 or 2×6 edgewise on top of the ledger. Hold the 2×4 against the side of one of the posts. Use a level to level the 2×4. Mark the bottom edge of the 2×4 (same as the top edge of the ledger) on the post. Repeat for each post. Note: If the braces are in the way, you'll need to adjust them. Remove all but one screw securing the brace to its stake. Lower the brace until it is out of the way, then resecure it by using two screws at each end.

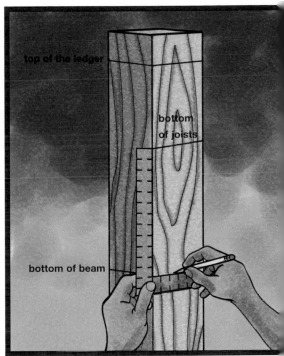

2 **FROM THE MARK,** measure down a distance equal to the vertical height of the beam and joists and mark the post. This is the finished top of the post. Use a speed square or combination square to transfer this mark to all four sides. Repeat this procedure for each post.

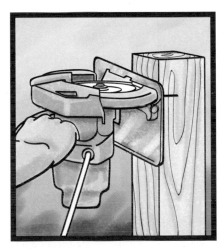

3 **CUT OFF THE TOPS** of the posts, using a circular saw and handsaw.

Beams are large, heavy pieces of lumber used to support joists. Beams are either solid lumber or are fabricated on site from two pieces of nominal 2× lumber sandwiched or "sistered" together. Solid beams longer than 16 feet are not readily available and may require a special order; a fabricated beam is a good alternative. The cost of the materials for a fabricated beam generally is less than for a piece of solid wood of the same dimensions, although making a beam requires additional labor.

Select wood that is straight and free of defects such as large knots or cracks. Do not use wood that is warped, twisted, or bowed. Select the correct galvanized metal post caps for installing beams. One type of post cap is made specifically to attach sistered beams (with an actual thickness of 3 inches) to solid posts (with an actual thickness of 3½ inches).

Make the beam at least 2 inches longer than required on each end. The extra length provides some flexibility when installing joists so that you can be sure the final framework is square. Once you install and square up the joists, trim the beam so that the end of the beam is perfectly flush with the outside edge of the outer rim joist (see Installing Joists, page 104).

Fabricating a beam

Check the span charts of pages 62–64 to determine the proper dimensions for fabricated beams made from two pieces of 2× lumber. When building the beam, use the longest pieces of wood available. Ideally, there should be no more than three offset seams, or butt joints, per beam—one on one side and two on the other. Measure post locations before building the beam. The placement of butt joints should correspond to post locations so that the post provides support directly beneath the joint. Butt joints should not be located within 3 feet of each other.

Build a beam in a location that provides continuous support for the wood and offers solid backing when nailing. A clean garage floor or driveway is ideal. Or use pairs of sawhorses. Move sawhorses so that nailing or driving screws occurs directly over a sawhorse.

Before beginning, "dry fit" the beam by placing it on a flat work surface. Butt joints should be square and tightly fitted. If not, trim the lumber to square the ends. Mark locations of all posts and check the butt joints to ensure they are supported by posts.

construction adhesive

1 OPEN THE DRY-FIT BEAM and use a caulk gun to spread a bead of exterior construction adhesive along the entire length of one beam in an S pattern that reaches within 2 inches of each edge. Reposition the second layer of 2× lumber. Align the top and bottom edges.

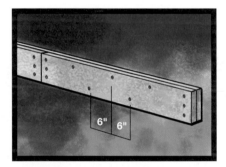

6" 6"

2 FASTEN THE LUMBER together, using 2¾-inch galvanized screws driven every 6 inches, alternating edge to edge. At ends and seams, use three screws driven no closer than 1½ inches from the end of the lumber.

Fabricated Beams

A fabricated beam is built of several pieces of 2× material fastened together. Butt joints must be supported by posts, so plan the length of each piece accordingly. Offset butt joints for maximum strength.

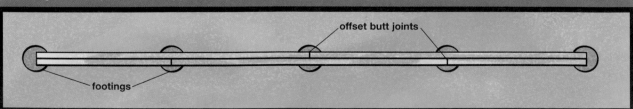

offset butt joints

footings

Installing beams

Beams are heavy. Have one or two helpers lift beams into position and hold them steady while they are fastened to the tops of posts. When setting a beam on top of tall posts-—such as for a second-level deck—keep safety first. Rent scaffolding to make the job easier and safer. Leave post braces in position until the joists are set.

Before setting the beam, sight along one edge to determine if the beam has a slight bend or "crown" to it. Always install structural lumber with the crown up.

1 BRUSH PRESERVATIVE or wood sealer on the top (the end grain) of each post. Fasten galvanized post caps to the tops of the posts, using galvanized joist hanger nails. Align all caps that will receive the beam.

2 SET THE BEAM into position. If necessary, loosen post anchors and braces and tap the posts into alignment. Plumb the posts, then tighten the post anchors. Reattach the braces. Align the ends of the beam with the ends of the ledger (making the beam slightly long ensures you don't make a mistake). Fasten the beam to the post caps, using galvanized joist hanger nails.

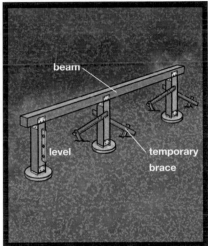

beam

level

temporary brace

Bracing

Permanent bracing attaches to posts and stiffens substructures so they won't move in high winds, during earthquakes, or under heavy loads of snow. Bracing may be required by local building codes, especially if deck posts are taller than 5 feet. Check with your building and planning department for specific bracing requirements in your area. Use 2×4s if the braces are 8 feet long or less. For longer braces, use 2×6s. Fasten the ends of braces to posts with pairs of lag bolts. Attach braces at 45-degree angles for maximum strength.

ledger

1

3

corner
bracket

3

1

beam

footing

2

header joists

4

Installing Joists

To install the joist system, begin with the perimeter joists. Install the outer rim joists (1) first, then the inner header joist (2). Next, install the inner rim joists (3). The last member of the frame is the outer header joist (4). Make the frame strong and rigid by fastening the paired joists together. Square up the frame and toenail it to the beam to secure it in position.

Joist installation begins with the outer or rim joists. Once this exterior frame is in place, square it up and nail it to the beam. The interior joists are installed inside this framework.

This method of joist installation uses a double outer rim joist to provide a particularly strong and rigid perimeter—a good system for attaching railing posts and stair stringers and for preventing flex or bounce in the deck floor. For aesthetics, consider making the outermost rim joist from 2× cedar, pine, or redwood stained or left natural. Using

cedar, pine, or redwood as an outer joist does not result in appreciable loss of strength in comparison to pressure-treated material.

Installing the rim joists

Check all measurements before cutting the joists to length. Before beginning, review the installation sequence and refer to the diagram, *above*. For clarity, the two rim joists parallel to the ledger are referred to as the inner and outer header joists.

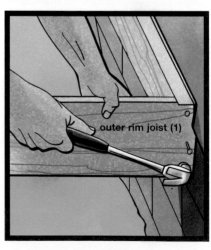

outer rim joist (1)

1 INSTALL THE OUTER RIM JOISTS
(1) by nailing them to the ends of

the ledger, using 16d galvanized box or common nails. Drilling pilot holes before nailing ensures that the nails won't split the ends of the joists.

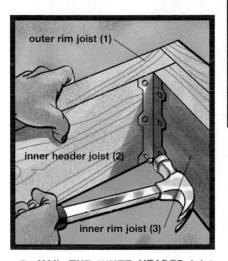

2 NAIL THE INNER HEADER joist (2) to the outer rim joists (1). The inner header joist is the same length as the ledger. Install the inner rim joists (3)—they fit between the inner header joist and the ledger. Attach the inner rim joist to the ledger using a galvanized metal corner bracket. Attach the outer header joist (4).

3 USE CLAMPS TO DRAW the joists together tightly. Fasten the paired joists to each other, using 2½-inch galvanized screws driven every 8 inches, alternating along top and bottom edges. If you prefer to

hide the screw heads from view, drive the screws only from the inside.

4 SQUARE THE RIM JOIST framing, measuring from opposite corners. Nudge the header joists until the corner-to-corner measurements are equal. Mark the top of the beam to indicate the proper location of the rim joists. Toenail the rim joists to the beam using 12d galvanized finish nails. If toenailing moves the rim joists off their marks, tap them back into position or move them by toenailing from the opposite side.

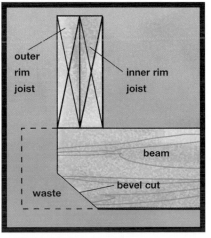

5 TRIM THE BEAM so it is flush with the outer edge of the outer rim joist. A bevel cut at the bottom of the beam creates a neat appearance. Use a circular or reciprocating saw.

Installing the interior joists

Install interior joists using galvanized joist hangers attached to the ledger and to the inside face of the inner header joist. Because hangers support joists from underneath, the interior joists do not have to be fitted tightly between the ledger and the header joists. Cut interior joists about ⅛ to ³⁄₁₆ inch shorter than the overall measurement to make them easy to slide into position.

As joists are installed, keep an eye on the header joist to make sure it remains straight. If the foundation wall has a bow (a defect that is difficult to detect), the interior joists will push the header joists, causing them to bow also. If interior joists are difficult to fit or if you see they are causing the header joist to bow, trim them to fit.

1 MARK THE POSITION of each interior joist on the inside of the header joist. These marks should correspond to the joist locations indicated on the ledger. To avoid confusion, indicate both sides of each joist. Align one side of a joist hanger along one mark. Nail the joist hanger using galvanized joist hanger nails.

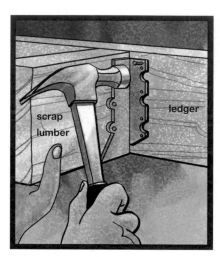

2 PLACE A SHORT PIECE of scrap joist lumber into the joist hanger and close the hanger until the fit around the scrap is snug but not tight. Nail the other side of the joist hanger into position. Install all joist hangers on the ledger and the header joist.

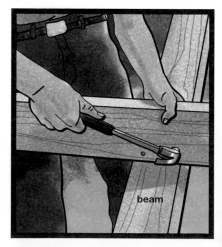

3 PLACE INTERIOR JOISTS in position; secure the ends with galvanized joist hanger nails. Toenail each joist into the support beam, with 12d galvanized box or common nails.

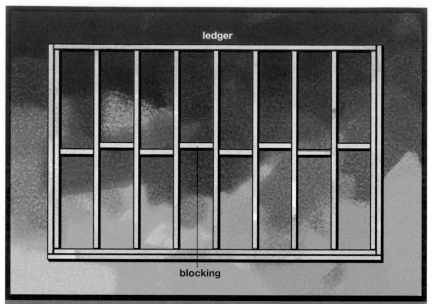

Install Blocking

Install blocking on joists that span more than 10 feet. Blocking keeps joists from twisting or warping over time and helps create a rigid framework that won't feel bouncy or springy underfoot. Blocking is made from short pieces of framing lumber cut to fit between the joists. This is a good way to use scrap lumber.

To position the blocking, measure out from the ledger along each side of the deck framing. Bisect the total distance—if the span is 12 feet, measure out 6 feet. Snap a chalk line across the tops of all joists. Install blocking along the line but alternate sides so that the blocking is staggered. Nail each piece of block with two galvanized 16d box or common nails driven into each end. For distances of 15 feet or more, plan a row of blocking every 5 to 6 feet.

Frame Around Trees

Frame around trees or other landscaping features by creating double joists on either side of the tree. Leave 4 to 6 inches between the framing and a tree to give the tree room to grow and expand. Complete the frame by installing headers between the joists. Headers should be the same dimensions as the joists. Because they carry the weight of interior joists, make headers from two pieces of 2x material "sistered" together. Attach headers to joists using double-size galvanized joist hangers, also called beam hangers. Attach interior joists to the headers using regular joist hangers.

Creating angled corners

If possible, make angled portions of the deck at 45-degrees. This basic angle is easy to work with, and 45-degree joist hangers are standard connectors available at home improvement centers. In this example, the interior rim joists are installed before the outer rim joists. Use corner brackets to attach the interior rim joists to the ledger.

1 INSTALL INTERIOR RIM JOISTS and square them to the ledger using 3-4-5 triangles (see page 92). Toenail the rim joists to the beam.

2 INSTALL THE INSIDE HEADER joist and attach it to the inner joists—you may have to support the header joist temporarily until the inner joists are attached.

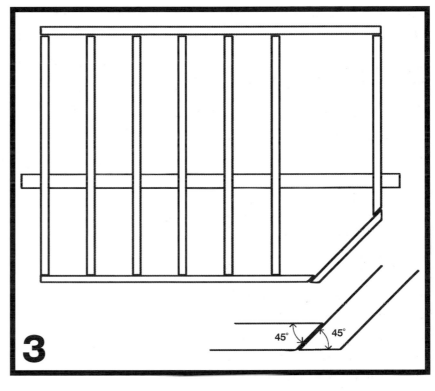

3 POSITION A STRAIGHT BOARD on top of the joists to indicate the proper location for the angled line of the deck. Mark the location on the tops of the joists. Use a combination square to draw a line down the face of the joist. Set the blade of a circular saw to a 45-degree angle and cut the rim joist and the header joist. Cut a piece of joist material at a 45-degree angle to fit against the cut ends of the interior rim joist and header joist. Cutting at a 45-degree angle exposes a lot of end grain—apply preservative or sealer to the ends of the boards before assembly. Use care when fastening the angled joist—predrill for nails to prevent splitting the wood. Use three 12d galvanized finish nails at each joint—the heads of finish nails are small enough to countersink easily, yet they provide plenty of holding power.

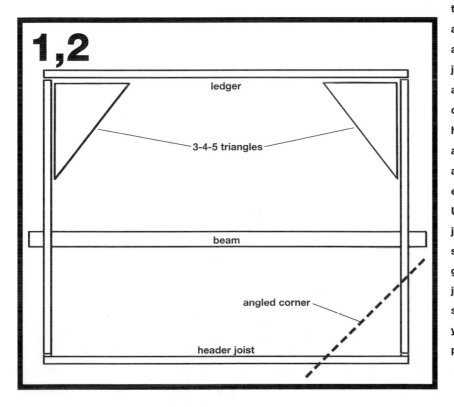

4 COMPLETE THE FRAMING by installing the outer rim joists and outer header joist. The key to this installation is to make closed miter joints at the angled corners. Closed miter joints present a neat appearance and will help prevent water penetration by concealing the end grain. Cut each end of the miter joint at 22½ degrees. This method allows the mitered joints on the outer joists to be offset from the 45-degree connections of the interior joists, creating a strong corner.

5 USE A FRAMING SQUARE to calculate the length of interior joists that will meet the angled header joist. Establish the distance between joists—for framing members 16 inches on-center, the distance is 14½ inches. Place the long leg of the framing square against the inside of the nearest full joist. Keep the shorter leg of the square above the angled header. Slide the framing square until the markings on the square indicate the distance to be 14½ inches. On top of the header, mark the intersection of the framing square and the header. Measure from this mark to the ledger to establish the length of the remaining interior joists. Add interior joists, using 45-degree angled joist brackets to attach the joist to the header.

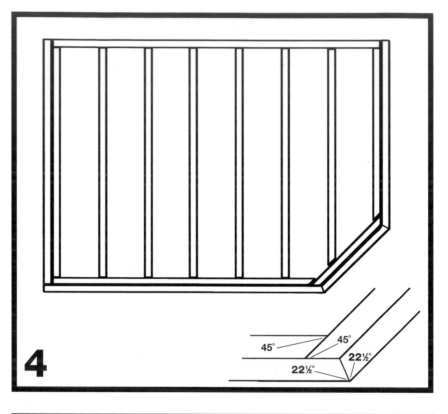

4

45° 45°
22½°
22½°

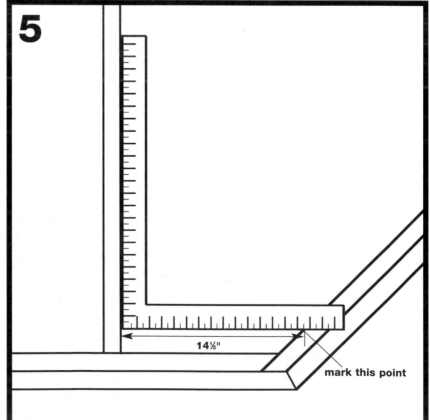

5

14½"

mark this point

Curved planting beds and meandering paths are popular in outdoor environments, and so are curved decks. Curves add style and interesting visual texture and they blend well with natural forms, which seldom have stiff, right-angled corners.

Building a curved portion of deck is time-consuming and requires moderate do-it-yourself skill. It also requires some specialized tools, such as a band saw, a thickness planer, and clamps—as many as two dozen of them. If you don't have these tools or can't borrow them, check availability at a rental store. If you need to buy them, building a curve may be cost-prohibitive. Professional contractors typically charge an additional $500 to $1,500 to build a curve.

The essence of a curved deck is a curved header joist. Because standard lumber is difficult to bend, create the curve from built-up layers of wood that is sawn and planed to a thickness of ½ or ⅜ inch, depending on the severity of the curve. These thin boards, called bender boards, are bent and glued together with waterproof glue—a process called lamination. You can use most species of wood to create a curve, but the boards must be free of knots and other defects, such as splits or checking. The wood species you select should match the species used for all the outer rim joists on the deck.

In general, use ½-inch-thick bender boards to laminate curves with a radius of 7 feet or greater and ⅜-inch-thick boards for curves with a radius of less than 7 feet. The object is to build a curved joist at least 1½ inches thick. You'll need three layers of ½-inch material and four layers of ⅜-inch material. For glue, use a top-grade, waterproof construction adhesive—available in tubes to fit caulk guns—or a urethane glue that is applied with a brush. Check with your local building and planning commission for guidelines or codes pertaining to curved decks.

Use full-length boards for laminating. It's possible to piece together shorter boards, but shorter boards are less flexible. Butt joints also weaken the finished joist. Refer to the deck plan to determine the length of the arc of the curve you will build. Cut boards at least 6 inches longer than this measurement. Split the thickness of each board in two, using a band saw. Nominal 2× lumber can be split into two boards about ⅝-inch thick. Plane each board to

final thickness, using a thickness planer. A cabinet shop will perform this operation for a fee. Make several extra boards in case a board breaks during the bending process.

To build a curve, install all straight joists first. Joists that butt the curve should be 6 to 12 inches longer than necessary—after all joists are installed, they will be trimmed to fit the curve exactly. To build a railing to match your curved deck, see Making Curved Railings, pages 127–129.

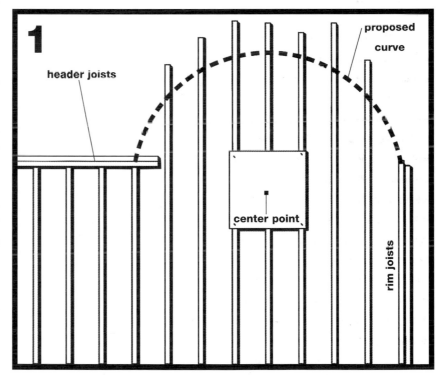

1 USE YOUR DECK PLAN to determine the center point of your curve. At this location, fasten a large piece of scrap plywood to the top of the joists. Using a piece of plywood at least 2×2 allows any necessary adjustment of the center point. Use screws to secure the plywood so you can remove it easily.

2 MAKE A PIVOTING SCRIBE STICK from a piece of straight 1×3 or 1×4. Drill a hole about 1½ inches from the end, and use a screw to fasten this end of the scribe stick to the center point (the screw should be exactly on the centerpoint). Make sure the stick swings freely. From the screw, measure along the scribe stick the length of the radius used to describe the planned curve. At that point drill a hole just large enough to push a pencil through.

3 SWING THE SCRIBE STICK over the inner joists and any rim joists that are included in the arc of the curve, marking the top edge of each joist. Check marks carefully—for curves that are an extension of one side of the deck, as shown in this example, the arc must meet rim joists precisely (see Examples A and B, *opposite*).

4 FROM THE MARK, use a combination or speed square to draw a line down the side of each joist. Set the blade of a circular saw to match the angle described on the top edge of each joist—each joist requires a slightly different blade angle. Follow the lines to trim the ends of the joists to the proper length and angle. Some of the joists may require cuts at angles steeper than a circular saw will allow. For these joists, set the blade square and as deep as it will go. Cut across the top of the joist, following the scribe line. Finish the cut with a reciprocating saw or handsaw.

NOTE: If your curve connects to rim joists as shown in Example A, *opposite,* then begin constructing the curve from that point. If the curve intersects rim joists as shown in example B, begin at the center or

saw kerf

4

"highest" point of the curve and work toward the ends. To begin in the middle, mark the middle point of all bender boards.

5 PUT A BEAD of construction adhesive on the ends of the joists. Predrill the bender board to prevent splitting, and secure it to the first joist with a single 8d galvanized box or common nail. The top of the bender board must be flush with the top of the joist. Check adjacent joists to make sure the bender board is flush with the top edges of the joists, and secure the bender board with nails. Go back and drive a second 8d galvanized nail into each joist. To prevent putting too much stress on the wood fibers, drive the nail heads just flush with the surrounding surface, but no deeper.

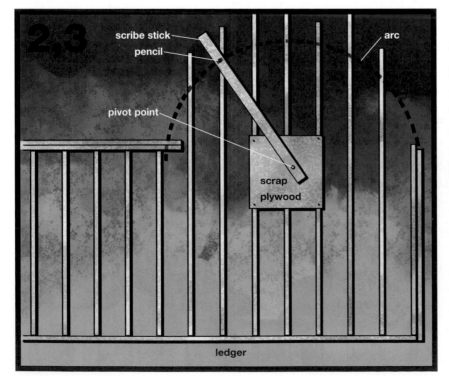

2,3
scribe stick
pencil
arc
pivot point
scrap plywood
ledger

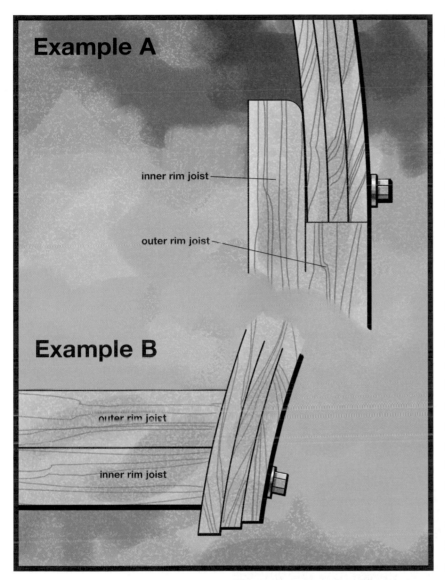

Example A

inner rim joist

outer rim joist

Example B

outer rim joist

inner rim joist

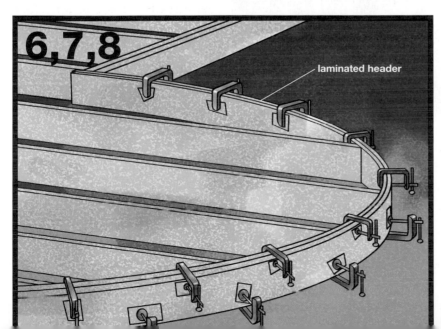

6,7,8

laminated header

6 WORK AROUND THE CURVE, driving nails square to the cut face of the joist. For joist ends cut at angles greater than 45-degrees, switch to 6d nails, nailing toward the thicker part of the joist. Check the glue manufacturer's recommendations for setting time and wait that amount of time before proceeding to the next layer of bender board.

7 COAT THE OUTER FACE of the first bender board with glue and apply the second layer of bender board, using clamps only—no nails. Attach C-clamps or sliding bar clamps every 6 inches, alternating at the top and bottom edge of the bender boards. Use pads or shims under the jaws to prevent marring the wood. Wipe up excess glue that appears between the joints. Leave clamps in place until the glue sets. Continue laminating until the final thickness is reached.

8 SECURE THE LAMINATED header joist to the interior joists by pre-drilling the header and driving three 16d galvanized finish nails into the ends of each joist. For added strength, use galvanized joist hangers at locations where the header meets a joist at 90 degrees and 45 degrees. To prevent knocking the header away from the ends of the joist, use 1-inch galvanized screws to fasten the joist hanger to the header. Predrill for screws.

AFTER THE SUBSTRUCTURE IS IN PLACE, complete the deck by installing the finish components. Most of these materials are lighter and smaller than those used for the substructure, but they require more precise measurements and more careful installation techniques. After all, the substructure is basically hidden, but finish components are there for all to see. Remember the carpenter's adage: measure twice, cut once. Double check measurements for accuracy. If in doubt, measure again.

Test the fit of finish components before installing them. Clamps are a great aid for test-fitting. Using clamps, hold pieces tightly together to check their fit or to mark their location before nailing or screwing them in place. Predrill whenever possible to prevent wood from splitting and to prevent wood fibers from crushing themselves against fasteners when wood swells during changes in humidity.

Most deck parts—including those made from pressure-treated wood—benefit from a coating of sealer or preservative prior to installation. This is especially true of end grain and freshly sawn wood. To ensure maximum protection of your deck, read Chapter 9, Finishing & Maintaining Your Deck, before installing finish components.

Installing decking, railings, and decorative touches requires precise measurements and careful work to get satisfying results.

ponents

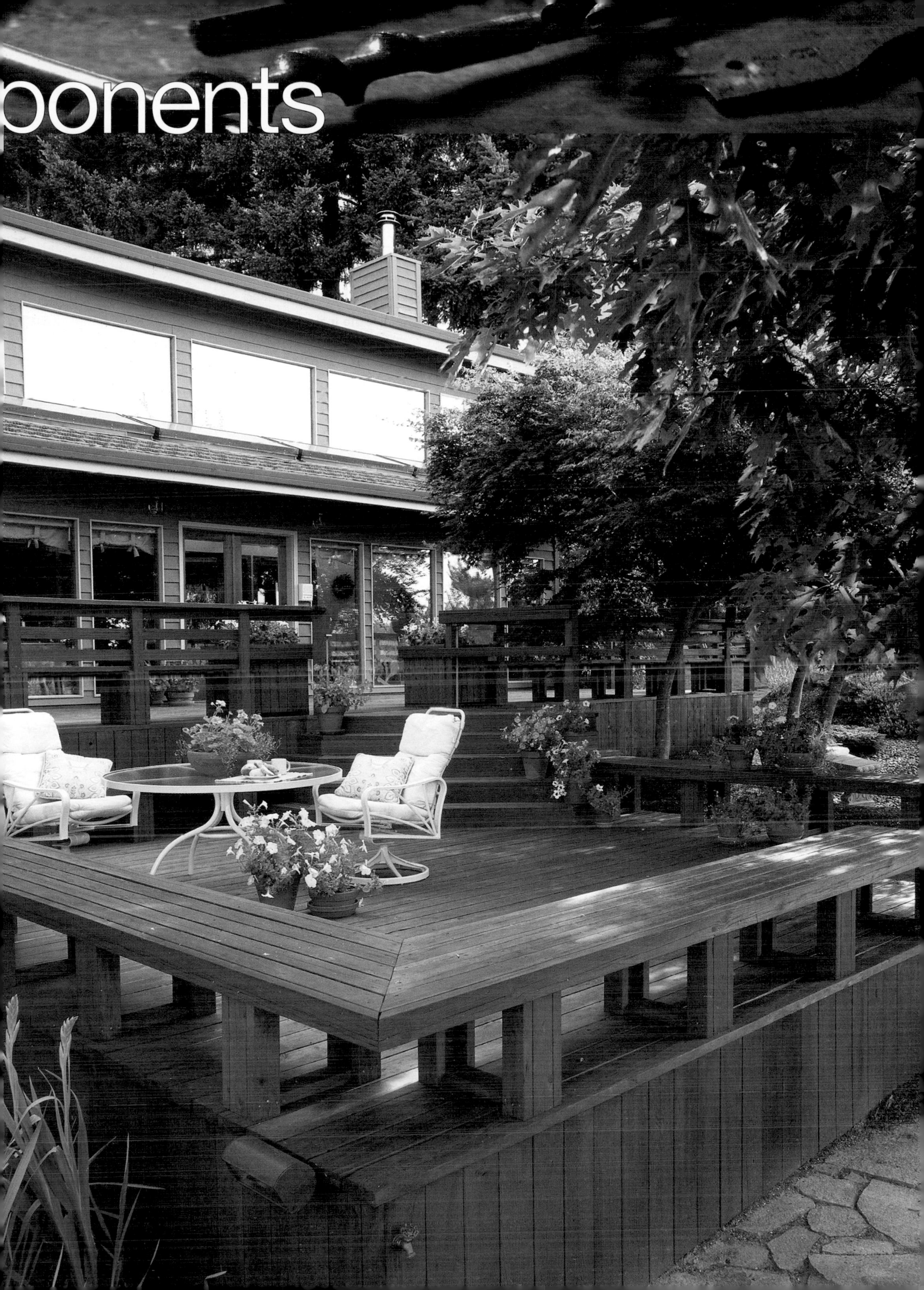

Installing the decking boards is one of the most enjoyable tasks of a deck-building project. Although the work is repetitive and time-consuming, you'll gain satisfaction as you see the deck take shape—and for years after.

The main objectives are to make sure the boards are straight, evenly spaced, and properly fastened. Along the way, monitor the alignment of boards so the rows remain straight. During installation, let the ends of the boards overhang the rim joists, then trim them all at once after the decking is completely installed. If space for the final piece of decking—the one installed against the side of the house—is too narrow or if the side of the house is not perfectly flat, scribe the last board so it fits snugly and precisely.

This basic installation assumes a rectangular deck with decking installed parallel to the house and butt joints randomly distributed throughout the field—a method that produces the strongest and most rigid decking surface with the least amount of waste. Other types of installations, such as patterns, are described toward the end of this chapter.

Brush preservative or sealer on the ends of boards prior to installation.

Installation techniques

Fasten decking boards to each joist with two nails or screws driven about ¾ inch from the edge of the decking. Sink nail and screw heads below the surface of the decking. For nails, use a nail set. Decking screws are self-countersinking— as they turn, they literally pull their heads below the surface of the decking.

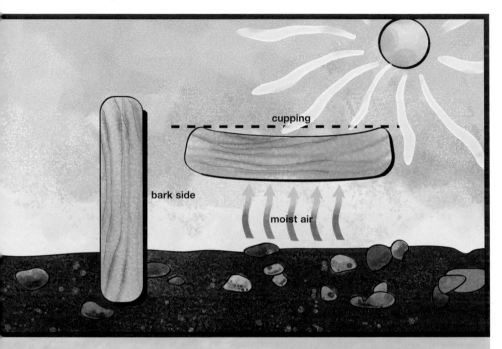

cupping

bark side

moist air

Which Side Up?

Even experienced deck builders disagree about which face of the decking should be installed up to avoid cupping—the tendency of the edges of decking material to bend upward over time, creating a "cup" that holds water and makes a bumpy decking surface. Some say the bark side of the board should be installed up; others say down. To understand the controversy, look at the growth rings on the end grain of a decking board. The "bark side" of the board means the side facing the outside of the tree.

The truth is, they're both wrong. The real culprit is the sun. Exposed to hot sun, the top surface of decking boards dry out faster than the underneath surface. This rapid drying causes the top layers of wood cells to shrink and contract, no matter which way the grain pattern faces. The problem is usually made worse by the fact that the bottom of the decking faces the shady ground and often is exposed to lingering damp conditions. A prime example is a sunny day shortly after a rain, when the top surface of the decking is in full sun while the ground beneath the deck is still soaked. The solution is to simply place boards with the most attractive face up and to use sound installation techniques to fasten the decking as securely as possible. Boards fastened with screws can easily be flipped over if cupping is excessive.

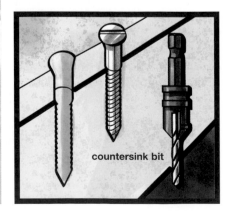

countersink bit

How deep they go is dependent on how much force is used to drive them. Most of today's electric drills feature clutch mechanisms with variable settings. When the drill encounters increasing force—such as the additional resistance met when a screw head enters the wood—the clutch disengages the drive. With a little practice, you can set the variable clutch to drive screw heads just below the surface of the decking but no farther.

However, as screw heads penetrate the surface of the decking they tend to tear the upper fibers of the wood. These wood fibers often stick up, creating little splinters. To prevent tearing the wood around screw heads, use a countersink bit to predrill holes for screws and screw heads. The method is necessary at the ends of boards to prevent splitting, but is also the best way to countersink screws without tearing wood fibers. To speed installation, use two drills—one outfitted with a countersink bit and the other with a power screw tip for driving the screws.

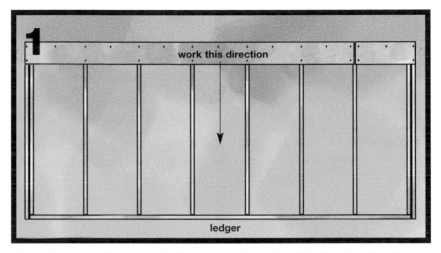

through a piece of scrap wood about 1 foot long. (A 16d nail is also the appropriate thickness to use as a spacer.) The nails should be about 8 to 9 inches apart. Place the spacer between decking boards and draw the boards together during fastening. Note: Never leave a spacer on the deck with the nails pointing up. When not in use, place the spacer with nails between decking boards. As a precaution, blunt the nail tips with a file.

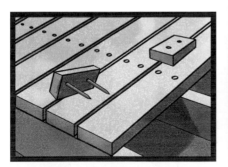

INSTALL DECKING with a gap of about ⅛ to ³⁄₁₆ inch between boards to allow for drainage. The best way to ensure even spacing is to use a spacer. Make a spacer by driving two 12d nails

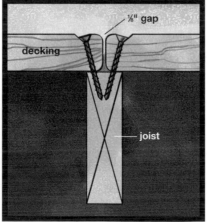

BUTT JOINTS MUST REST on a joist. Where butt joints occur, leave a ⅛-inch gap between the ends. Use a piece of coarse sandpaper to slightly chamfer the top edge of the ends to

reduce the likelihood of splinters. Angle fasteners so they fully penetrate the joist.

Installing decking

Begin installation along the outside edge of the deck and work inward (toward the house). This method ensures a full piece of decking in a highly visible location. Start with straight boards. Not every board will be *perfectly* straight, however. Bring boards that are slightly warped into alignment with clamps using the techniques described below.

1 INSTALL THE FIRST ROW of decking along the header joist. The outside edge of the decking should be flush with the outside face of the header joist. Drive a screw into each interior joist. Drive screws every 8 inches along the outside edge of the decking. Let all ends run long—trim after all decking is installed. Use a spacer to maintain even spacing between boards. Stagger butt joints throughout the field. Thoroughly fasten each piece of decking before moving to the next piece.

2 **AFTER INSTALLING** every third or fourth row of decking, sight along the edge of the decking to make sure the rows are straight. For visual reference, stretch a mason's string along the edge. If the rows appear warped or wavy, bring the rows into alignment by snapping a chalk line on top of the joists as a reference. Measure out from the high point of the decking a distance equal to the width of one piece of decking plus a ⅛-inch space and mark the joist. Have a helper stretch a chalk line from one side of the deck to the other. Measure out from the house along the rim joists. Adjust the chalk line so it passes over the marked joist and so the two measurements along the rim joists are equal. Snap the line. Install the next row of decking so that its edge is flush with the chalk line.

Scribing to fit

When the decking is within 6 to 8 feet of the house, measure the distance to the house along the rim joists to calcu-

late how many rows of decking remain. Remember to include the width of the decking plus all gaps between boards. If the last piece of decking is narrow—less than an inch—eliminate the partial piece by increasing the gaps between remaining rows of decking by ¹⁄₁₆ of an inch. If the last row of decking is wider than 1 inch but narrower than a full decking board, scribe it to fit. A narrow row against the house will not be readily noticeable.

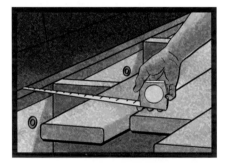

1 **WITH THE NEXT-TO-LAST ROW** of decking fastened in place, measure from the edge of the row to the house in several places to determine the largest distance. Subtract ¼ inch (the size of a ⅛-inch gap plus a ⅛-inch allowance between the house and

the boards to prevent moisture from being trapped) from this measurement and transfer it to a caliper or compass.

2 **MEASURE FROM THE OUTSIDE** edge of one rim joist to the outside edge of the opposite rim joist. This is the total length of the last row of decking. Cut a row of boards to fit this length—you want to have the last row fit precisely for length because once it is fastened in position it will be too close to the house to cut without damaging the ledger board. Place this full row of decking on top of the second-to-last row. Align the ends of the decking so they line up with the outside edges of the rim joists. Hold the compass so the jaws are at right angles to the decking, with the pencil on the decking and the point against the house. Draw the compass along the length of the house, tracing the outline on the loose decking.

3 **PLACE THE LAST ROW** of boards on sawhorses and cut the scribe line, using a jigsaw. Put the last row in position, set the correct spacing, and fasten it in place.

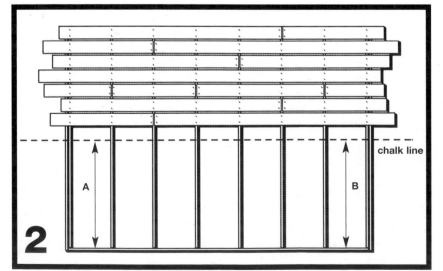

chalk line

A

B

2

4 SET THE DEPTH of the blade of a circular saw to match the thickness of the decking. Snap a chalk line across the decking flush with the outside face of the rim joists. Trim the decking boards. Brush preservative or sealer on the freshly cut ends of the decking.

Diagonal decking

Begin installation of 45-degree diagonal decking at an outside corner and work toward the house. If you work the other way, you risk having a tiny, odd-looking piece of decking in a conspicuous location.

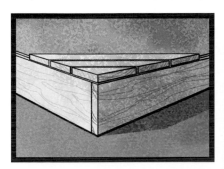

Start with a full-width piece of decking and cut the ends to 45 degrees so the resulting piece is triangular. To maintain a consistent 45-degree angle,

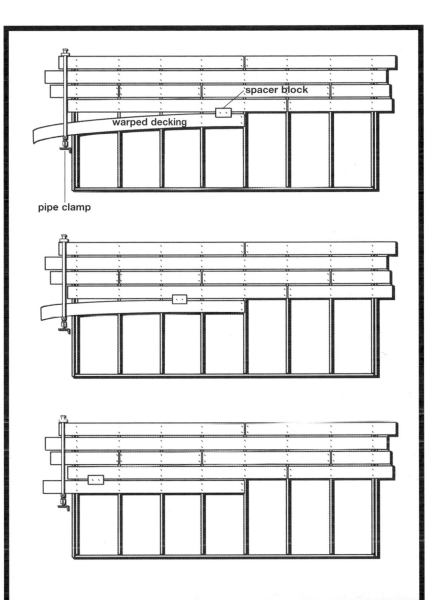

Straighten Warped Decking

As decking boards dry, some invariably bow or curve. Install these otherwise sound boards, using pipe clamps. The process straightens the decking board a bit at a time, fastening it into position as you proceed along its length. For this method to work, the decking is placed with its curve as shown above. Fasten one end of the warped decking to at least two joists so that the end is firmly anchored. Position a spacer block between the next pair of joists. Put a pipe clamp on the outward ends of the decking to provide maximum leverage. Tighten the clamp until the gap between the decking boards at the spacing block is correct. Fasten the warped piece of decking to the next joist. Reposition the spacer block and continue tightening and fastening the decking. To prevent the clamp pressure from twisting the decking off the joists, stand or kneel on the decking as you drive the screws or nails. If two pieces of decking are too tight, tap a wooden shim between the boards to force them apart before fastening.

install the first three or four pieces with ends cut flush to the outside edges of the rim joists. Use spacers to ensure a proper ⅛-inch gap between boards. Measure from the corner of the deck to the ends of each cut piece. If the decking is installed correctly, the measurements will be equal. After installing the first several boards and checking measurements, let the ends of the decking overhang the rim joists. Trim them as described in Step 4 of Scribing to Fit. Decking that butts against the house must be cut to fit before installation.

Building stairs

Building stairs requires exact measurements and careful layout. Thoroughly review your deck plan and determine

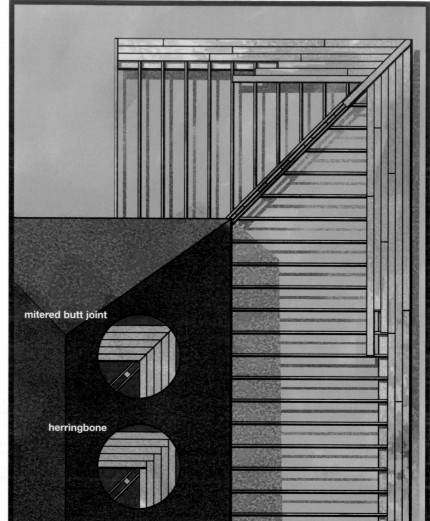

mitered butt joint

herringbone

Decking Around Corners

To install decking around two sides of a house, frame the joists as shown. The key is a double header joist installed at a 45-degree angle. Doubling this joist allows it to support interior joists and permits a variety of decking joints.

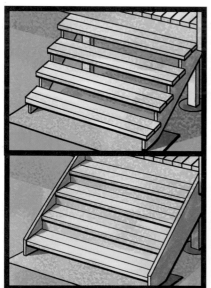

Open Stringers and Closed Stringers

A stair system with an open stringer, *top*, features notched stringers and treads supported by the notches. A closed stringer system uses solid boards at the sides with treads supported by metal or wood cleats.

how stair stringers, railing posts, and stair treads are designed. Detailed construction drawings ensure the stairs fit properly and are built without errors.

This section provides instruction for building open stringer stair systems. An open stringer is slightly more difficult to build than a closed stringer, but it allows easy cleaning of leaves and other debris, is less likely to trap moisture, and is aesthetically pleasing. This system does not use a closed or solid riser. Instead, the backs of the treads are open for cleaning and to simplify construction. If you prefer closed risers, they are simple to build. Suggestions for closed risers are given near the end of this section.

Stringers

Stringers are notched pieces of lumber used to support stair treads. Use 2×12 pressure-treated lumber for stringers. After cutting the stringers—but before they are installed—brush preservative or sealer on the stringers to prevent moisture damage.

Stringers attach to the deck one of three basic ways:

1 THE TOP OF THE STRINGER is flush with the top of the joists and the stringer fastens to the face of the rim joists with angle brackets or joist hangers. In this method, the tread material for the top stair is flush with surrounding deck material.

2 THE STRINGER ATTACHES to the front of the rim joists. However, because the rim joists usually do not provide enough vertical height for proper attachment of the stringer, an extension must be added to the bottom of joists. This method is good for novice stair-builders, but you must take into account the aesthetics of the extension and the fact that the bracket forms a closed riser on the last step.

3 THE STRINGER ATTACHES to the back of the rim joists with angle brackets. This methods works only if the vertical height of the rim joist equals the height of the risers in the stair system. Also, consider the thickness of the double rim joists needs when laying out and cutting the stair stringer—the uppermost tread of the stringer needs an additional 3 inches of width.

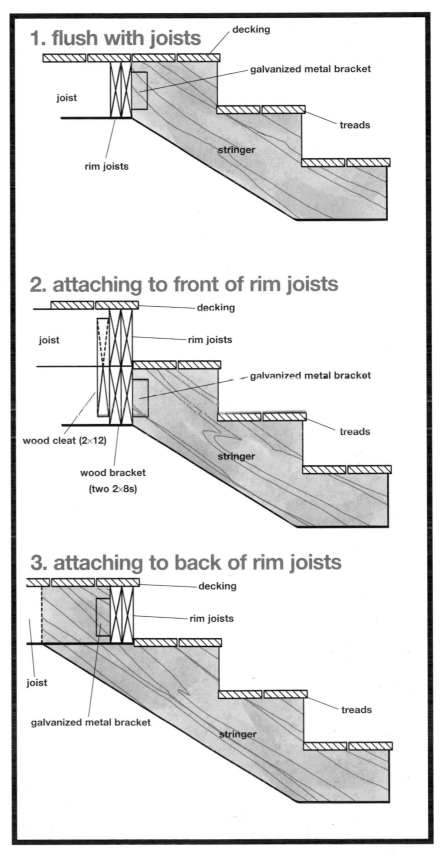

1. flush with joists

decking

galvanized metal bracket

joist

treads

stringer

rim joists

2. attaching to front of rim joists

decking

joist

rim joists

galvanized metal bracket

wood cleat (2×12)

treads

wood bracket (two 2×8s)

stringer

3. attaching to back of rim joists

decking

rim joists

joist

treads

galvanized metal bracket

stringer

Nosings

Letting the front edge of the stair tread hang over the tread cutout creates a small lip—a nosing. Nosings are not a necessity but they do help protect the stair stringer from moisture and sun damage, and they are details that lend an air of professionalism to the finished stairway. Because nosings have rounded edges, they resist cracking and splintering. Radius-edged decking (RED) material is ideal for creating treads with nosings. If you use standard 1× or 2× material, use an electric sander or a router with a round-over bit to shape the front of the tread. Remember that a nosing subtracts from the length of the tread below it. Compensate by adding the length of the nosing to the

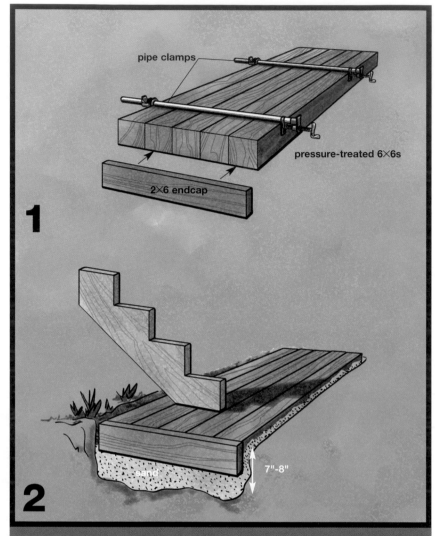

1

2

Making a Wood Landing

Make a low-cost wood landing from pressure-treated 6×6s. Gather the 6×6s together using pipe clamps, and secure them by capping the ends with a piece of 2×6 cut to length. Drive at least two fasteners into each end of every 6×6.

overall length of the tread cutout, and positioning the tread material toward the front of the step. Nosings should protrude no more than ¾ inch beyond the stringer.

Making a wood landing

The base or foot of the stairway needs to rest on a solid base—either a con-

crete landing (see Pouring a Landing, pages 97–98) or a simple wood pad made from pressure-treated 6×6s rated for ground contact.

Use the deck plan to determine the location and size of the landing—it should be at least six inches wider than the stairway on both sides and large enough to provide about 2 feet of wood in front of the base of the stairs.

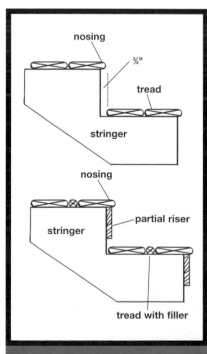

Nosings

Use nosings with any type of tread design. Unsupported nosings should not be longer than ¾ inch to prevent breaking the edge of the tread.

The pad rests in a pit 7 inches deep filled with 2 inches of smooth, level sand. Cap the ends of the 6×6s with pressure-treated 2×6s rated for ground contact. If you cannot obtain ground-contact 2×6s, use regular pressure-treated 2×6s brushed with liberal amounts of preservative.

1 MAKE THE LANDING BY lining up 6×6s. Cut 2×6 end caps equal in length to the combined width of the timbers. Use pipe clamps to hold the 6×6s together, and nail the 2×6 end caps onto the 6×6s, driving at least 2 16d galvanized box or common nails into the end of each 6×6.

2 DIG A PIT 7 TO 8 INCHES DEEP of appropriate width and length to hold the wood landing. Put sand in the pit to fill it within 5 inches of the top. Smooth the sand and level it, checking the surface with a level. The pad will be heavy—have a helper assist you in placing the landing into the pit. After positioning the pad, backfill around the edges.

Closed risers

Add closed risers to give your stairway a more formal, finished look. Risers can be full, covering the entire rise, or partial, covering only a portion of the rise. Partial risers don't trap debris and moisture and allow air to circulate along the back of the tread. Make risers from 1× or 2× material. Because riser boards take up the same amount of space from step to step, there's no need to recalculate the run of the tread to compensate for the added thickness.

Cutting stringers

To determine the approximate length of the lumber needed for a stringer, start with the number of steps in the stairway. On the legs of a framing square, establish the height of the riser, the rise, and the width of the tread, the run. Use a tape measure to measure the distance between the rise and run. Multiply this number by the number of steps plus 1.

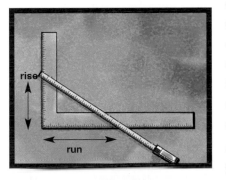

1 PLACE A 2×12 of appropriate length on a pair of sawhorses. Sight along the edge of the lumber to determine if there is a crown. Make sure the crown side is the upper edge of the stringer. Using a framing square, begin at a top corner of the lumber and mark off the rise and run of the first step, measuring from the edge of the stringer.

2 CONTINUE ALONG THE LENGTH of the stringer, marking off each

The Framing Square

A simple framing square, also called a carpenter's square, is an invaluable tool for laying out stairs. The square has two legs set at a right angle—the long leg is called the tongue; the shorter leg is the blade. Both inside and outside edges of the tongue and blade are marked for measuring. To avoid confusion, use only the inside or outside edge for measuring to lay out stairs.

step. At the last step, shorten the rise by the width of the tread material. At the top and bottom of the stringer layout, mark cutoff lines.

3 USE A CIRCULAR SAW to make cutouts in the stringer. Make sure the saw is not plugged in. Fully extend the blade and square the blade to ensure it is at a right angle to the foot of the saw. Cut off the ends of the stringer at the cutoff marks. Cut out the steps, running the front of the blade just to the intersection of the marks for risers and treads. Because the blade is circular, there will be a bit of wood remaining on the underside of the stringer. Cut this with a saber saw or handsaw held perpendicular to the surface of the stringer. As you make the final cuts, support the cutout to prevent the wood from tearing.

4 HAVE A HELPER HOLD the first stringer in position against the deck with the base or foot of the stringer resting on a concrete landing. Check the treads with a level to make sure they are level. If so, use

the first tread as a template to mark out the remaining treads. Use a sharp pencil so that the lines you draw are tight to the original tread. Cut out the remaining stringers.

Installing stair stringers

Use care when fastening risers and treads to stair stringers. Cutting stair stringers exposes the end grain. Brush preservative on freshly cut wood. Pre-drill holes for nails and screws.

1 PUT THE STRINGERS on a solid surface and nail an angle bracket flush to the back of each stringer. Hold the outside stringers in posi-

tion against the rim joists and nail the brackets to the joists. Place a straight 2×4 across outer stringers and use it to align the inner stringers before nailing them into position. Use a framing square to make sure the stringers are square to the rim joists.

2×4 cleat

2 ATTACH THE BOTTOMS of the stringers to the landing by using angle brackets or 2×4 cleats. Attach the cleats to concrete using concrete nails or lag screws and shields. Attach to a wood pad using galvanized screws. Install the treads.

framing square

building railings

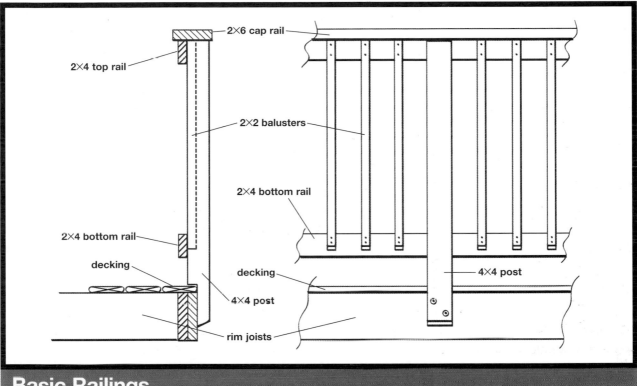

Basic Railings
Make a strong but simple railing system using 2×4s on edge for rails. Attach the rails to the back side (facing the deck) of the posts. Attach balusters to the front of the rails. A 2×6 cap rail goes over the top rail and the tops of the posts.

Making railings

Railings come in many styles and configurations (see Railings, page 71). Study the method for installing the basic railing described in this section, then modify the construction techniques to fit the style of railing you build. Thoroughly work out details on paper before beginning. Check the layout by measuring and drawing in post locations along the edge of the deck. That way, you have the opportunity to make adjustments between posts before cutting lumber. Adjustments of an inch or less are virtually undetectable.

Build a simple, strong railing system using notched 4×4 posts and ordinary lumber—2×4 top and bottom rails, a 2×6 cap rail, and square, 2×2 balusters with beveled ends. In this system, the rails are installed along the inside of the posts—not butted between them—minimizing the time required for construction. For a decorative touch, attach finials to the cap rail directly above each post. To make railings that match curved portions of deck, see Making Curved Railings at the end of this section.

Join long pieces of lumber together with scarf joints. Form scarf joints by cutting the ends of the boards at 45 degrees, then fitting them together. Drive fasteners through the joint so that both boards are pinned together—

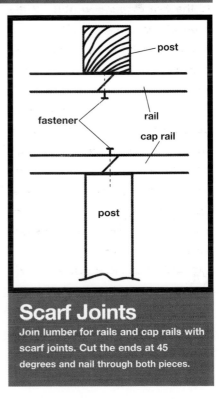

Scarf Joints
Join lumber for rails and cap rails with scarf joints. Cut the ends at 45 degrees and nail through both pieces.

this prevents the joint from opening up during changes in temperature and humidity. Before joining the pieces, brush preservative or sealer on the freshly cut ends. Position scarf joints at posts to supply a solid backing for the fasteners and always predrill for fasteners to prevent splitting the wood.

At outside corners, use a corner post or two regular posts positioned within a few inches of each other (see page 71, Planning Railings). Some lumber suppliers have precut corner posts. Otherwise, make one by cutting a 4×4 to length and notching it with a saw and chisel so the bottom of the post fits around the corner. Using two regular posts is easier—these posts can even be adjusted to somewhat account for minor errors in the layout of the railing system. However, the placement of the two posts must conform to codes—the distance between them must be no more than 4 inches.

At stairs, the railing must turn to follow the angle of the stairway. This is one of the trickiest parts of railing construction—the rail that descends along the stairway is angled. A miter joint involving an angled piece of wood is called a compound miter. Instructions for making a compound miter are given later in this section.

Some codes require that the handrail be "graspable," small enough for the human hand to fit around comfortably. The 2×6 cap rail used in the deck railing may not fit that description. Instead, install a standard handrail with galvanized hardware.

Where deck railings meet stair rail-

ings, take care to ensure that details of construction are thoughtfully designed.

Setting posts

1 USING YOUR DECK DESIGN as a guide, lay out post locations along the edge of the deck. If necessary, adjust the layout so posts and balusters are evenly spaced.

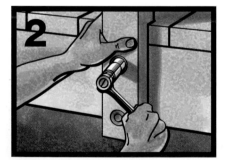

2 POSITION AND LEVEL POSTS individually. Place the post on the layout marks. Mark the tail of the post (the part that hangs down along the rim joist) for two carriage or lag bolts. When you use carriage bolts, the area behind the rim joist must be unobstructed so the nuts can be tightened. Drill and install one of the bolts. Use a level to set the post

plumb, then drill and install the remaining bolt. Continue around the perimeter of the deck. Install posts along the stairway according to the deck design.

Altering a corner post for a stairway

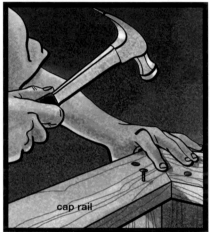

cap rail

Clamp a regular notched post to sawhorses for cutting. Use a combination square to mark one-half the tail of the post for removal. Position the marks so the post fits against the stringer as shown. Use a circular saw to cut away the waste portion of the tail. Secure the post using two fasteners—one driven into the rim joist and the other driven into the stringer.

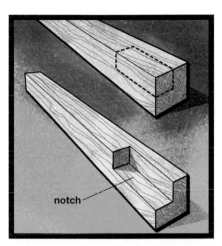

notch

Altering a post for an outside corner

Clamp a 4×4 to sawhorses for cutting. Cut the post to a length equal to the other railing posts (including the tail). Use a combination square to mark the post for notching. Make the length of the notch equal to the length of the tails of the other posts. Make the depth of the notch equal to the depth of the notch in the other railing posts. Mark this depth in two directions as shown above. Set the blade of a circular saw to

this depth. Cut along the lines but do not extend the cut past the lines indicating the length of the notch. Because the blade is circular, a small portion of wood will remain uncut. Use a sharp chisel to cut and remove the waste.

Installing rails

1 **INSTALL THE BOTTOM RAILING** by clamping it in position. Drive two fasteners through the rail into each post. Install the top railing flush with the tops of the posts. Use scarf joints to join long pieces of lumber, placing scarf joints at posts. Use miter or butt joints at corners.

2 **INSTALL THE CAP RAIL,** using scarf joints to join pieces of the cap. At outside and inside corners, miter across the width of the cap. On top of the post where the deck railing meets the stair railing, run the cap over the top of the post and allow it to overhang the sides of the post and top rail by about ¼ inch on all sides. Sand the corners slightly.

3 **INSTALL BALUSTERS** between the posts with the bevel end pointing down. For each section of railing, install a single baluster, using a level to make sure it is plumb. Refer to your deck design to determine the spacing between balusters. Use this

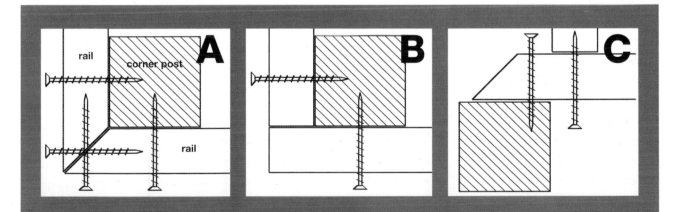

Attaching Rails at Corners

Decks may have a combination of inside and outside corners. At inside corners, miter the rails (A) for a clean appearance. Keep the joint closed by nailing the rails to the posts and adding fasteners through the joint. Butt joints (B) are simpler. Joining rails at outside corners (C) requires fastening the end of one rail to a post and butting the joining rail into it.

balusters

spacer block

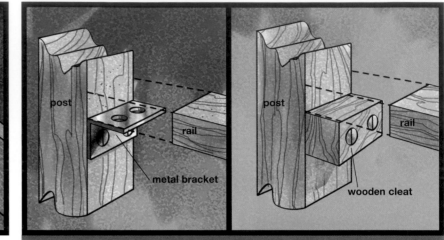

post

rail

metal bracket

post

rail

wooden cleat

Butting Rails to Posts

Butt rails to posts by supporting the ends of the rails from underneath. Use metal angle brackets or wooden cleats. Screw or toenail rails to the posts.

measurement to cut a spacer block from a scrap piece of wood. Using a spacer block to install balusters makes the job much faster and ensures accuracy. Use at least three fasteners per baluster—two in one end and another in the opposite end.

Butting rails between posts

Butt horizontal rails inside posts using wooden cleats of galvanized metal brackets to attach the rails to posts. Cut the rails to length and install the cleats or brackets as shown. Slide the rails into position and attach them. If you are using wooden cleats, drive two 8d galvanized finish nails at an angle from the top of the rail into the posts. If using metal brackets, drive galvanized screws into the rails from below.

Joining deck and stair rails

Use a compound miter joint to join deck and stair rails. First, make a dry run of the layout by clamping boards in position before cutting. A dry run allows you to visualize the necessary

cuts, especially the complex compound miters, and to mark pieces appropriately.

Ideally, the stair rails meet the deck rails at a single compound miter. However, depending on the rise and run of the stairway design, the rails will intersect at various angles. Using short filler blocks that wrap partway around the corner post gains some leeway and allows you to change the point where the deck and stair rails meet.

1 MARK THE LOCATION of the deck rails on the corner post. Use a combination square to extend these marks around two sides of the post.

2 CLAMP THE STAIR RAILS into position and mark the outline of the rails on the face of all posts. On lower posts, use a combination square to transfer the marks to the opposite side of each post. Cut off the post tops with a circular saw. At the post where the deck railing meets the stair railing, use a bevel

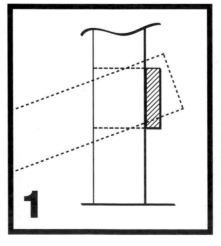

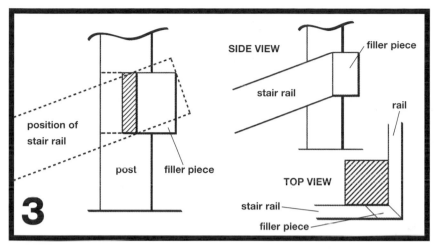

3

position of stair rail

post   filler piece

SIDE VIEW

filler piece

stair rail

rail

TOP VIEW

stair rail

filler piece

gauge to capture the angle between the rail and the post. Use this angle to mark a rail for cutting a compound miter. Clamp the rail to sawhorses. Set the blade of a circular saw to 45 degrees, and follow the bevel line to cut the compound miter. Note: The miter on the beveled piece will be longer than the miter on the level deck railing. The miters should be joined flush at their bottoms and the top of the taller miter trimmed with a hand saw to match the upper edge of the deck rails.

3 IF NECESSARY, MAKE A FILLER piece to wrap partway around the post. Measure the distance from the back side (facing the deck) of the deck rail to the marks on the post that indicate the intersection of the deck and stair rails. Make a filler piece to length that is mitered on both ends. Install the deck rails, filler pieces, and stair rails.

Installing cap rails on stairways

At the corner post where the deck railing meets the stairway railing, the cap

rails are not joined. The 2×6 cap for the deck railing ends over the top of the post, and the 2×6 cap for the stair rail is cut at an angle to butt against the post. Use a bevel gauge to capture the correct angle for butting the stairway cap rail to the post. Set the blade of a circular saw to this angle, and cut the bevel. Install the stairway cap rail.

Installing stairway balusters

After the cap rail is fastened in position, install the balusters. Because the balusters are plumb but the railing is angled, you must trim the upper ends of the balusters to meet the cap rail. Trim all balusters to the same length. Install one baluster, making sure it is plumb. To speed installation and create even spacing between balusters, use a spacer block.

Making curved railings

Curved railings require special considerations. Although the vertical members—the posts and balusters—are the same as those used for straight railing systems, the horizontal rails of a curved railing system are bent to match the arc

Installing Cap Rails on Stairways
Where railings turn from the deck and follow stairways, the cap rails do not meet. Instead, the deck cap stops at the post and the stair cap butts into the post.

2×6 cap for deck railing

2×6 cap for stair railing

scribe onto 2×12

under the header joists. Scribe the curve of the header joist on the lumber. Indicate the edges of each post. This mark indicates the outside edge of the rails—the surface that rests against the inside (the side facing the deck) of the posts.

of the deck. Make curved rails by cutting 1½-inch-wide arcs from pieces of 2× lumber, such as 2×8s or 2×10s. To match the curve, use the curved header joist (see Building Curves, pages 109–111) as a template.

To create the thickness necessary for rails, stack and laminate two pieces of curved 2× material together, using weatherproof glue and fasteners. Because two pieces of 2× material have a thickness of 3 inches (and standard 2×4 rails are 3½ inches wide), modify rails for the remaining portions of the deck by trimming ½ inch from the width of the rails.

1 USING YOUR DECK DESIGN as a guide, mark locations for all posts on the edge of the curved deck. Use a combination square to extend the marks across the face of the header joist.

2 HAVE A HELPER ASSIST YOU in holding a piece of 2× lumber

3 USE A SABER SAW TO CUT 1½-inch-wide curved rails. The pieces should be long enough to reach from post to post, with enough length to allow scarf joints on the ends of the pieces for joining. Cutting tight-fitting scarf joints on curved pieces may require two or three attempts before the fit is exact. Stack two curved sections on top of each other to produce a rail 3 inches wide. Laminate the pieces using weatherproof glue and fasteners driven every 6 inches. Clamp the sections together and predrill for fasteners, driving them up through the bottom of the rail sections to hide the heads. When the laminations are dry, remove the clamps and sand the faces flush.

4 INSTALL ALL POSTS, using a level to ensure the posts are plumb. Use two lag bolts or carriage bolts to secure the post tails to the curved header joist. Starting at one end of the curved portion of deck, cut scarf joints in one section of rail. Secure the railing in position, using a single finish nail through the open scarf. Cut a corresponding scarf joint in the next section of rail, but leave the opposite end long. Match the scarf joints, recutting if necessary. When the joint fits tightly, mark the opposite end and cut the next miter

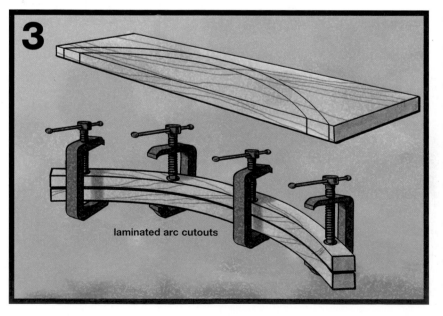

laminated arc cutouts

4

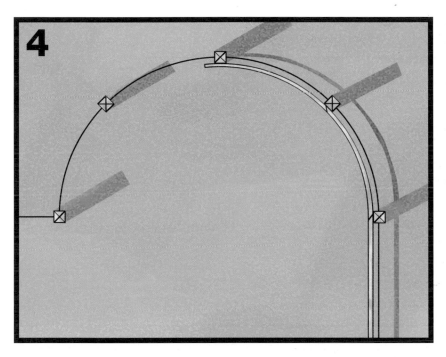

Making Tight Radii

Cut wood for pronounced curves by cutting a crescent-shape from a piece of 2×
lumber, then gluing the crescent to the back of the original lumber using
waterproof glue. When dry, mark and cut the glued board.

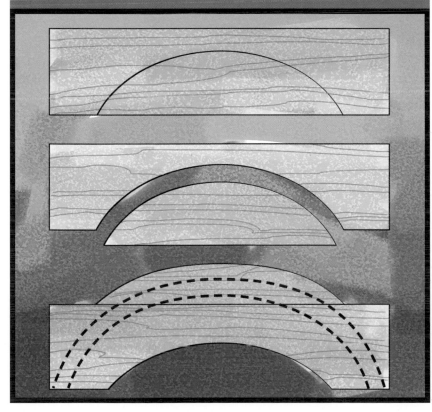

for a scarf joint. Secure the rail, driving two fasteners through the finished joint and a single nail through the next open scarf joint. Continue around the curve, carefully fitting one joint before moving to the next post. Install top and bottom rails.

5 WITH THE RAILS SECURED, install the balusters, using a level to make sure they are plumb. Use a spacer block to ensure even spacing between balusters. Screwing the balusters is preferable to nailing them—hammering produces shock that may loosen the rails or separate the laminations. Set the tops of the balusters flush with the top edge of the top rail. Predrill for screws to prevent splitting the balusters.

6 Out 5½-inch-wide cap rails to match the curve of the railing from 2×8s, 2×10s, or 2×12s. Set the cap rail lumber on top of the rails and use a pencil to mark for cutting. Mark each baluster along the front (away from the deck), then connect the lines to form a curve as a guide for cutting. Join the cap rail with scarf joints over the tops of posts.

Making tight radii

If the curve is pronounced, it may be difficult to cut tall rail arcs from a piece of standard lumber. Make tall arcs by cutting out a moon-shaped piece of lumber and reattaching it to the opposite edge of the board with glue. Trace the arc of the curve on the joined lumber, then cut out the pieces for the rail.

installing skirting

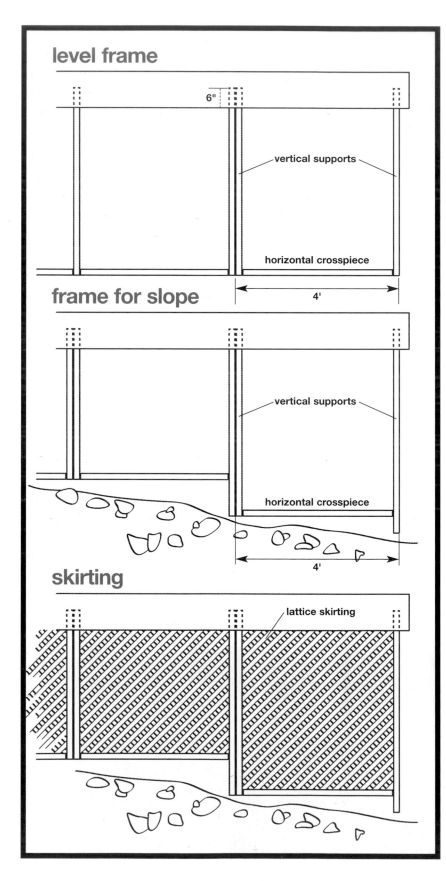

level frame

6"

vertical supports

horizontal crosspiece

4'

frame for slope

vertical supports

horizontal crosspiece

4'

skirting

lattice skirting

The plastic or wood lattice used for skirting typically comes in 8×2- and 8×4-foot sheets. Install skirting around the perimeter of the deck by constructing a frame to support the lattice material. Make the frame from pressure-treated 2×2s, which are lightweight and easy to cut and handle. When the framework is complete, however, it will be rigid enough to hold the lattice firmly in place. If 2×2s are not available from a lumber supplier, make them by ripping 2×4s to 1½ inches wide. Each section of framework consists of two vertical supports and a horizontal crosspiece. Attach the vertical frame members to the inner face of the rim joists; allow 6 inches of frame for attaching to the joists.

Make each section of frame 4 feet (48 inches) wide. This allows installing the lattice panels horizontally, 8 feet long. If the skirting is taller than 4 feet, install the lattice material vertically. The calculated height of each section should be within 1 inch of grade.

Because the square-cut 2×2s are 1½ inches thick, each horizontal member will be 45 inches long (45 + 1½ + 1½ = 48). An exception is at a corner. Here, one section is a full 48 inches wide. The frame that abuts is only 46½ inches wide, but it supports a lattice panel that overhangs the frame by 1½ inches. This happens because both sections count the same vertical member—the one that is fastened directly in the corner—in their overall width. The overhang of the one panel attaches to the frame of the abutting panel.

If there is a section at an end of the deck less than 4 feet wide, make a frame to fit it. Fasten adjacent sections together by clamping vertical supports together and driving two ⅜-inch galvanized screws through one vertical frame member into the next.

Shape the bottom of the skirt to match changing grade levels by cutting the skirting material to match the contours. The vertical 2×2 frame supports can be different lengths, depending on the vertical distance from the rim joist to grade. However, install the horizontal cross member square to the supports as shown.

rim joist

1 MEASURE THE VERTICAL distance from the bottom of the rim joist to grade. Add 6 inches to this measurement for attaching the vertical frame members to the inside face of the rim joist. Cut vertical and horizontal members to length.

2 FOR EASIER INSTALLATION, make each three-piece frame section separately and install them one at a time. Fasten horizontal crosspieces to the inside edges of

the vertical supports by pre-drilling and driving a 2¾-inch galvanized screw through the vertical support into the horizontal crosspiece.

3 BEGINNING AT ONE CORNER of the deck, install a section of frame, securing each vertical support to the back of the rim joist with two fasteners. The vertical supports must be plumb and the horizontal crosspieces square to the supports.

4 CONTINUE INSTALLING support sections along the perimeter of the deck. Fasten sections together by clamping adjacent vertical supports to each other and driving 2¾-inch galvanized screws through one support into the other every 12 to 18 inches.

5 SUPPORT A SHEET OF LATTICE material on sawhorses. Mark the bottom edge to fit the space between the rim joist and the grade, allowing about 1 inch of clearance at the bottom to prevent moisture damage. Cut the lattice to fit, using a saber saw or circular saw. If cutting wood lattice with a circular saw, use caution. The pieces of crisscrossing lath are held together with staples at every intersection. Remove any staples in the path of the saw before cutting. To prevent splitting wood lattice, pre-drill for screws. Butt the lattice tight to the undersides of the rim joists, and fasten it to the vertical supports and horizontal crosspieces using 1-inch galvanized screws driven every 8 to 10 inches. At the sides of the deck, the rim joists rest on one or more beams. Cut out the lattice to fit around the ends of the beams. For a finished appearance, install trim around the outside of the cutout, fastening the trim to the beam.

skirting frame

building an overhead

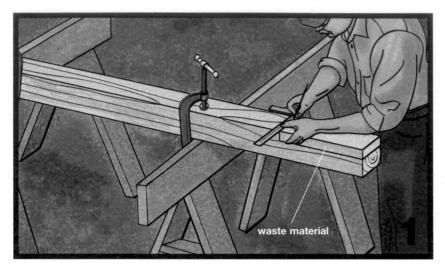

waste material

1 MEASURE THE LENGTH and depth of the notches in the posts used for the railing. Use a combination square to transfer these dimensions to the lumber for the overhead supports.

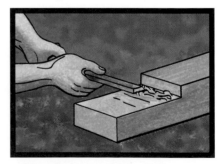

2 PLACE THE SUPPORT POST on sawhorses or an appropriate work surface and secure it with clamps. Set the blade of a circular saw to the depth of the notch. Cut across the post at the mark for the length of the notch. Follow this cut with a series of cuts across the end of the support post, spacing the cuts about ¼ inch apart. Make smooth, even passes with the circular saw. Keep the shoe of the saw flat and avoid rocking the saw when entering or exiting the cut.

Build an overhead to provide shade and to define specific areas of the deck. A typical overhead consists of tall posts that support a grid of beams, rafters, and 2×2s fastened to the rafters. The tighter the spacing between the 2×2s, the more shade the overhead will cast.

Design the posts for the overhead as extensions of the railing system or as part of an independent structure. If they are part of the railing system, use single corner posts in the design rather than a two-post corner configuration (page 71). A single post significantly simplifies the design and construction of the overhead.

Even though they do not support a live load, the size of the beams and rafters should conform to the sizes specified in the span tables on pages 62–64 (for rafters, refer to the span tables for joists, page 63). This ensures the lumber won't sag over time under its own weight.

In the basic design described here, the beams are made from two pieces of 2× material attached to the sides of the posts with carriage bolts, rather than being set atop the posts and secured with galvanized metal post cap connectors. This provides support for structural members that are not expected to bear live loads.

For decorative flair, use a saber saw to shape the ends of beams and rafters, and cut semi-circles from the bottoms of braces. Brush preservative, sealer, or stain on all parts prior to assembly. Bevel the tops of posts to shed water or add post caps.

Cutting notches in posts

If the overhead is integral to a railing system featuring notched posts, the supports for the overhead also must be notched. The notches should be the same depth as the notches in the railing posts so the rails will be in alignment.

Mark the post and indicate the waste material. Use a circular saw to cut a series of kerfs through the waste material and a chisel to clean out the notch. For cutting notches in corner posts, follow the procedures described on page 125.

3 USING A SHARP CHISEL held flat, bevel side up, remove the waste material from the notch. Smooth notch interior with the chisel.

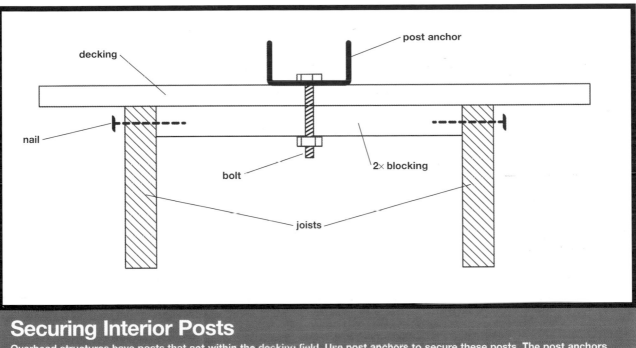

Building a simple overhead

Take care when setting tall posts—temporarily brace them upright until beams, joists, and permanent braces are attached. Screw blocks of wood to the decking to provide temporary anchors for the ends of braces. Fasten permanent braces at a diagonal between the joists and the posts. They give the overhead the stiffness and strength needed to prevent flexing during high winds.

To make installation easier and more accurate, mark all beams and rafters prior to construction. Place the beam lumber on edge on a pair of sawhorses. Make sure ends are aligned and draw the lumber together with clamps. Use a framing square to indicate the location of posts on the bottom edges of the beams. Flip the beams over and indi-

cate the position of all rafters on the top edges. Indicate both sides of each rafter to avoid confusion.

This construction method calls for toenailing the rafters into the beams, using galvanized finish nails. However, building codes may require a different fastening system, such as a metal connector specifically designed to withstand high winds. Be sure to check with

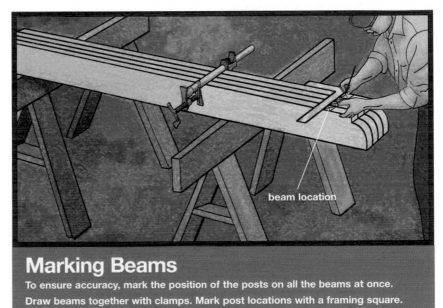

Marking Beams

To ensure accuracy, mark the position of the posts on all the beams at once. Draw beams together with clamps. Mark post locations with a framing square.

your local building department about requirements for fastening rafters on outdoor structures.

All overheads have freestanding posts—posts that occur in the midst of the decking field. Secure freestanding posts with galvanized post anchors. To ensure a solid connection, fasten the post anchor to a joist beneath the decking with a lag bolt. If the post falls between two joists, install a piece of flat blocking directly beneath the post location. Drill through the decking and the blocking and secure the anchor with a through bolt. Hide the post anchor by trimming the bottom of each post with 1× material. Note: Because post anchors slightly elevate posts on metal plates called "stand-offs," carefully calculate the difference in length between perimeter posts and those secured with post anchors. Cut posts to length accordingly.

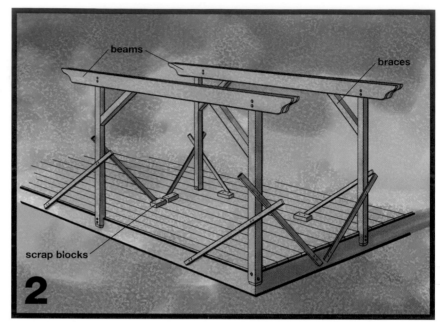

beams

braces

scrap blocks

2

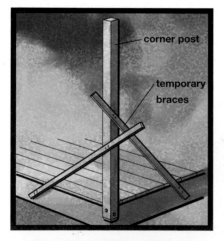

corner post

temporary braces

1 SET THE CORNER POST in position. Use a level to make sure it is plumb in all directions. Brace the post temporarily, using 1×4 boards attached at an angle of about

45 degrees from the middle of the post to the rim joists—using screws to attach the temporary braces makes them easy to remove. Fasten temporary braces to the decking by screwing scrap blocks of wood to the decking boards. Use two fasteners at each end of the braces. Set and brace the remaining posts.

2 SET ONE PAIR OF BEAMS into position and secure them temporarily by driving a single screw through the middle of the beam into the posts. Drill holes for carriage bolts. Install the bolts and tighten the nuts until the washers just begin to crease the surface of the wood. Drill the remaining holes and install all carriage bolts.

3 MAKE PERMANENT BRACES from pieces of 4×4 material. Cut the bottom end of the brace at a 45-degree angle and bolt it to the support post. Leave the other end of the brace square. The brace should be

about 2½-feet long and extend from the post through the double beam. The squared end of the brace should extend about 6 inches past the bottom edges of the beams but should not protrude past the top edges of the beams. When installed at an angle, the squared top of the brace creates a peak that sheds

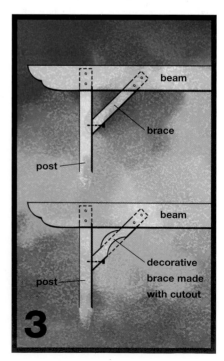

beam

brace

post

beam

post

decorative brace made with cutout

3

2×2 lath

rafters

4

water. Secure the brace with two fasteners driven through the sides of the beams; drive a lag bolt or two long screws driven through the base of the brace into the post.

4 SET RAFTERS IN POSITION on top of the beams. Toenail the rafters to the beams, using 12d galvanized finish nails. Set 2×2 lattice pieces on top of the rafters. Secure the 2×2s to the rafters by driving a 2¾-inch galvanized screw through the top of the 2×2 into each rafter.

5 INSTALL THE RAILING POSTS, rails, and balusters. Cut the cap rail to fit around the inside face of the support posts.

5

ALL WOOD—EVEN PRESSURE-TREATED WOOD—NEEDS PROTECTION from the elements. Left unfinished, wood will split, crack, discolor, and even pull away from fasteners. Regular applications of sealer, stain, or paint minimize damage and extends the life of the deck, protecting your investment.

Because wood is a natural material, even regular maintenance cannot keep it in perfect condition indefinitely. Decks, especially decks five years or older, require periodic inspection for defects and damage, such as rot, insect damage, and cracked boards, that could reduce the structural integrity of the structure and lead to costly repairs. A do-it-yourself inspection takes minimal time and quickly reveals the condition of the structure. This chapter shows how to monitor the condition of a deck by inspecting possible problems areas. If the deck does have some deterioration, the section on deck repair advises how to remove and replace damaged parts without disturbing other areas of the deck.

In some instances, the damage may be so widespread that a complete remodeling of the structure is in order. If that's the case, a redesign may be in order. If so, you may be able to keep portions of the deck or salvage usable materials to reduce costs.

A quality finish and periodic maintenance will keep your deck beautiful and trouble-free for years.

ing your deck

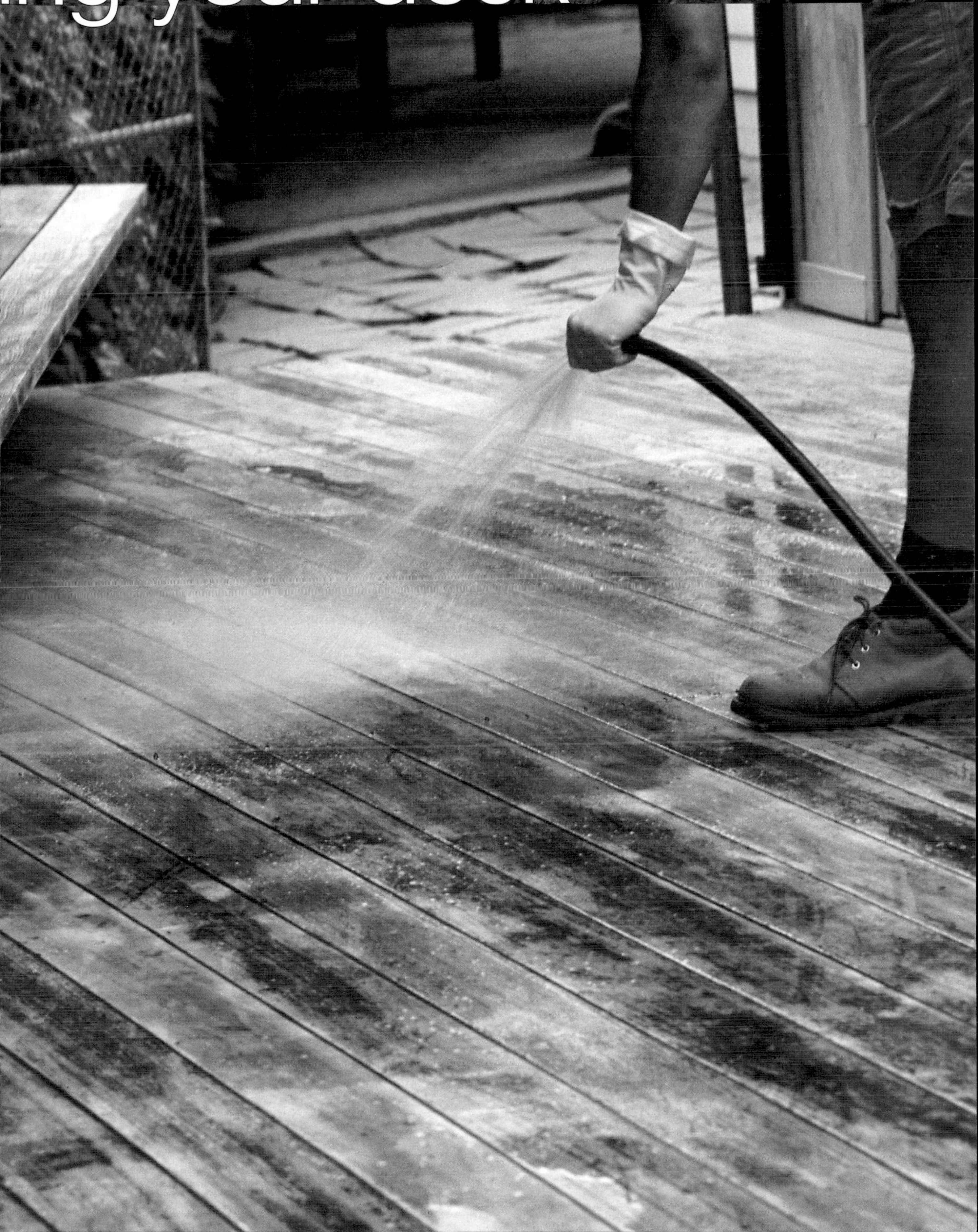

finishing decks

Finishing a deck means applying a protective coating, a finish, that helps protect from damage by the sun, moisture, fungi, and insects. There are many types of finishes made specifically for decks, each one offering unique abilities and formulas. All these treatments can be divided into two basic types.

Penetrating finishes seep into wood fibers and form protection below the surface of the wood. Typical penetrating finishes include water repellents, preservatives, clear wood finishes, and semitransparent stains. Penetrating finishes tend to enhance grain patterns.

Nonpenetrating finishes form a protective coating over the surface of the wood. Examples include paints, opaque stains, and polyurethane. Paints and opaque stains hide grain patterns but are available in many colors for design flexibility. Polyurethane comes in clear or tinted versions.

Protecting decking boards is particularly challenging for any finish. The broad, horizontal surface of the decking is exposed to the harshest conditions—direct sun, pounding rains, and heavy abrasion caused by dirt and grit ground into the wood from foot traffic. A finish that is fine for railings, overheads, and skirting may not be practical for decking boards. One solution is to apply a penetrating finish designed specifically for decking. Use more colorful finishes on other deck parts.

Remember that the end grain of wood is especially absorbent and susceptible to damage from moisture. Protect wood by applying a penetrating finish to the end grain and to freshly sawn pieces prior to assembly. Some penetrating finishes can be used to pretreat wood before applying a non-penetrating finish, such as paint. To make sure this will work for your project, check the manufacturer's recommendations on the container.

How wood ages

Left untreated, wood exposed to the elements weathers to soft, silvery gray. Exposure to sunlight and photochemical changes that occur in the top layer of wood fibers produce this natural color shift. Many people find this light gray attractive and manufacturers even offer finishes that mimic the color. The color reaches only a few thousandths of an inch into the wood surface, however, and is easily removed with a deck wash product or mild bleach solution.

Wood color is also affected by mildew growth. Mildew and fungi are persistent organisms found in most regions and are particularly troublesome in damp or coastal areas. However, they do not destroy wood and should not be confused with rot. Mildew may occur as dark gray or black splotches and speckles on wood surfaces. Remove mildew by scrubbing with a deck cleaner or mild bleach; prevent mildew by using a deck finish that includes a mildew retardant called a mildewcide.

Changes in humidity cause more serious problems. As wood swells and shrinks, cracks develop. Sunlight, especially ultraviolet (UV) light, dries out wood fibers, making them brittle. The fibers break off and wash away when it rains. Over time, wood splits and warps, and the surface becomes increasingly rough and pitted.

Poorly Maintained Decks

Decks that are not maintained with periodic refinishing display deterioration within two or three years. Some common problems include cracking and splitting of the wood, particularly at fastener locations; excessive shrinking that opens up the spacing between boards and creates hazardous gaps; and discoloration caused by mildew and other wood-loving fungi.

CRACKED BOARDS   EXCESSIVE SHRINKING   MILDEW AND DISCOLORATION

Graying Wood

Even though this five-year-old deck has been faithfully maintained with yearly applications of clear sealer, it appears gray compared to a brand new decking board.

Finishes protect against the general degradation of wood by preventing moisture from entering wood and slowing dimensional changes. Finishes with added UV protection block harmful sunlight. The same natural forces that degrade wood, however, also degrade finishes. To achieve maximum protection and to keep a deck looking clean, refinish the deck every one or two years. Even so, the natural tones of even carefully maintained wood will gradually fade after years of exposure to the sun.

Penetrating finishes

Penetrating finishes, also called sealers, repel water and won't peel or crack. They are absorbed into the wood where they solidify yet remain flexible, allowing the wood to shrink and expand with climactic changes while providing protection. Penetrating finishes work well with all types of wood, including pressure-treated lumber.

WATER REPELLENTS usually contain water-shedding wax; a drying oil, such as tung or linseed oil to seal the wood;

and a binder that allows the finish to adhere to wood fibers. Most water repellents are clear and have a thin, watery consistency to make them easily absorbed by wood. After the repellent dries, it decreases the amount of moisture that wood is able to absorb, thus keeping shrinkage and swelling to a minimum and helping to prevent cracking, warping, and splitting. Clear water repellents have no protection from UV light. A repellent with a UV inhibitor will contain a colored chemical compound that acts like a stain on wood.

Water repellents are easy to apply and need only a few hours to dry. However, some water repellents contain non-drying oils, such as paraffin-based oil, that penetrate the wood but require several days to dry completely. Both types work well and are easy to apply, but they generally are not as durable and long-lasting as semitransparent stains. Read and follow the manufacturer's recommendations for application and drying time.

Some water repellents, called preservative sealers, contain a mildewcide. They help prevent the growth of mildew and slow the discoloration of natural wood tones. Other types contain additives that offer protection from ultraviolet light.

SEMITRANSPARENT STAINS are, basically, water repellents or preservative sealers containing pigments. Semitransparent stains work well with all types of woods. The stain enhances wood grain patterns, and the pigments offer superior protection from sunlight damage and fading. Stains especially formulated for use on decks have superior resistance to moisture and abrasion caused by foot traffic. Manufacturers of stains produce an ever-increasing variety of colors but the final hue always depends on the type of wood being used. When selecting a semitransparent stain, base your decision on the look of stain samples applied to specific woods. A semitransparent stain is a good way to disguise the dull-green color of pressure-treated wood.

PRESERVATIVE SEALERS contain chemicals to kill mildew and mold and to help extend the life of wood used outdoors. These finishes are particularly helpful for protecting decks built in damp or coastal climates. You'll find specially formulated water repellents and semitransparent stains containing mildewcides on the shelves of most home improvement and hardware stores.

Nonpenetrating finishes

Non-penetrating finishes form a protective coating on the top of the wood, preventing moisture from seeping into wood fibers. They include exterior-grade paints, opaque stains, and polyurethane. Use these products for coating posts, railings, balusters, risers, and other decorative deck elements. However, most are unsuitable for decking because abrasion from foot traffic quickly wears away the protective layer, exposing the wood.

EXTERIOR-GRADE PAINTS are either oil-based or latex (water-soluble). Both block sunlight and offer superior protection for deck elements in a wide selection of colors. Top-quality exterior paints are slightly flexible when dry, allowing the paint to accommodate the inevitable shrinking and swelling of wood. Although they seal the wood from moisture penetration, paints also seal in existing moisture and cannot prevent mildew and mold from forming on the wood underneath the paint, a condition which may cause the wood to deteriorate or the paint film to discolor. For decks built in damp or coastal climates, choose paints specially formulated with mildewcides to reduce the growth of microscopic fungi.

Some manufacturers produce durable paints designed for use on decking and porch floors. As tough as these products are, however, they eventually are no match for the wear and abrasion caused by foot traffic combined with everyday dirt and grit. For colored decking boards, a semitransparent stain is preferable.

Most paints perform best when used with a primer. Look for a high-quality, stain-blocking primer that will prevent resins and other naturally occurring solvents from seeping out of knots and bleeding through the paint.

If paint is not properly applied and routinely maintained, it will crack and peel. Repairing damaged paint is usually a tedious, time-consuming job that requires sanding, scraping, patching, sealing, and repainting. Inspect paint jobs regularly for signs of wear, and repair cracked, blistered, or peeling paint immediately before the problem spreads.

OPAQUE STAINS are closely related to paints and form a coating on top of wood surfaces. Both paints and opaque stains mask grain patterns, but opaque stains are thinner than paint formulas and tend to reveal wood texture. They are effective finishes for textured woods such as rough cedar and fir.

Opaque stains effectively block deterioration and discoloration of the wood caused by ultraviolet light. Some are formulated for use on decking boards—look for brands guaranteed to withstand foot traffic. Opaque stains are available in a limited number of colors.

POLYURETHANES, varnishes, and lacquers are clear or slightly tinted top coat finishes. Versions of these products are rated for exterior use, but require vigilant maintenance and generally are not recommended for decks. Because these finishes are particularly hard and stiff when dry, they do not easily withstand the rigors of outdoor climates, especially in

Paints and Stains
This stylish deck includes a railing system with two kinds of finishes—a penetrating stain for posts and a crisp white exterior latex paint for rails and balusters.

cold northern regions. Should they crack or peel, they are difficult to repair or remove.

Preparing to apply finish

Applying a finish properly is a matter of timing. Don't apply finish if the temperature is below 60 degrees. The wood must be dry enough for a penetrating finish to soak into wood fibers and for a nonpenetrating finish to adhere tightly to wood surfaces. The best method is to allow wood to dry in controlled conditions, such as a garage, for two weeks prior to use. An exception is wood rated as "kiln dried" or marked KDAT. This wood has been dried at the factory to a low moisture content and is ready for finishing. Test the moisture content of the wood by placing the wood in a horizontal position out of the sun and sprinkling water over the surface. If the water droplets are absorbed within half a minute, the wood is dry enough for finish application.

Wood that is dirty, is splintered, displays uneven surfacing (chatter marks), or has a reflective mill glaze caused by factory machinery should be sanded smooth before finishing. Finishes will not hide surface imperfections and may enhance them. Sand wood with a medium-grit sandpaper and a belt or heavy-duty finish sander. Always sand with the grain. Remove loose sawdust by brushing sanded lumber with a soft bristle brush. When sanding pressure-treated lumber, wear a respirator. Sweep up sawdust, place it in a plastic bag, and dispose of it in the trash.

Pretreat all pieces with finish before construction begins. This is especially important for pieces that have hidden surfaces, such as the backs of post notches or lumber that butts or rests against other pieces of wood. Usually, you do not need to treat these areas again during the life of the deck. Hidden surfaces also tend to be the places where moisture may be trapped and eventually cause damage. It is important that these surfaces receive a protective coating before installation. This guideline includes pressure-treated wood and moisture-resistant woods such as redwood, cedar, and cypress. It is often impractical to completely treat all surfaces of pressure-treated lumber used for the substructure, but take care to coat end grain and freshly made cuts with a penetrating finish or preservative sealer to extend its serviceable life.

Decking boards should be treated before installation. Although decking should receive periodic refinishing over the years, the bottoms and sides of the boards are nearly impossible to finish (or refinish) once fastened in place. Set up sawhorses or a suitable work area and coat all surfaces of decking boards. Allow the finish to dry according to the manufacturer's recommendations before installation. After cutting boards during construction, coat the exposed wood with finish before nailing each board in place.

Applying finishes

Clean loose grit and dirt from the wood surfaces. Apply finishes out of direct sun or during the hottest part of the day. Otherwise, some finishes, such as latex paints and opaque stains, may dry so quickly that they don't bond properly to wood surfaces. Use proper tools for applying finishes— brushes with natural bristles for alkyd- and oil-based finishes and brushes with synthetic bristles for latex finishes.

Liberally apply clear finishes and preservatives with a brush, roller, pad, or sprayer. Allow the sealer to penetrate the wood completely before flipping boards over and coating other sides. Work any remaining puddles into the wood with a brush or roller. If a section of wood absorbs finish much more rapidly than surrounding areas, recoat it.

Apply semitransparent stains with a brush, roller, pad, or sprayer. For a uniform look, allow the stain to sit on the surface of the wood for several minutes, then even out the stain by rubbing it with a rag. If the color appears too light, reapply the stain and allow it to sit on the wood for several more minutes before rubbing it. Don't allow stain to drip along adjacent sides—it will be difficult to remove the drip mark even if wiped up immediately. Handle stain-soaked rags properly—spread them out in a safe location so that they can dry properly. Bunched-up rags are a fire hazard because the heat caused by evaporating solvents may spontaneously combust.

Paints may be brushed or rolled on. It's best to pretreat the wood with a top-quality primer before applying the finish coat of color. Make sure the primer is compatible with the type of paint you'll be using. Apply a second coat of paint according to the manufacturer's instructions.

To keep deck lumber in good condition, clean and refinish a deck every year or two. While periodic maintenance and refinishing is necessary for all deck elements, the decking boards require special attention. Decking boards are directly exposed to harsh sunlight, heavy rains, accumulated dirt and grit, foot traffic, and stains from plant material settling on the surface of the deck. Ultraviolet light often breaks down the cellulose in wood fibers, causing the top surface of decking to fray and fuzz. Cleaning removes accumulated dirt and gray, damaged wood fibers. Refinishing adds a protective sealer to prevent deterioration caused by sunlight and exposure to the weather. Refinishing also restores your deck's original beauty.

Cleaning

Rejuvenating deck boards begins with a thorough cleaning. Inspect the boards closely for dirt and plant material accumulated between boards, especially at butt joints and where decking crosses joists. This material traps moisture, which leads to decay. Remove dirt, leaves, and seeds by prying them out with a narrow-bladed screwdriver or similar tool. Sweep the deck thoroughly to remove loose dirt and grit.

Apply a deck-cleaning solution according to the manufacturer's directions. Several types of cleaners are available at home improvement centers and hardware stores. A chlorine-based solution contains sodium hypochlorite—a compound that kills mildew and lightens the color of the wood. This type can drain wood of its natural color, leaving it looking pale and washed out, and is not as effective at lifting and removing ground-in dirt. It also is harmful to nearby plants.

Trisodium phosphate (TSP) is a good general-purpose cleaner but does little to brighten and rejuvenate deck wood. Note that water runoff containing phosphates has been linked to environmental damage occurring in lakes and streams. The stain remover oxalic acid helps eliminate blotches caused by resins and natural tannins, such as those that leach out of damp oak leaves, but it has little overall cleaning power.

The latest generation of deck brighteners combines ingredients that remove dirt, kill mildew, and brighten decks by aiding the removal of grayed wood fibers. Some formulas combine detergents, bleach, and mild acids. Others include solutions of disodium peroxydicarbonate—an oxygen-based whitener found in clothing detergents and toothpaste. These cleaners do a good all-around job of cleaning and brightening decks and are safe for use near plants.

Apply the cleaner with a brush with stiff nylon bristles to remove the top layers of wood. The amount of wood scrubbed away is microscopic, and the deck's appearance will be greatly improved. Wear eye protection and gloves when working with cleaners. Some solutions may bleach fabric, so wear old clothes. If instructed by the manufacturer, protect nearby shrubbery and plants from overspray by draping tarps over them.

Clean all parts of your deck. Clean painted surfaces and parts covered with opaque stains with a mild solution of trisodium phosphate or common household detergent. Rinse parts thoroughly and let all surfaces dry before refinishing. Clean hard-to-reach areas, such as the spaces between balusters, with a toothbrush dipped in cleaner.

Combating Insects

Termites and powder post beetles typically live in the ground and use damp wood for food. Big, black carpenter ants do not use wood for food but join termites and powder post beetles in boring up through the bottoms of posts and other structural members, destroying wood from the inside out. Occasionally, termites reveal themselves by building dirt tunnels along the sides of foundation walls so they can reach wood without being exposed to sunlight. In many cases, the destruction caused by insects is invisible until it's too late.

If you live in an area where insect damage is likely, or if a neighbor reports problems, take precautions. Pressure-treated wood is a deterrent but no guarantee against insect attack. The best solution is to treat substructure parts with a preservative that contains an insecticide. These strong chemicals are strictly regulated by the Environmental Protection Agency—use caution to prevent children and animals from exposure. Follow the manufacturer's guidelines for application. If necessary, have the area around your home treated by a professional exterminator. Look in the Yellow Pages under "Pest Control Services."

Caring for decking

Before applying sealers or finishes to decking materials, use a screwdriver or awl to clean out debris from the spaces between boards. This is especially important at butt joints *left* where joists underneath the decking help trap twigs, seeds, leaves, and dirt. Freshly sealed decking *left* shows the characteristic beading of moisture after a rain—a sure sign the sealer is working. The long puddle sitting in the middle of the board indicates the board is cupped.

Use care when cleaning surfaces coated with latex-based stains. These water-soluble stains are easily damaged by vigorous scrubbing. Use a soft sponge and mild detergent such as dish soap. Don't continue if you see the stain is coming off on the sponge. Rinse all parts thoroughly.

Using a power washer

If you are cleaning a large deck, consider renting or buying a power washer. Use a power washer to rinse the deck after applying a deck-cleaning solution. Power washers deliver water at high pressure that sweeps away dirt and frayed wood fibers, saving you the labor of hand scrubbing.

Use caution when working with a pressure washer. If the pressure is too high or the nozzle of the washer held too close to the wood, the water will easily gouge and damage soft decking boards such as cedar. Use a pressure of 500 to 1,000 pounds per square inch (psi). Use a nozzle that delivers the spray in a 30-degree to 40-degree arc. Hold the nozzle no closer than 6 inches from the surface of the deck, and move the nozzle slowly and evenly without stopping. Wear eye protection when operating a power washer.

Refinishing

Clean decks before refinishing; trapped dirt and grime limit the ability of the finish to penetrate or to adhere to wood surfaces. If the deck has more than one finish, refinish each portion separately and protect adjacent surfaces with masking tape.

Sand rough or weathered boards to remove splinters, gouges, or sharp edges. Before sanding, check that fasteners are countersunk, then sand using a finish or belt sander with 80- to 100-grit sandpaper. When sanding pressure-treated wood, wear a respirator. Don't sweep sawdust from pressure-treated wood off the deck; use a shop vacuum.

After cleaning the deck, allow it to dry for several days in warm weather before applying a finish. Sweep the decking boards just before refinishing. Apply finishes with a brush, roller, pad, or sprayer according to the techniques described in Applying Finishes, pages 141–142.

For painted sections of the deck, use classic techniques for repairing paint. Inspect surfaces for cracking, blistering, or peeling. Remove damaged paint with a scraper, a wire brush, or by hand sanding. Prime sanded areas with quality exterior stain-blocking primer. When the primer is dry, repaint the damaged areas.

Tools for finishing

Useful tools for finishing decks include a sprayer (A), roller and pan (B), 24-inch-wide pad applicator made especially for decking (C), 6-inch-wide pad for cutting in around posts (D), and bristle brushes (E).

Maintaining and repairing an older deck begins with a thorough inspection of deck parts. The primary concern is rot—the destruction of wood fibers caused by certain fungi. Rot-producing fungi are not the same organisms that cause harmless mildew spotting and discoloration. However, the presence of mildew signals that conditions are ideal for wood-destroying fungi to infect deck parts. Rot softens wood and reduces structural integrity. In worst-case scenarios, rot may weaken decking, posts, ledgers, and stairs enough to make a deck susceptible to collapse, therefore dangerous to walk on.

Once you have identified rotten deck elements, either remove and replace them, or treat the rot with a fungi-killing preservative and reinforce the rotten lumber with a second board of nearly equal dimension and strength. This method, called "sistering," is necessary when the infected lumber cannot be easily removed, such as a joist that carries decking boards.

Check for rot by probing deck parts with a small-bladed screwdriver, a sturdy knife, or an awl. Wear old clothes and be prepared to spend time underneath the deck. The most likely places for rot to develop are the ends of posts, joists, beams, and ledgers where vulnerable end grain is exposed, or where wood comes in contact with concrete and the ground. Poke around probable spots with the tool—if the wood is rotten, it will be soft and the probe will penetrate with little resistance. Use a bright crayon or piece of chalk to mark rotted deck parts for replacement.

From the underside, check the tops of joists. The many fasteners used to secure the decking penetrate the tops of the joists and make them vulnerable to moisture penetration. Moisture tends to run along nail and screw shanks and find its way into the upper edges of the joists, creating conditions that foster rot growth.

On the outside of the deck, check joints where wood comes together, such as where railings meet posts and where railing posts rest on decking boards. Pay particular attention to areas against the house where moisture may have been trapped. Check the ledger and ends of stair stringers. Look for discoloration that indicates mold, mildew, and other fungi have started growing on the deck.

Replacing small parts

For many smaller deck parts, such as railings and balusters, replacement is relatively straightforward. The infected board is simply unfastened and a replacement board retrofitted. You may also need to remove adjacent deck parts to free the infected board; the task is time-consuming but not difficult. The job is vastly simplified if screws have been used for construction because they can be removed with a reversible drill and, in many cases, reused. Once you unfasten the adjacent deck parts, take this opportunity to re-coat end grain with sealer or preservative before reinstalling the parts.

If nails are the primary fastener, the job is more complex. Nails, especially galvanized nails, have tremendous holding power. Use a crow bar, preferably two of them working in opposition, to pry apart stubborn deck parts. To prevent damage to the deck, place a sturdy shim between the bar and the work surface. Use caution working with large prying tools—they may slip or suddenly loosen pieces. Never position yourself directly in line with a crow bar and wear a hard hat and safety glasses.

If all else fails, try to cut stubborn nails (or screws with broken heads). Equip a reciprocating saw with a nail-cutting blade, and slip the blade between deck parts to sever fasteners. The drawback of this method is that the blade may trim the surrounding wood. When removing substructure parts this minor damage does not show and does not affect the strength of the deck. On finish parts, however, the damage may be noticeable. Limit the damage to the part needing replacement. Once you cut the fasteners, use a hammer and nail set to drive cut shanks below the surrounding surface of the wood. Alternatively, you can cut apart the damaged piece in two or three places to make it easier to remove.

Replacing posts and beams

Removing large deck parts and key structural components requires careful planning. If in doubt, consult or hire a professional builder to do the job.

Removing a post requires lifting the deck slightly, using a hydraulic jack or

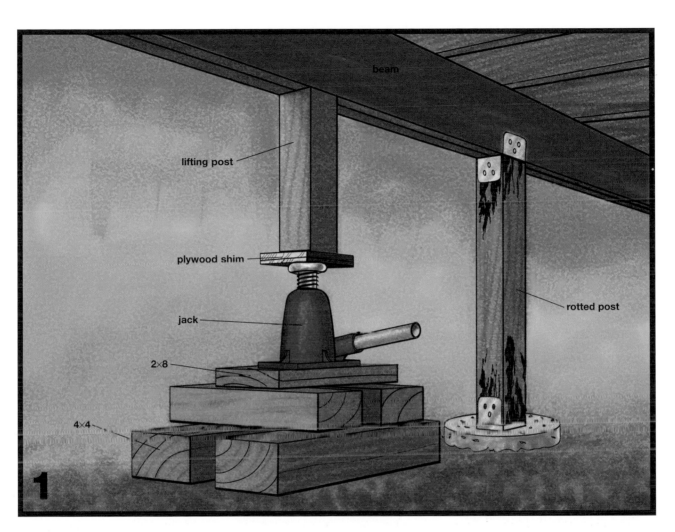

beam

lifting post

plywood shim

jack

2×8

4×4

rotted post

1

screw-type car jack, to relieve weight from the rotten post so it can be taken out and replaced. Positioning the jack is critical—it must be set on a level, firm surface, such as pairs of 4×4s.

Before removing the damaged post, measure it and cut a new post to match. Have the new post ready to install. Brush preservative on the ends of the new post to help prevent rot. To remove the damaged post, you'll need to remove the metal connectors. This requires flexing the connector plates slightly to extract the nails. Leave the connectors in place and reuse them to fasten the new post.

1 SET A HYDRAULIC JACK on a firm, level surface directly under the beam within 2 feet of the damaged post. Leave space between the jack and the post so you can work comfortably. Place a 4×4 lifting post between the top of the jack and the beam. Do not use a post longer than 2 feet—longer posts may suddenly turn out under pressure if they are not plumb. Instead, build up the base under the jack, using pairs of 4×4s. Place a metal plate between the top of the jack and the post so that pressure from lifting does not crush the end grain of the post. If you do not

have a metal plate, use a piece of ¾-inch plywood. Don't use regular 1× material because it may crack under pressure.

pry bar

2 CLOSE THE JACK'S hydraulic valve and apply pressure until the lifting post is firmly seated against the beam and can't be moved by hand. Give the jack an additional pump to lift the beam slightly. Remove the metal connectors holding the damaged post by prying back the sides of the connectors slightly to extract the nail heads. Use a claw hammer, pry bar, or cat's paw to remove the nails. Bend the connector as little as possible.

replacement post

3 **REMOVE THE DAMAGED POST.** If it is still held in place by pressure, use a jack to relieve the pressure. Don't pump the jack too vigorously and lift only enough to free the post. Slip the new post into position, make sure it is plumb, and lower the jack until pressure holds the new post firmly. Drive joist hanger nails through the connector plates into the new post. When you finish nailing, lower the jack completely.

Sistering joists

Often, it is too difficult to remove a joist and replace it. Galvanized joist hangers secure the ends of joists, and many nails or screws are driven through the decking boards into the upper edge of the joist. Joists may also be toenailed into beams. The best remedy is to stop further deterioration of the damaged joist by applying a rot-killing preservative, then adding another structural member alongside the damaged lumber to restore structural integrity to the deck. This method is called sistering. If the damaged joist is not badly deteriorated, a new joist can be screwed or bolted to it to gain strength. Secure the ends of the sistered joist to the ledger and rim joists using galvanized corner brackets. If the joist is in poor condition, use joist hangers to install a new joist about 6 inches away to prevent rot from spreading.

It may be impossible to slide a new, full-length joist into position because the space is too cramped. In that case use two shorter joists and allow their free ends to run past each other by 3 feet where they cross over a beam. Bolt the free ends together using five carriage bolts arranged in a W pattern.

1 **MEASURE THE LENGTH** of the damaged joist and cut a sister joist to match. Slide the new joist alongside the damaged joist. Clamp the two joists together, checking that the top edge of the new joist is flush with the top edge of the damaged joist. It may be difficult to "stand" the new joist upright because the space between the beam and the decking is tight. Use large C-clamps to help squeeze the new joist into position. Don't clamp too forcefully. Use firm pressure and tap the upper edge of the joist with a hammer to move it. Retighten clamps and tap with a hammer until the joist is upright.

Sistered Joints

Where it is not possible to slip a new joist into position, use two shorter joists joined over a support beam. Run ends of joists past each other 3 feet, and secure the ends to each other with five carriage bolts arranged in a W pattern.

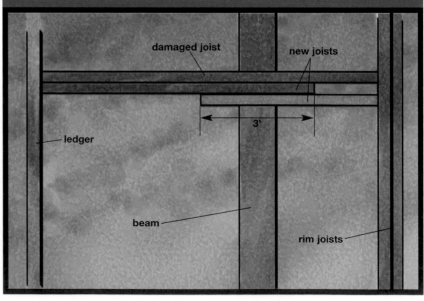

damaged joist

new joists

3'

ledger

beam

rim joists

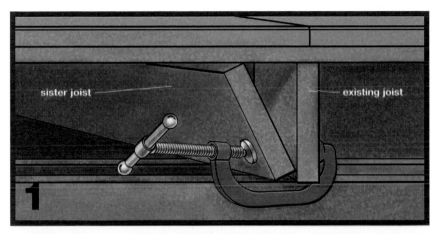

sister joist   existing joist

1

2

2 **ATTACH CORNER BRACKETS to the ends of the new joist. Use the brackets to fasten the ends of the new joist to the rim joist and ledger. Bolt or screw the sistered joists together. If using carriage bolts, install a bolt every 3 feet, alternating between upper and lower edges of the joists. If using screws, drive a 2¾-inch galvanized screw every 16 inches, alternating between upper and lower edges of the joists.**

Replacing decking

Decking has a hard life because it is installed horizontally and exposed to sun, harsh weather, and foot traffic.

Even diligent maintenance may not prevent decking boards from cupping or cracking until they are hazardous underfoot. In addition, accidental spills or sparks from barbecue grills may discolor and permanently mar the decking. The remedy is to replace damaged decking boards.

If the board is not structurally damaged, simply flip it over and reinstall it. This is a cost-effective solution with the added advantage that the board is already cut to the correct length. If it was installed with screws, the process is easy—remove the screws with a reversible drill. Reuse the existing screw holes. At the ends, predrill new guide holes before installing screws.

If the decking was installed with nails, removing it will require more labor and time. Resist the urge to slip the end of a crow bar between decking and pry up the damaged board as this is likely to ruin adjacent boards. Instead, go beneath the deck and loosen the board with hammer blows—make sure you strike the correct board. If the fasteners refuse to let go, you may be able to lift the heads far enough so that you can pry them out from above. However, apply prying force only against the damaged board—not against its neighbors. This combination of hammering and prying will likely further damage the board so it cannot be reused. As a last resort, slip the blade of a saber saw alongside the damaged board and cut it apart.

A replacement decking board will look much newer than surrounding decking. Match the color of the surrounding decking by applying a stain. Be sure to test the stain color on a piece of scrap before you commit to using it. To lighten a board, try a deck cleaner with a bleach solution. To achieve a realistic gray, try applying a solution made from 1 cup baking soda dissolved in 1 gallon of warm water. Let the solution sit on the board for several minutes, then rinse the board and let it dry. Remember that it is better to make the board too light than too dark. You can always deepen a stain color with a second application, but it is difficult to reverse a too-dark board.

Renovate older, deteriorated decks by removing weathered, cracked finish components including railings, stairs, and decking. Inspect the structural components carefully—if they are sound, well-fastened, and free of rot, consider leaving them in place to save the cost of tearing them out and rebuilding the substructure. Rejuvenate the deck with newer parts featuring a different style, and paint or stain parts to add color.

To reconfigure a deck, add on to the existing substructure or alter only a portion of it, preserving as much of the substructure as possible. Architects and other professional designers usually are accustomed to the challenge of reconfiguring existing structures and may prove helpful in reinventing decks.

Tall decks and second-level decks present a common dilemma—the space beneath the deck is generous but unusable for weatherproof storage. Solve this problem by adding a ceiling system designed for use underneath decks. These systems divert water and debris that fall through the gaps in the decking boards, creating dry, usable space beneath the deck.

Removing old parts

If you plan to preserve the style of your old deck, carefully inspect handrails, posts, and other parts to determine if they can be salvaged. Note how the parts are fastened to each other. Look on all sides of joints for nails, screws, clips, or brackets. Screws and lag bolts often can be reversed and removed. If posts are secured with carriage bolts, go underneath the deck and apply penetrating oil to the nuts. Give the oil a few minutes to work, then loosen nuts using a wrench or ratchet set. To remove decking, see Replacing Decking on page 147.

If the parts are nailed together, use a reciprocating saw equipped with a nail-cutting blade to sever fasteners. Otherwise, pry apart components with a pry bar, or knock parts loose using a 2- or 3-pound sledge hammer. Take care during vigorous demolition work—wear safety goggles, work gloves, and a hard hat.

If the deck is badly weathered or damaged, trying to save parts usually is not a cost-effective strategy. It's usually better to move through the demolition full-speed and get on with reconstructing the deck.

Covering old rim joists with fascia

Old, cracked rim joists may be unsightly, but chances are they are structurally sound. If joists do not have rot and do not have cracks that extend through the thickness of the board, plan to keep them in place. To hide blemishes, install fascia to cover the outer surfaces of the rim joists.

Make fascia from 1× material. Because fascia is exposed to harsh sun and temperature fluctuations, choose sound, #2 or better grades of lumber. Better grades of lumber have fewer defects and are less likely to crack and split over time. Brush preservative, sealer, or stain on all surfaces prior to installation.

Install the fascia so its upper edge is flush with the top surface of the decking. Choose fascia boards a full size wider than the rim joists. For example,

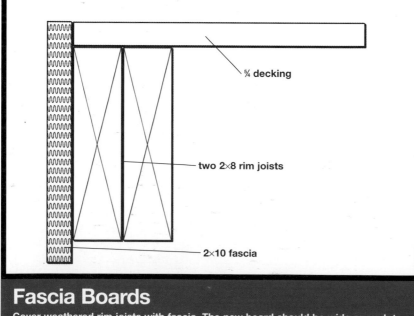

¾ decking

two 2×8 rim joists

2×10 fascia

Fascia Boards

Cover weathered rim joists with fascia. The new board should be wide enough to completely conceal the rim joists and the edges of the decking.

to cover 2×8 joists, use 1×10s. So that the fascia has enough width to fit flush with the top of the decking.

Installing a deck ceiling

Deck ceilings systems vary in design and the methods used to install them, but most employ flexible vinyl insets fastened between joists to prevent water from reaching the area beneath the deck. Installing the insets at an angle allows gravity to divert rain water, melted snow, and debris to a gutter at the end of the system. Usually, the insets are white to reflect light and create a bright, dry space beneath the deck. Look for do-it-yourself deck ceiling systems at home improvement centers.

Deck Ceilings

Deck ceiling systems consist of flexible vinyl panels that fit between joists. The panels form channels to divert water and debris toward gutters.

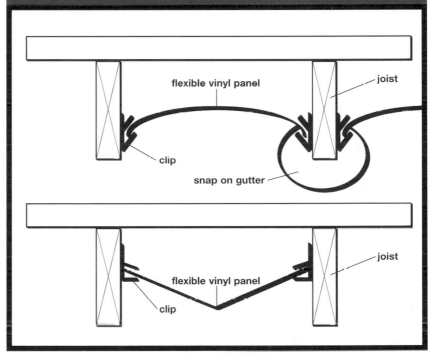

Overhead Awning

Retractable overhead awnings are an increasingly popular way to increase the liveability of deck spaces. The awnings fold way against the house when not in use and are extended by an electric motor or hand crank when needed. They provide plenty of shade when the sun is overhead but fold up at night or when days are cool and the sun is welcome. Some types have wind sensors that monitor air currents and retract the shade automatically when strong breezes are detected—a helpful feature when owners aren't home.

Reinventing an existing deck uses many of the same planning and building techniques as those required for completely new construction. The goal is to create deck space that fits the size and slope of the yard and accommodates the needs of the homeowner. If possible, the new deck should incorporate the existing substructure, resulting in savings of time, materials, and costs.

Of course, you may prefer to completely redo the deck, building new substructure to do so.

Begin by removing all finish components including decking, railing, stairways, and ancillary components, such as planters, benches, and arbors. Measure the structural components, and transfer all measurements to working drawings that include elevations

and plan views. Use the planning and drawing techniques described in Chapters 2, 3, and 5. Use these drawings as the basis for a new design.

Many older decks were constructed without concern for establishing architectural harmony. Take this opportunity to make sure your newer deck is integral to the overall design of your house and landscaping scheme.

Basic Deck

Built in the 1990s, this dinky, bland 12x10-foot deck typifies basic deck design and construction—it is intended to provide a small outdoor living area without much thought to blending with the house. As a result, it looks tacked on. Without significant increase in size or materials, the substructure can be reused to support a deck of similar size. However, a more attractive decking material, such as cedar, along with a cedar rim joist or fascia, provides a significant upgrade in appearance. In addition, the cedar can be stained to complement the siding of the house. Dividing the stairway with a small landing will give the deck horizontal definition, allowing it to be more harmonious with the overall shape of the house.

Choice 1

This multilevel deck winds its way to the yard and features a conveniently built-in cooking area near the kitchen door. Nearby worksurfaces and storage areas increase functionality. The storage wall next to the door directs traffic, is a safety feature, and firmly but gently separates the first two levels. Down one level is a generous eating area, and a third level incorporates a potting and gardening work surface and steps to the yard. A fourth level leads to the yard.

Choice 2

This elaborate solution creates an outdoor room. The railings are made from an open material, such as wire or safety glass, to preserve views in all directions. Three areas are created by the changes in the arbor structure. A half-arbor over a portion of the deck creates plenty of private, usable space, similar to an interior room attached to the outside of the house. The room breaks up the large expanse of the decking surface and provides a sense of grandeur.

10. great deck solutio

DECKS ARE AS VARIED AS THE PEOPLE WHO USE THEM. Shade patterns, degree of slope, and access to views influence the shape and location of a deck. Add the individual preferences and goals of the homeowners, and finished decks differ greatly, even if attached to houses of similar size and architectural style.

Examining plans for completed decks is an excellent way to begin the design process. By seeing how the experts integrate decks into a home you will see how to create a deck that best suits your home, and find solutions for dealing with site problems.

About these projects

Archadeck, a world leader in deck design and construction, provided the projects for this chapter. To find the Archadeck builder in your area, go to the company's website, archadeck.com, call 800-722-4668, or look under *Patios, Decks, Porches, and Enclosures* in the business listings of a phone book.

This chapter presents working drawings of nine deck designs, including framing details, elevation and plan views, and lumber lists, from Archadeck (see box at left). These projects are chosen because they show several basic construction techniques, and they depict a variety of smart solutions for several typical site concerns. So while you won't be able to simply build a deck directly from these designs, you'll gain a better understanding of the process. The price estimates provide ballpark figures for use as a guideline only; actual costs will vary. As you study these designs, make note of the particulars that apply to your situation. Then, get ready to build the outdoor space of your dreams.

A well-chosen deck increases living area, offers a comfortable outdoor environment, and looks beautiful.

THIS MULTILEVEL DECK PROJECT adds an abundance of outdoor living area and smoothly integrates a number of entry points to the back of the house. The original rear entrance—a small raised concrete stoop featuring a portico cover—was left intact. Tearing it out would have been expensive. Instead, the upper level of the new deck is flush with the top of the stoop, creating a seamless walking surface. The lower level of the deck wraps neatly around a walk-down basement entry. The railing system that protects the walk-down also screens the entry from view.

A key benefit of this deck design is access. The deck provides many points to step into the backyard in several directions. The lower deck is only two steps from grade and except for the portion surrounding the basement stairway, railings are unnecessary around most of the perimeter of the lower deck. Built-in bench seating defines one corner.

This 380-square-foot deck is constructed entirely of pressure-treated Southern yellow pine and was constructed for a cost of $8,000 to $10,000.

Lumber cut list

Basic lumber requirements for this deck including substructure, railings, stairway parts, and decking.

1x4		1x6			5/4x6 decking				2x2	
12	14	12	14	16	10	12	14	16	8	12
18		11			1	10	10	66	72	

2x4					2x6					2x8				
8	10	12	14	16	8	10	12	14	16	10	12	14	16	18
2		14	2	4			6	1		9	5	16	7	

2x10					2x12			4x4			4x6		
10	12	14	16	18	8	10	12	10	12	14	10	12	14
		4	4		1	4	1	5	8				

Substructure framing

Angled corners tie the design of both levels together. The deck is not attached to the existing concrete stoop with a ledger. Instead, the joists bear on a beam placed 2 feet from the stoop. A short ledger attached to the house supports the small wraparound portion of deck alongside the stoop.

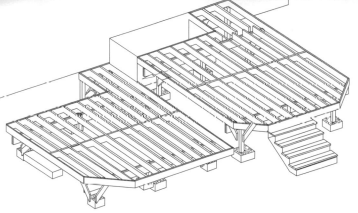

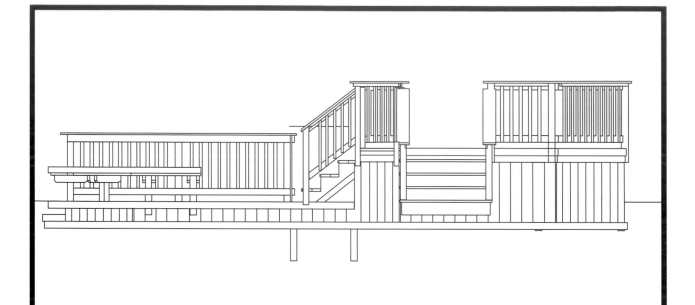

Front Elevation

Solid board skirting visually anchors this deck. For solid skirting, the support frame (see page 157) includes a second horizontal member installed an inch or two below the rim joists. Use regular board lumber for solid skirting—not tongue-and-groove. Joints on tongue-and-groove boards tend to trap moisture and make breeding areas for rot-producing fungi.

Side Elevation

Steps leading from the upper level deck to the lower level are wide—almost as wide as the entire deck. This stairway has a handrail protecting the edge near the open yard but nowhere else. Wide stairways usually do not require handrails at locations other than those above grade. Always check your local building codes concerning the placement of handrails.

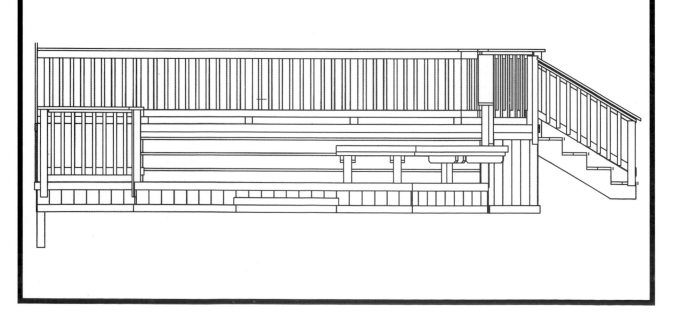

156   complete decks

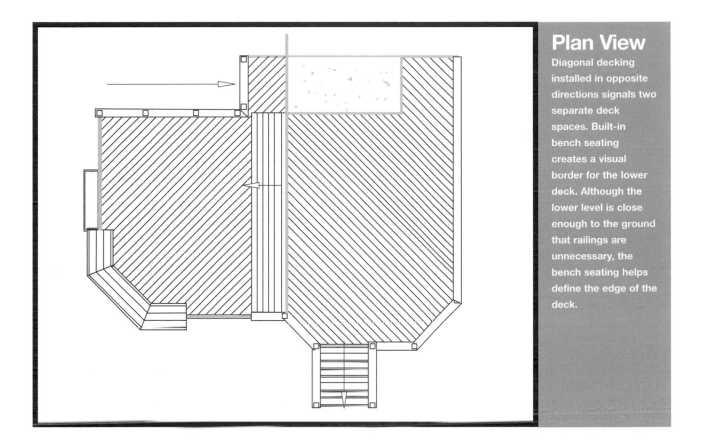

Plan View

Diagonal decking installed in opposite directions signals two separate deck spaces. Built-in bench seating creates a visual border for the lower deck. Although the lower level is close enough to the ground that railings are unnecessary, the bench seating helps define the edge of the deck.

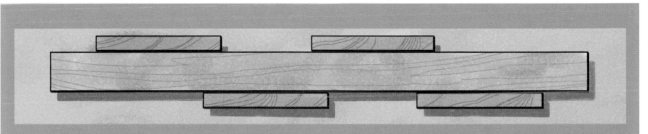

Solid Skirting

Skirting of solid board lumber instead of lattice gives a deck heft and substance—a useful design feature for small decks or decks built low to the ground. Resist the temptation to use tongue-and-groove lumber for solid skirting—the tight-fitting tongue-and-groove joints make breeding grounds for rot-producing fungi.

To prevent the lumber from twisting or warping and causing unsightly gaps, use the support framing for the lumber with horizontal crosspieces every 2 feet. Secure each board to the framing using two galvanized deck screws driven into each horizontal support. To ensure a tight fit, temporarily clamp the board to the crosspieces before driving the screws. To hide the screw heads, drive the screws from the rear—through the cross-pieces into the boards. Predrill the crosspieces to prevent splitting and be sure to select screws of the correct length that won't poke through the outside sur-faces of the boards.

Another method is to offset the boards, *above*, installing one board in front of the supports and the next board behind, overlapping edges by 1 inch. This method allows air circulation underneath the deck.

DUE TO A SLOPING LOT, the rear entrance of this house is nearly 7 feet above grade. To create access to an in-ground pool farther out in the yard, the owners built a deck that descends gracefully in two levels. The stepped design gives each level a view of pool activities, and doesn't block the view from the double windows next to the entry door.

On the upper deck, traffic cuts directly across the deck toward the stairway, making this portion public and functional. It's the perfect place for the barbecue grill—right off the kitchen and handy to cooking and cleaning facilities. At the lower level, the stairway is off to one side, creating a much more private and intimate area. Bench seating around the perimeter provides extra room for guests to relax, yet there's ample floor space for a sizeable table and chairs. To emphasize the differences between the levels, the upper portion features solid board skirting; the lower portion has lattice skirting.

This 480-square-foot project is built of pressure-treated Southern yellow pine and costs between $8,000 and $10,000 to construct.

Lumber cut list

Basic lumber requirements for this deck including substructure, railings, stairway parts, and decking.

1x4		1x6			5/4x6 decking				2x2	
12	14	12	14	16	10	12	14	16	8	12
32		37			2	11	2	81	47	

2x4					2x6					2x8				
8	10	12	14	16	8	10	12	14	16	10	12	14	16	18
		26	4	11			3	2		9	23	11	3	

2x10				2x12			4x4				6x6		
10	12	14	16	10	12	14	10	12	14	16	10	12	14
8	3					3	2	3		1	1	5	

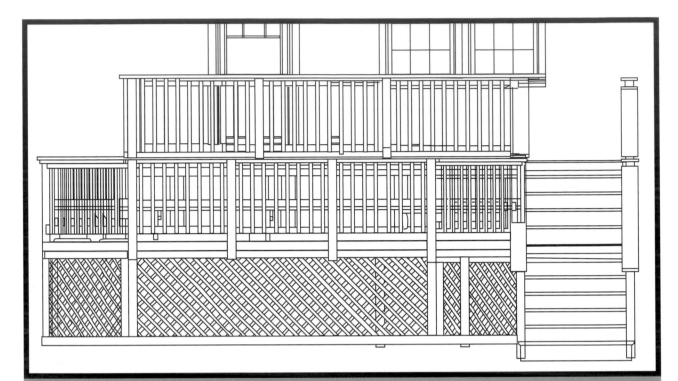

Front Elevation

The front elevation has substantial vertical mass—lattice skirting adds visual weight to the bottom of the structure and keeps it anchored to the ground. The clearly defined stairway leads directly to the pool from both levels.

Side Elevation

Skirting made from vertical board lumber visually separates the upper deck from the lower. The board skirting gives substance and heft to the taller structure and more closely associates it with the main house. The bottom of the upper stairway rests toward the middle of the lower deck, leaving a portion of that surface to act as a landing—a good feature for long stairways.

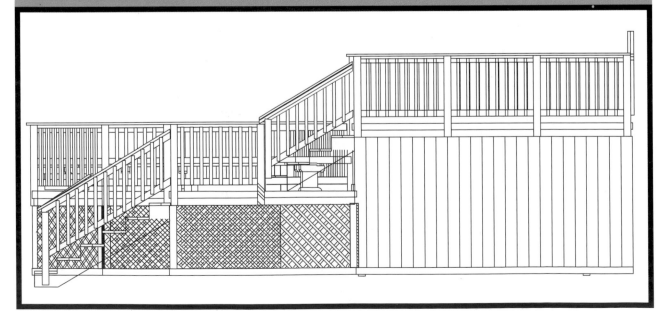

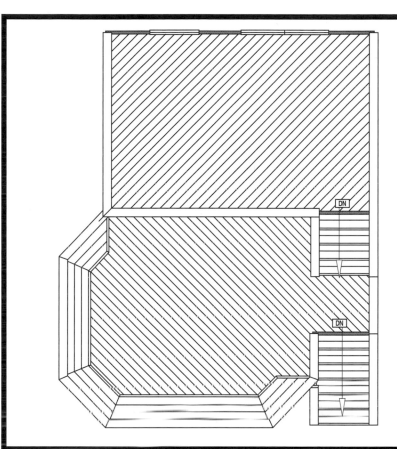

Plan View

Simple changes in shape differentiate the upper deck from the lower deck, *left.* The upper portion is rectangular and plain, giving it a utilitarian appearance. The lower deck, with its angled corners and perimeter bench seating, is a natural invitation to sit, relax, and enjoy the company of friends or family.

Substructure Framing

Positioning the posts of the upper level toward the front of the deck, *below,* allows the ledger of the lower deck to be firmly secured. Because they are nearly 7 feet tall, posts for the upper deck are well braced to prevent shifting or flexing. In this example, the posts rest on square blocks of poured concrete.

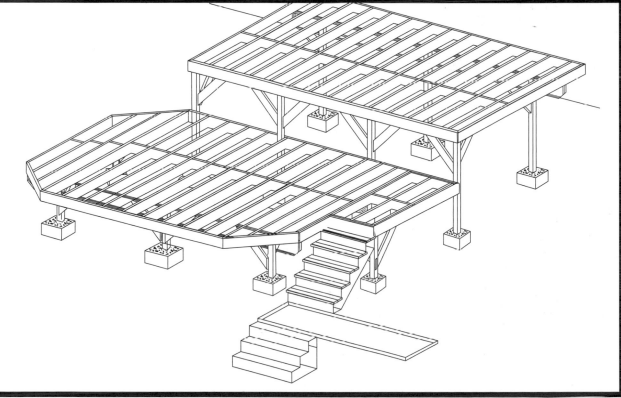

THIS MULTIFACETED DECK HAS two levels: An inset spa, generous space for patio furniture, and outdoor storage under built-in benches provide a thoughtful arrangement of space within a compact design.

The upper level features a partial octagon with an 11-foot diameter—a size ideal for a round table and chairs. A small 5-foot-wide deck near the octagon makes a convenient nook for a barbecue grill. Although only five sides of the octagon shape are constructed, the entire shape is preserved in the pattern of the decking boards.

The focus of the lower deck is a built-in spa resting on its own foundation and inset at one side of the deck. Access to the backyard is provided by a single stairway directly in line with the rear entrance to the house and the short run of stairs connecting the upper and lower levels.

This 600-square-foot-deck is built entirely of pressure-treated Southern yellow pine. It cost between $14,000 and $16,000 to build.

Lumber cut list

Basic lumber requirements for this deck including substructure, railings, stairway parts, and decking.

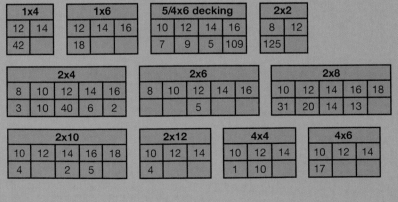

1x4	
12	14
42	

1x6		
12	14	16
18		

5/4x6 decking			
10	12	14	16
7	9	5	109

2x2	
8	12
125	

2x4				
8	10	12	14	16
3	10	40	6	2

2x6				
8	10	12	14	16
		5		

2x8				
10	12	14	16	18
31	20	14	13	

2x10				
10	12	14	16	18
4		2	5	

2x12		
10	12	14
4		

4x4		
10	12	14
1	10	

4x6		
10	12	14
17		

Substructure framing

Normal deck framing isn't strong enough to support the weight of a spa full of water and people. A good solution for an inset spa is to create an independent foundation for the tub and butt the surrounding deck framing to the sides of the spa. Have a local building department representative review foundation details for supporting a spa.

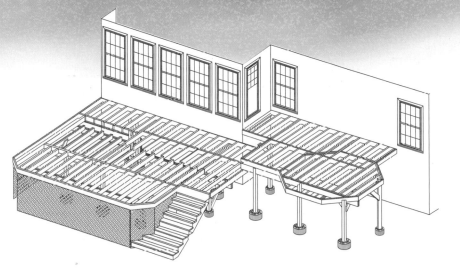

Side Elevation

A lattice privacy screen built into the railing system appears as the tallest part of this elevation view. Installed along one side of the lower deck, it effectively blocks the spa from the view of next-door neighbors. The screen features solid boards along the lower portion and latticework that extends 2 feet above the height of the cap rail. The stairway is designed so it doesn't protrude beyond the edge of the deck structure. Access doors allow storage underneath the deck.

Front Elevation

A subtle change in height from one deck to the other follows the gradual slope of the yard. The elevation change keeps the railing system from obstructing views from large living room windows and prevents the skirting from appearing too massive.

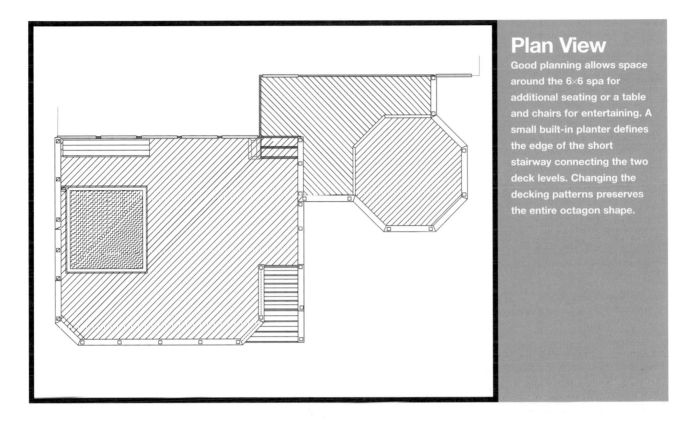

Plan View

Good planning allows space around the 6×6 spa for additional seating or a table and chairs for entertaining. A small built-in planter defines the edge of the short stairway connecting the two deck levels. Changing the decking patterns preserves the entire octagon shape.

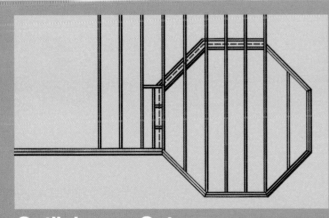

Outlining an Octagon

An octagon is a popular shape for decks. All angles are 45 degrees. Boards that meet with mitered joints, such as the outer rim joists, require their ends cut at an angle that is one-half of 45 degrees, or 22½ degrees. This angle—22½ degrees—is a common setting often marked on circular saws and power miter boxes.

Most octagon deck shapes, however, are not complete octagons. Instead, a portion of the deck projects out as part of an octagon; the remainder is incorporated within a traditional rectangular deck area. For a stylish touch, create a full outline of the octagon, using perimeter trim. Emphasize the shape of the octagon by altering the decking pattern inside the trim.

Make trim from lumber the same thickness as the decking, but a different width. For common 1×6 or ⁵⁄₄×6 decking, make the trim piece about 3 inches wide. If you rip a piece of decking to produce the trim boards, the edges will be square. Square edges are not recommended for decking as they break off and splinter too easily. Round off the edges using a sander or a router equipped with a round-over bit before installing them.

Install the trim pieces before installing the remaining decking. Where trim crosses joists at right angles or at 45 degrees, installation is straightforward. Installing trim parallel to joists requires blocking between the joists to support the trim. The ends of the decking that butt the trim pieces also require full support. In this case, the homeowners installed a system of blocking designed to support the trim as well as the ends of the decking.

AT FIRST GLANCE, this 650-square-foot deck looks complex, with various levels and a variety of unusual shapes. The main deck, however, is built on a single level. It looks more complex than it actually is because of varied decking patterns.

The main deck stretches 46 feet, 8 inches and follows the contours of the house. Two rear entrances open to this level. There is a single step to the octagonal portion of the deck and one more step from the octagon to the lowest level. Although the levels are close enough to grade that railings are unnecessary, a railing encircling the octagon provides a protective sense of enclosure and intimacy. Designing individual spaces—even if separated only by decking patterns—gives each area its own personality.

This deck features a substructure of pressure-treated Southern yellow pine and finish components—including the cedar decking. The deck was completed for a cost of $12,000 to $14,000.

Lumber cut list
Basic lumber requirements for this deck including substructure, railings, stairway parts, and decking.

1x4	
12	14
37	

1x6		
12	14	16

5/4x6 decking			
10	12	14	16
5	13	9	113

2x2	
8	12
43	

2x4				
8	10	12	14	16
6	48	9	2	14

2x6				
8	10	12	14	16
1		7		

2x8				
10	12	14	16	18
33	12	7	5	

2x10				
10	12	14	16	18
2	1	2		

2x12		
8	10	12
2	1	1

4x4		
10	12	14
	2	3

4x6		
10	12	14

Substructure framing

Ledgers for this deck are complex—they must fit around the changing shape of the house, and each piece of the ledger must be firmly fastened to the foundation walls or band joists. Angled joist hangers secure joists to the ledger.

Front Elevation

A low platform design and minimum of vertical components are much in keeping with the general appearance of this single-story house. The configuration presents few obstructions to block views from the many windows. This deck ties together the two rear entrances into the house.

Side Elevation

Here, built-in bench seating plays an integral role in defining the edges of the platform-style deck. The bench straddles a level change with one end resting on the step leading from the upper deck to the lower.

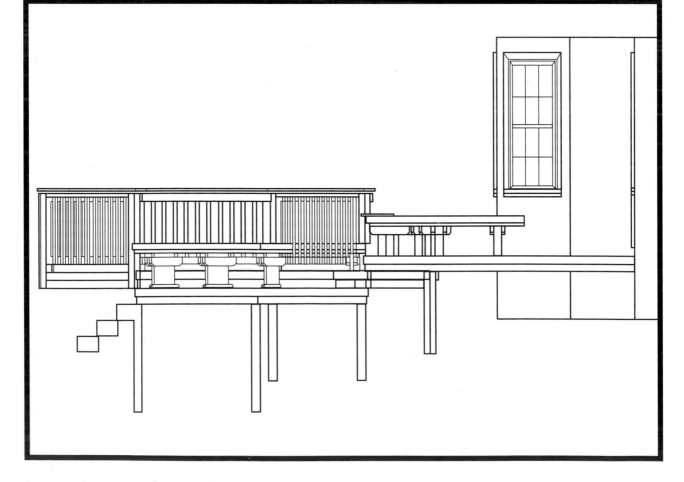

Plan View

Changing decking patterns creates individual sections of deck. There are three areas within the upper level alone. Freestanding furniture can be moved from place to place and changed according to shade patterns at various times of day. A small portion of deck adjacent to the octagon is designed as a tree cutout—it's protected by a short section of railing and a built-in bench.

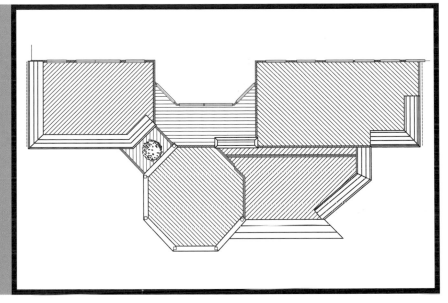

Posts in Concrete

Some building codes allow posts set into the ground. This method is helpful when building platform decks because it eliminates having to install short posts on post anchors. Posts installed into the ground are stable, although care must be used so that the posts are plumb and aligned with one another. Once the posts are set in concrete, they cannot be adjusted.

Dig footing holes just past frost lines. Fill the bottom of the footing holes with 2 to 3 inches of gravel and compact the gravel by tamping it with a heavy piece of lumber. For posts, use only pressure-treated posts rated for ground contact. Saturate the bottom ends of the posts with preservative before installation. Set posts in the centers of the holes and brace them plumb. If necessary, leave posts long so that they can be braced properly. Check alignment of posts using a mason's string. Make any adjustments prior to pouring concrete.

Mix the concrete according to the manufacturer's instructions and pour it into the holes, taking care not to disturb the posts. Pour one-third of the depth of the hole at a time; then pause to ream the concrete with a stick to remove any air bubbles and ensure total settling of the concrete around each post. Continue pouring and reaming the concrete until the hole is full.

made in the shade

JUST 300 SQUARE FEET, this modest second-level deck accomplishes big goals. It provides easy access to the backyard by way of a handsome stairway placed well to the side of the deck. The long vertical traverse from the back entryway to the ground is eased by a two-level deck design and a stairway that descends 5 steps to a landing before making a 90-degree turn to complete the journey to grade level. Tucking a portion of the stairway behind the deck is a compact design feature that prevents the bottom of the stairs from jutting into the yard.

The deck also provides generous amounts of shade. The deck doubles as a shade structure for the existing grade-level patio, and the structure has a generous pergola over half the deck. A closely spaced grid of 2×2 lattice ensures cooling shade. The pergola attaches to the main house with a ledger board fastened to the top plate of the wall framing.

This deck is built of Southern yellow pine. It cost $8,000 to $9,000 to build.

Lumber cut list

Basic lumber requirements for this deck including substructure, railings, stairway parts, and decking.

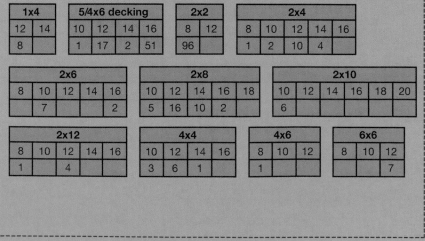

1x4	
12	14
8	

5/4x6 decking			
10	12	14	16
1	17	2	51

2x2	
8	12
96	

2x4				
8	10	12	14	16
1	2	10	4	

2x6				
8	10	12	14	16
	7			2

2x8				
10	12	14	16	18
5	16	10	2	

2x10					
10	12	14	16	18	20
6					

2x12				
8	10	12	14	16
1		4		

4x4			
10	12	14	16
3	6	1	

4x6		
8	10	12
1		

6x6		
8	10	12
		7

Substructure framing

Using 6×6 supports reduces visual clutter underneath the deck by keeping the number of posts required to a minimum. Knee braces are positioned as high on the posts as building code allows. Posts bear directly on an existing concrete patio—check with local building departments to ensure such a foundation system meets approval.

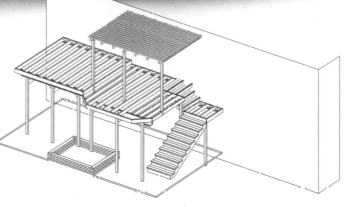

Side Elevation

This second-level deck has a stairway inset into the rear of the deck. The stairway descends to a landing before turning to complete the distance to grade. The design keeps the long expanse of stairway from extending awkwardly into the backyard.

Front Elevation

Second-level decks occasionally must take into consideration lower-level entrances. This deck employs a stepped design. The upper deck is raised so light reaches the sliding glass patio doors below. The deck steps down and enlarges to create a separate living area with its own personality. Tall support posts must be braced to stiffen the structure.

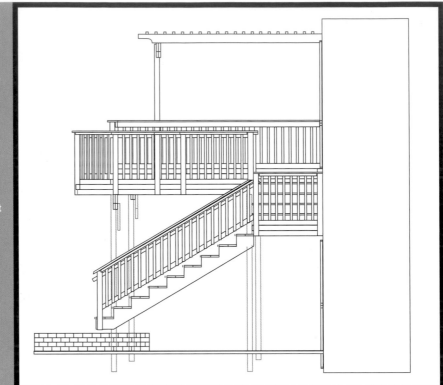

Plan View

Varying the pattern of the decking boards differentiated the separate deck levels. A bump-out design gives the lower deck slightly more space and presents an apron for a barbecue grill. The footprint of the deck is within the outline of the existing patio.

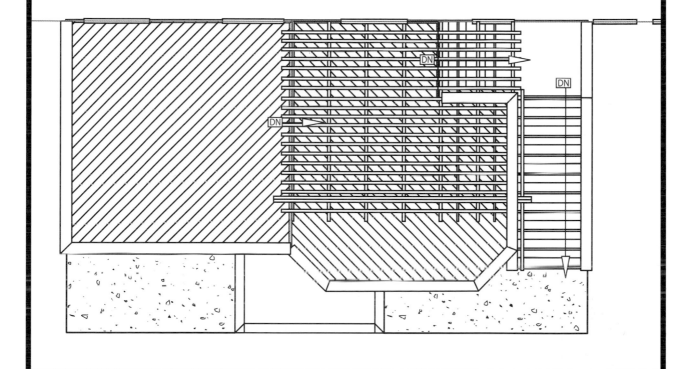

Graspable Handrail

Some building codes require handrails to be "graspable." That is, they must fit the human hand comfortably. Railing designs that use a 2×6 cap rail do not readily fit that description. Check your local building code requirements and discuss your plans with a building official before proceeding.

To accommodate building codes without altering the design of stairway railings, add a handrail. Purchase traditional handrails and mounting brackets at home improvement centers. Ensure long life for the handrail by prefinishing it with several coats of preservative, sealer, or stain. Mount handrails to railing posts. Wax the mounting hardware and screws with automobile wax prior to installation to resist corrosion.

DECKS ARE PERFECT COMPLEMENTS to above-ground swimming pools. They provide access to the edge of the pool, and offer convenient places to sit, relax, dry off, and store pool toys. Plan a freestanding poolside deck so that it hides motors and pumps from view.

Build a poolside deck using the same techniques as any deck, with one important consideration. Because they are not attached to a substantial structure, such as a house, the posts of a freestanding deck should be solidly braced (see Bracing, page 103) to resist flexing and vibration. Strengthen the foundation system of a freestanding deck by adding more posts rather than designing the substructure to the span limits for joists and beams.

For safety reasons, most building codes strictly limit accessibility to pools. The deck shown here includes a locking gate at the top of the stairs. Note how the wide stairway narrows toward its upper steps, which makes designing, building, and operating the gate much easier.

This 350-square-foot deck is built of pressure-treated Southern yellow pine and costs between $6,000 and $8,000.

Lumber cut list

Basic lumber requirements for this deck including substructure, railings, stairway parts, and decking.

1x4	
12	14
9	

5/4x6 decking			
10	12	14	16
5	4	3	62

2x2	
8	12
97	

2x4				
8	10	12	14	16
1	1	4		

2x6				
8	10	12	14	16
		1		3

2x8				
10	12	14	16	18
3	13	8	8	2

2x10					
10	12	14	16	18	20
2	1	2	3		

2x12				
8	10	12	14	16
2		1		

4x4			
10	12	14	16
	3		2

4x6				
8	10	12	14	16
		2		4

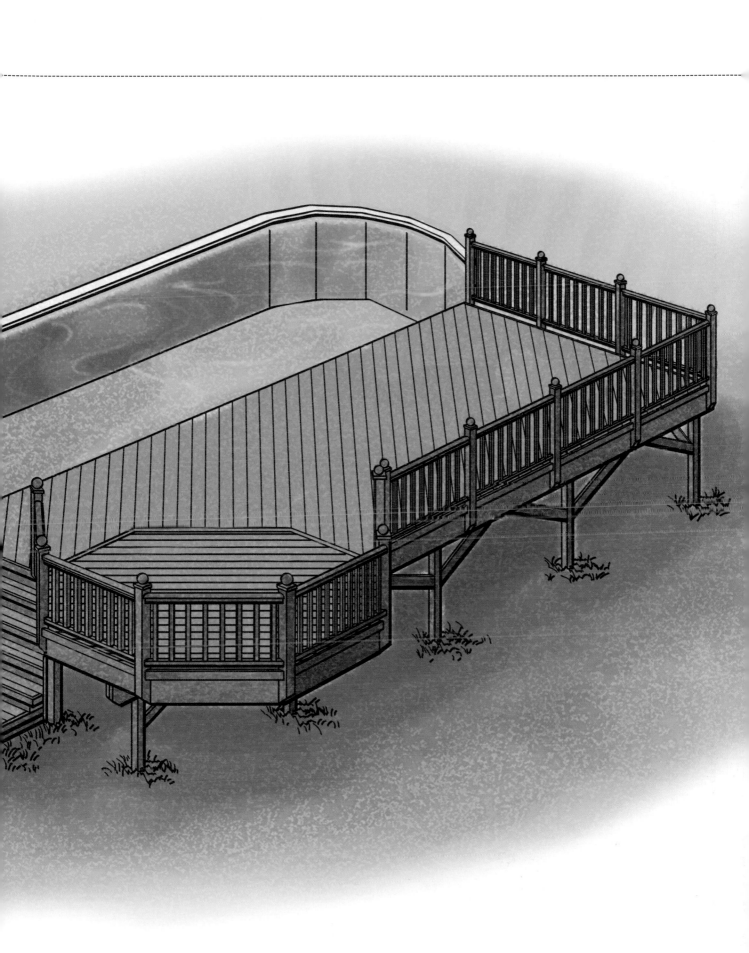

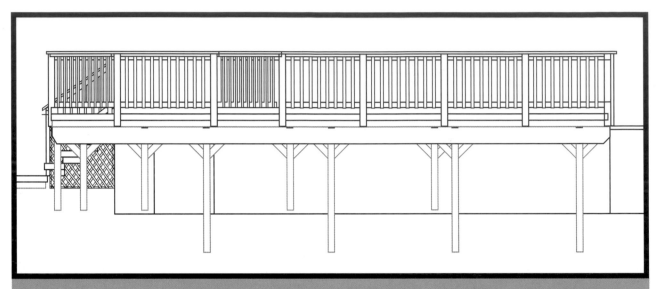

Front Elevation

Keeping skirting to a minimum allows access to the sides of the pool for cleaning and repairs. Use skirting to hide poolside equipment such as pumps and filters. Knee braces are a must for freestanding decks to ensure the structure stays rigid.

Side Elevation

The decking surface is constructed with a short lip overhanging the edge of the pool to make getting in and out of the pool easy. The inner beam is within 8 inches of the pool to provide superior stiffness and rigidity at the edge of the pool and to ensure strength for attaching the poolside ladder.

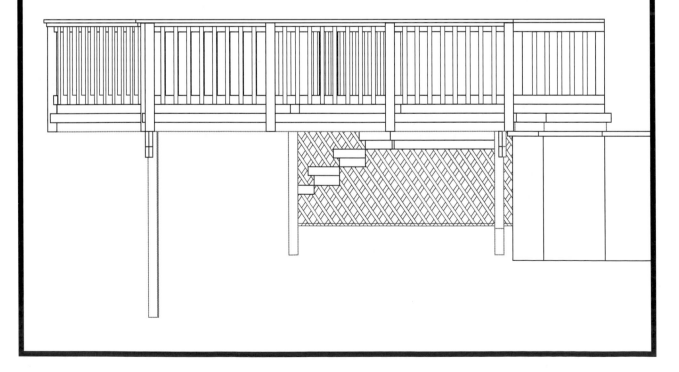

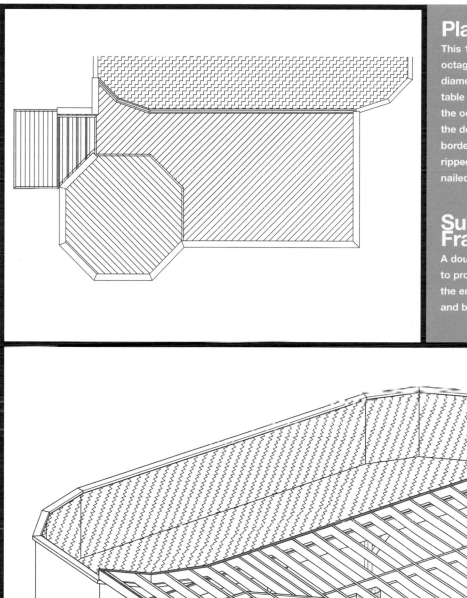

Plan View

This 12×27-foot deck includes an octagonal bump-out with an 11-foot diameter—an ideal size for including a table and chairs. The interior edges of the octagon are defined by altering the decking pattern and adding a strip border made from decking material ripped to a width of 1½ inches and nailed to the joists.

Substructure Framing

A double row of blocking is necessary to provide a firm backing for securing the ends of the decking that form—and butt against—the octagon.

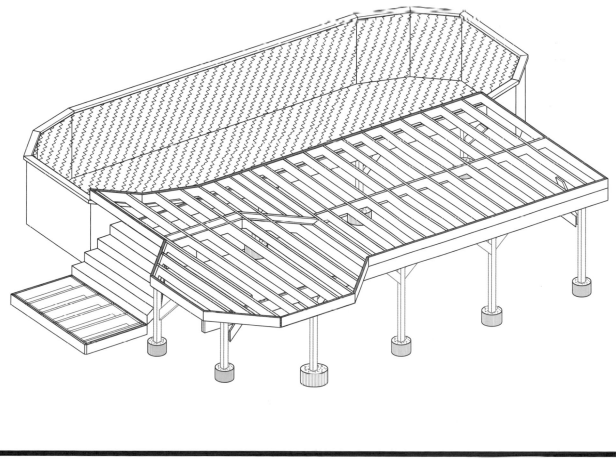

making the grade

ALTHOUGH AN EXISTING SCREENED PORCH
affords this split-level home an open-air venue, the
homeowners wanted to increase their outdoor living area
with deck space. They planned a two-level deck that makes
a gradual transition from the second-story porch to the
ground. The design incorporates two existing concrete
patios—one at the intermediate level and one at the
walk-out level of the house basement. The lowest level deck
exits from the back onto an intermediate-level patio. Existing
steps complete the descent to the lower walk-out patio.

Each of these decks features angled outside corners and
diagonal decking for a bit of flair. Both decks are generously
sized for patio furniture, barbecue grills, and freestanding
hammocks. The substructure is made from pressure-treated
Southern yellow pine, and the decking and railing system is
constructed of synthetic composite material. The
380-square-foot project cost between $9,000 and $11,000.

Lumber cut list

**Basic lumber requirements for this deck including
substructure, railings, stairway parts, and decking.**

1x4	
12	14
9	

5/4x6 decking			
10	12	14	16
	14		63

2x2	
8	12
121	

2x4				
8	10	12	14	16
		18		

2x6				
8	10	12	14	16
		3		

2x8				
10	12	14	16	18
4	7	13	15	

2x10					
10	12	14	16	18	20
8	2				

2x12				
8	10	12	14	16
4				

4x4			
10	12	14	16
	7		2

4x6				
8	10	12	14	16
		6	1	

Substructure framing

Instead of bearing on a ledger attached to the support posts of the upper deck, the lower deck uses an independent support system. The method allows a small gap between the decks that is bridged by the short stairway.

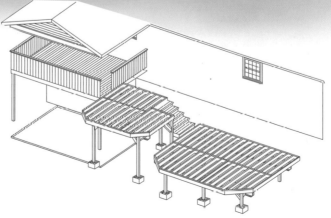

Front Elevation

Although the new deck is bolted to the covered porch, its weight does not bear on the existing support posts. Instead, new beams carry the entire load of the added decks. While the existing porch bears on an old concrete patio, the new decks bear on foundation footings.

Side Elevation

Because they do not share railings, joists, or beams, the portions of a multilevel deck can be subtly—or extremely— different from each other. Here, the lower deck extends about 18 inches past the upper deck to gain its own distinct personality. In turn, the upper deck extends 6 feet beyond the edge of the existing porch.

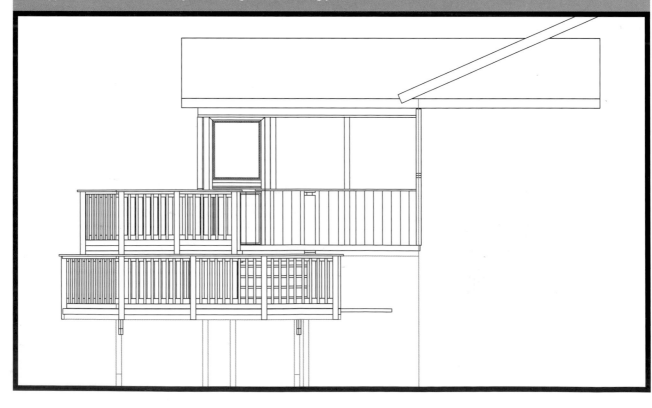

Plan View

A main goal of the homeowners was to incorporate the two existing patios into the design. The solution called for the lower deck to be constructed flush with the upper patio surface. A short flight of existing stairs provides entry to the walk-out basement. Traffic pathways are kept toward the back of the decks, away from furniture areas.

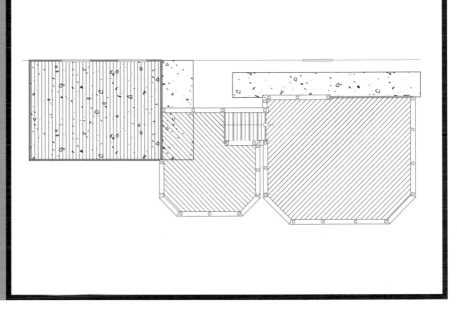

Attaching to Existing Concrete

If your local building officials approve, you may be able to attach posts directly to existing concrete slabs, such as a patio. Using a galvanized metal post anchor makes this type of connection relatively simple.

Use your deck plan to determine the location of posts. Mark the center of each post on the concrete slab. Secure the anchors to the slab using lag shields and galvanized lag bolts at least ¼-inch in diameter.

1 Drill for lag shields, using a hammer drill equipped with a carbide-tipped masonry drill bit.

2 Use a shop vacuum to remove residual dust from the inside of the holes.

3 Tap the shield into the hole with a rubber mallet. Bolt the post anchor into position.

TAKING THEIR DESIGN CUES from the shape of their house, the owners of this single-story home designed a large platform-style deck with three sections meandering around the back of the house. Two main areas located at both ends of the structure provide access from the interiors to the outside through sets of sliding patio doors. A middle deck area connects the two ends. Two-thirds of the deck is built on the same level and is completely encircled by a three-step stairway that provides access to the backyard. Changing decking patterns help define the three areas.

The design of the deck is deliberately low-key and low-profile, in keeping with the modest architectural intent of the house. Minimum use of railings and a moderate vertical mass prevent the deck from imposing itself on the overall scheme. The most elaborate part of the deck is raised a single step from the lower deck areas. This upper deck connects to a living room and offers space for a comfortable grouping of outdoor furniture. The project is built entirely of pressure-treated Southern yellow pine and costs between $10,000 and $11,000 to construct.

Lumber cut list

Basic lumber requirements for this deck including substructure, railings, stairway parts, and decking.

1x4		1x6			5/4x6 decking				2x2	
12	14	12	14	16	10	12	14	16	8	12
22		18			13	6	3	118	62	

2x4					2x6					2x8				
8	10	12	14	16	8	10	12	14	16	10	12	14	16	18
	9	13	2		1	4	2	3	8	13	11	19	23	

2x10					2x12			4x4			
10	12	14	16	18	12	14	16	10	12	14	16
	1	4	2				1	1	7		3

Side Elevation

A close look at the deck elevations reveals the general intent of this deck—much of it serves as a transition space between the interior rooms and the backyard. Steps accompany most of the perimeter so that the yard is accessible from any point. Nevertheless, there is ample room for lounge chairs and other patio furniture.

Front Elevation

A slightly raised section of the deck meets a set of sliding patio doors leading to the living room. This raised deck is encircled by a railing that lends a sense of intimacy and privacy to outdoor gatherings. A small stairway at one end leads to the side of the house.

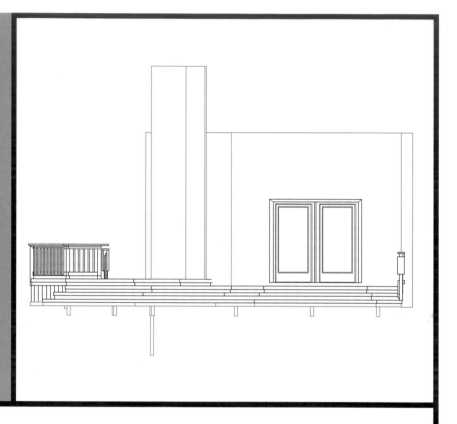

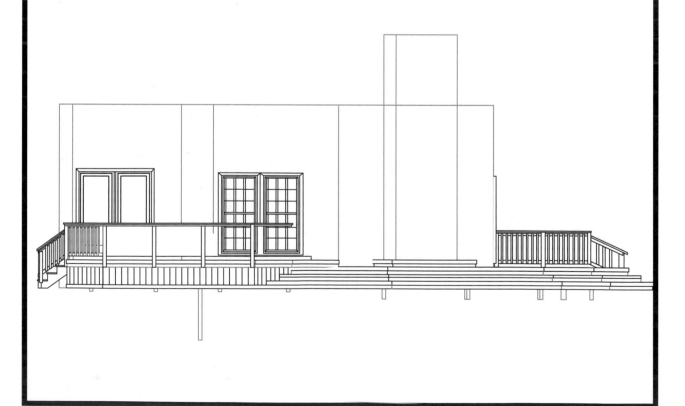

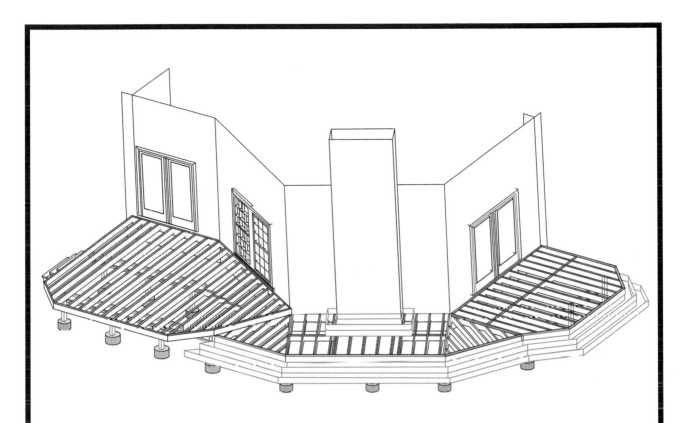

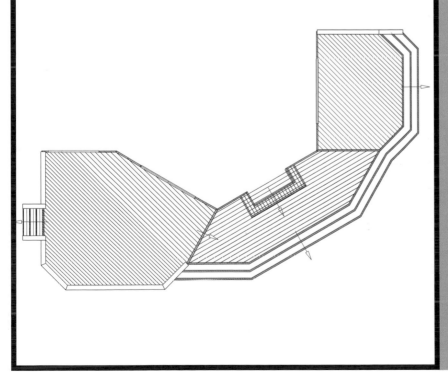

Substructure Framing

A view of the framing shows the deck is divided into three portions—two larger decks set at either end of the house and a narrower portion connecting the two. The design unifies the back of the structure with a flowing walkway that gives clearance to a fireplace chase.

Plan View

A continuous, flowing stairway makes it easy to enter and exit the deck system from any point in the backyard. Angling the corners and changing the shape of the perimeter keep the design of this simple deck visually intriguing. Diagonal decking defines each area of the deck.

NESTLED IN THE CROOK of an added-on family room and a bump-out window, an existing 15×15-foot deck was well-positioned for shade and privacy but lacked size. The homeowners wanted to expand the deck but preserve the intimacy of the original scale. A second deck located on the opposite side of the family room addition was added, and the two decks connect via a series of small 4×4 platforms that cascade around the back of the house and follow the gently sloping grade of the property. The new deck also camouflages an old patio. Without laborious removal of the old patio, the new deck simply bears directly on it. The platform-style construction is close enough to the ground that safety railings are unnecessary.

This deck—including the decking—was built entirely of pressure-treated Southern yellow pine. To ensure the new portion matched the old, the older decking was removed and replaced with new 5/4 RED decking. A small built-in bench seat (see page 190) and a planter (see page 34) help give the edges of the lower deck definition and substance. The total usable area increased to 450 square feet. The cost of this North Carolina deck is between $8,000 and $10,000.

Lumber cut list

Basic lumber requirements for this deck including substructure, railings, stairway parts, and decking.

1x4	
12	14
22	

1x6		
12	14	16

5/4x6 decking			
10	12	14	16
4	11		85

4x4			
10	12	14	16
3		1	1

2x2	
8	12
12	

2x4				
8	10	12	14	16
2	3		1	4

2x8					
10	12	14	16	18	20
26	9		3		

Side Elevation

Seen from the side, the new deck is compact and subdued. Built-in bench seating and a board-sided planter along the left side of the deck give pleasing visual mass that blends well with the stepped platform decks and offer a sense of shelter to the otherwise unadorned decking surface.

Front Elevation

Besides adding usable space, the lower deck is well below nearby windows and does not obstruct views to the backyard from inside the house. The series of four smaller platform decks descend at the consistent rate of one step per deck. The deck at the left-hand portion of the elevation offers access from the driveway to the rear entrance of the house and the nearby kitchen—when there are groceries to unload, no more muddy feet tracking inside.

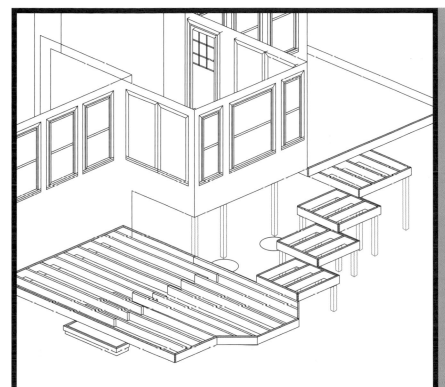

Substructure Framing

Joists made from 2×8s form the basic substructural framing, *left.* To gain length, the joists run past each other and bear on an existing raised concrete patio. Consult your local building department when planning to use an existing concrete structure to bear the weight of a portion of your deck. Your plans may require an initial check of the concrete from a building inspector.

Plan View

The decking is installed on the diagonal, and changes directions at each individual deck, *below.* The four stepped decks move away from the house, creating an alcove for plantings and ensuring nature is integral to the overall design.

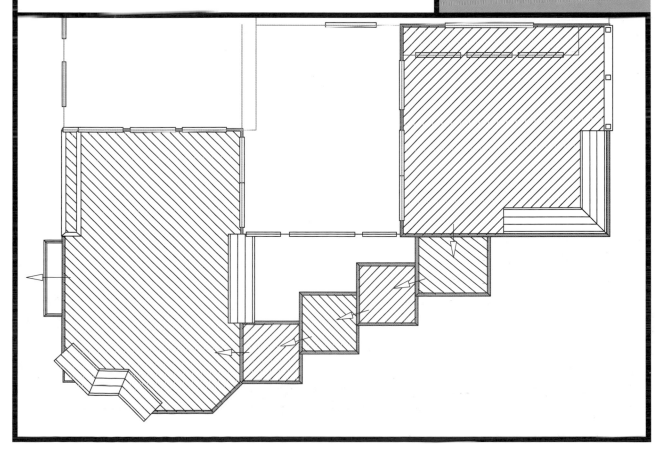

Built-in bench

This built-in bench features T-shape supports with sturdy 4×4 posts for vertical members. The basic design makes it easy to cut decking to fit against each post and keeps posts to a minimum to simplify cleaning underneath the bench. Use your deck plans to determine the location of the bench posts.

Notch the 4×4s to fit around joists, using the techniques described on page 132. Secure them to the joists with carriage bolts. Install a post every 32 to 48 inches. On low platform decks that do not require railings, consider installing benches at the perimeter of the deck by fastening support posts directly to the outside of the rim joists.

To support the ends of decking that butt against the posts, wrap each post with short 2×4 blocks installed flush with the top edges of the joists. Install the decking before installing the bench seats to make it easier to work around the posts. Plan for seats 18 to 24 inches wide.

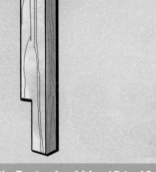

1 Cut posts to length. Posts should be 15 to 16 inches long plus the width (vertical height) of the joist. Notch the bottom of the post to fit around the joist. The depth of the notch should equal the thickness of the joist—1½ inches. Install the post, using two ⅜-inch diameter carriage bolts in each tail. Keep the uppermost carriage bolt 4 inches below the top of the joist to provide room for the blocking.

3 Install bench seat supports made from 2×6s or 2×8s. Fasten two supports to each post, using 2-inch diameter carriage bolts. Make sure the ends of the seat supports are flush to each other and that all bench seat supports are aligned.

2 Install 2×4 blocking around each post to support the decking. Pre-drill to prevent cracking the blocking during installation. Install the decking.

4 Install 2×4 or 2×6 edging by driving fasteners through the edging into the ends of the bench seat supports. The top of the edging should be higher than the seat support by a distance equal to the thickness of the seat material. Use a block of the bench material as a gauge. Miter the corners of the edging and install the bench seat material.

index

Numbers in bold indicate photographs.